Rachel Della Ratta

Research Methods in Human Development

Research Methods in Human Development

PAUL C. COZBY
PATRICIA E. WORDEN
DANIEL W. KEE
California State University, Fullerton

Mayfield Publishing Company
Mountain View, California

Copyright © 1989 by Mayfield Publishing Company

All rights reserved. No portion of this book may be reproduced in any form or by any means without written permission of the publisher.

Library of Congress Cataloging-in-Publication Data
Cozby, Paul C.
  Research methods in human development.

  Bibliography: p.
  Includes index.
  1. Social sciences—Research—Methodology.
I. Worden, Patricia E.   II. Kee, Daniel W.
III. Title.
H62.C675   1989   300'.72   88-13714
ISBN 0-87484-788-5

Manufactured in the United States of America

10 9 8 7 6

Mayfield Publishing Company
1240 Villa Street
Mountain View, California 94041

Sponsoring editor, Franklin C. Graham; production editor, Sondra Glider; manuscript editor, Cici Teter; cover designer, Cynthia Bassett. The text was set in 10/12 Zapf International Light by Compset and printed on 50# Finch Opaque by Arcata Graphics Company.

Contents

Preface   xi

CHAPTER 1
The Scientific View   1

Career Profile: Un Chu Kim, Community Center Program Aide   1
Use of Research Methods   2
Objectives of the Scientific Approach   3
Advantages of the Scientific Approach   6
Basic and Applied Research   8
Summary   11
Study Questions   11

CHAPTER 2
The Origins of Scientific Inquiry   12

Career Profile: Linda P. Acredolo, Journal Editor   12
Sources of Ideas   13
How Scientists Communicate   17
Summary   26
Study Questions   27

CHAPTER 3
Studying Relationships Between Variables 28

Career Profile: David K. Slay, Child Guidance Center Clinical Director   28
Scientific Variables   29
Operational Definitions   30
Types of Relationships   31
The Correlational Method   34
The Experimental Method   36
Independent and Dependent Variables   38
Choosing a Method   38
Conclusion   40
Summary   41
Study Questions   42

CHAPTER 4
Measurement   43

Career Profile: Camilla Freitag, Social Worker   43
Self-Report Measures   44
Behavioral Measures   47
Physiological Measures   48
Projective Measures   48
Evaluating Measures of Behavior   49
Scales of Measurement   53
Summary   55
Study Questions   57

CHAPTER 5
Designing Experiments   58

Career Profile: Donna Chafe, Elementary School Teacher   58
Confounding and Internal Validity   60
External Validity   60
Poorly Designed Experiments   61
Well-Designed Experiments   65
Quasi-Experimental Designs   68

Summary 69
Study Questions 70

CHAPTER 6
Types of Experimental Designs 71

Career Profile: Jerriann M. Wilson, Child Life Specialist 71
Independent Groups Designs 72
Repeated Measures Designs 74
Longitudinal Versus Cross-Sectional Designs 77
Time-Series Experiments 82
Summary 87
Study Questions 88

CHAPTER 7
Complex Experimental Designs 89

Career Profile: Kathleen C. Guy, Bereavement Counselor 89
Factorial Designs 90
Additional Complexity 98
Human Development and Family Relations Questions and Complex Experimental Designs 103
Summary 107
Study Questions 108

CHAPTER 8
Nonexperimental Methods 109

Career Profile: Juan Castanon Garcia, Marriage and Family Counselor 109
Why Conduct Nonexperimental Studies? 111
Field Observation 112
Systematic Observation 116
Case Studies 118
Survey Research 119
Archival Research 125

Summary 128
Study Questions 129

CHAPTER 9
Preparations for Conducting Research 130

Career Profile: Maryhelen Campa, Montessori Teacher 130
Research Proposals 131
Fine-Tuning Manipulations, Measures, and Controls 133
Obtaining Subjects and Sampling 140
Setting the Stage 145
Pilot Studies and Manipulation Checks 147
Working with Children and Other Special Populations 148
Summary 149
Study Questions 150

CHAPTER 10
Understanding Research Results 151

Career Profile: R. Max Learner, Department of Health Coordinator 151
Descriptive Analyses 153
Inferential Statistics 157
Issues in Decision Making 163
Selecting Statistical Tests 168
Summary 169
Study Questions 170

CHAPTER 11
Correlation Coefficients 171

Career Profile: Jocelyn S. Carter, Convalescent Hospital Administrator 171
Correlation Coefficients and the Correlational Method 172
Indexing the Strength of a Relationship 173
Graphing Correlations with Scatterplots 174
Interpreting Correlations 176
Partial Correlation 178

Correlation Coefficients and Prediction of Behavior   178
Multiple Correlation   179
Summary   180
Study Questions   180

CHAPTER 12
Ethical Concerns   **181**

Career Profile: Melanie J. Ingle-Nelson, Psychosocial Coordinator   181
The Principle of Psychological Risk   182
The Principle of Informed Consent   185
Debriefing   190
The Issue of Nontreated Controls   192
Institutional Review of Research   192
Summary   194
Study Questions   197

APPENDIX A
A Sample Research Paper   **198**

APPENDIX B
Statistical Tests   **213**

Descriptive Statistics   213
Statistical Significance Tests   216
Measures of Strength of Association   231
Conclusion   234

APPENDIX C
Statistical Tables   **235**

Random Number Table   236
Critical Values of Chi-Square   238
Critical Values of the Mann–Whitney U 238

Critical Values of t	240
Critical Values of F	241
Critical Values of *rho*	244
Critical Values of r	245

Glossary   247

References   257

Index   267

Preface

Our objective in writing *Research Methods in Human Development* was to produce an undergraduate-level introduction to basic research techniques and methodology for the "consumer" of research—someone who is not necessarily going to become a researcher, but who needs to know the basics to be effective in his or her career. The book will help undergraduates understand what they are reading and what their professors are saying about the research foundations of their fields of study. It also will alert students to common problems and misconceptions about research. Students who become teachers, social workers, or counselors will be confronted with the findings of social science research throughout their careers. This book presents the concepts that are needed to evaluate such research.

The audience we have in mind includes students of child development, education, family relations, life-span human development, psychology, sociology, gerontology, and other social science fields that study human development. We present the concepts of research methodology in the context of these areas, but our intent is not to present a comprehensive coverage of the content of any specific area. Rather, we illustrate basic research questions with examples from a wide variety of fields: child development, marital and family relations, sex roles, and adulthood and aging. However, we frequently focus on research with children because there is a substantial body of literature on this subject, and such research often presents special problems that students should be aware of.

This book is not designed to be a statistics text. Although we present the basic statistical ideas and concepts that a student may encounter in the course of his or her readings, this text is not meant to teach students to perform sophisticated statistical analyses of their own. In courses that require students to do so, we recommend that instructors assign a statistics text in addition to this one.

PREFACE

This text differs from many methods texts because it presents basic research methods with an emphasis on human development research. Chapter 1 introduces the scientific method and its objectives. Chapter 2 explores what variables are and how they are chosen for study. This chapter also covers how research is communicated and gives practical information about literature searching. Chapter 3 introduces types of relationships between variables and distinguishes experimental and correlational research. Chapter 4 explores issues in measurement in human development research. Chapters 5, 6, and 7 discuss designing experiments. Chapter 5 presents the features that distinguish poorly designed from well-designed experiments. Chapter 6 compares independent groups and repeated measures designs. This chapter also compares cross-sectional and longitudinal designs and briefly covers time-series experiments. Chapter 7 explores complex factorial designs and their interpretation. Chapter 8 examines nonexperimental methods, including field observation, case studies, surveys, and archival research. Chapter 9 covers the practical aspects of conducting research, including writing research proposals, obtaining subjects and sampling, preparing instructions, and debriefing. Chapters 10 and 11 discuss research results and ways they are typically analyzed and presented in research reports. Chapter 10 focuses on results from experimental studies, and Chapter 11 covers correlational results. Chapter 12 presents the ethical concerns involved in conducting research in human development and family relations. The book is designed to allow instructors flexibility to assign chapters in the order that best suits the goals of their classes.

Finally, we know that some students expect research methodology to be a dry, uninteresting, technical subject. We have used interesting examples that challenge the students' curiosity. After all, research is exploration, and we hope that students will come to appreciate the excitement involved in the process as well as in its outcome.

Paul C. Cozby
Patricia E. Worden
Daniel W. Kee

Research Methods in Human Development

CHAPTER 1

The Scientific View

CAREER PROFILE

Un Chu Kim / Community Center Program Aide

Un attended Mt. San Antonio Junior College in Southern California. She is currently employed at the Delhaven Community Center as a Program Aide working with developmentally disabled adults. She also serves as a Club Advisor for a group of children with behavioral and/or emotional problems.

"As a Program Aide for disabled adults, I follow a program designed to foster self-esteem and independent living skills. Some of the basic skills I teach include showing disabled adults how to tie their shoes and clean up after meals. Mastery of these basic skills helps my clients develop a more positive image of themselves and increases their ability to interact in the community. As a Club Advisor for kids, I meet with children twice a week. The club is a place for them to forget about their troubles and come and be themselves. The program is a combination of group rap sessions designed to foster positive thinking and self-image and highly structured recreational activities. One-on-one attention is also provided."

Un is one of the many consumers of research knowledge. She consults regularly with licensed clinical social workers. She finds that they "are a valuable resource for written articles and books," and she reports that she occasionally uses reference lists for further library research. "By taking information from these consultation sessions and my own library research, I can incorporate them into the program and hopefully better serve my clients."

This book discusses research methods for the study of human development and family relations. Research is the cornerstone of our scientific knowledge—past, present, and future. The scientific methods used in research are the tools that help us understand behavioral changes that occur with age and evaluate processes associated with families. Such tools facilitate our understanding of existing information, help us identify important issues, and provide us with the means for seeking answers to questions about human development and family functioning.

This introductory chapter discusses how an understanding of research methods will be useful to you as a student and future specialist in human development and family relations. Further, it examines the characteristics of the scientific approach to studying human behavior, and it reviews the general kinds of research activities associated with the approach.

USE OF RESEARCH METHODS

Understanding research methods helps you assess the value of information about human development and family relations. Many articles concerning these topics appear in daily newspapers and in magazines such as *Time*, *Newsweek*, *Parents*, and *Psychology Today*. For example, headlines may read: "TV viewing time linked to poor grades," "Teach your two-year-old to read," "Stress in home harms children," "Pets ease adjustment in retirement homes," or "Reentry women excel in college classrooms." How can you evaluate the stories that accompany these headlines? Should you simply accept the conclusions presented because the report is presumably based on scientific research? A background in research methods will help you appraise the contents of the articles and provide you with the skills to seek further information on the topic.

A variety of activities in human development and family relations rely on research findings. For example, counselors need to know about the latest advances in family or play therapy techniques. Assessment specialists need to know about new testing procedures and how to interpret test results. Educators must keep current with recent advances in instructional technology such as computer uses in classrooms. Thus, your knowledge of research methods, regardless of your speciality, will give you the ability to read and evaluate research reports. In turn, the information you gain from research will provide the basis for your professional activities and decisions you make. To illustrate, each chapter of this book opens with a profile of someone who uses knowledge of research methods in his or her human development and family relations careers, even though the person being profiled may not actually be a researcher. For example, Un Chu Kim relies on research articles and books to keep her up to date in her work with developmentally disabled adults.

Your knowledge of research methods may motivate you to conduct a research project. Term papers in future classes can be supplemented by findings from your own research. You also will gain the expertise to advise a child on his or her science fair project. With an appreciation of the methods of science, you will discover that many aspects of your personal and future professional activities are open to systematic study. A counselor may wish to determine the best age and group size for recreational activities. A pediatric nurse may wish to discover if "medical play" helps children better understand medical procedures. A gerontologist may examine the most effective way to help elderly adults improve their memory skills. Solutions to these types of problems can be found through research. In addition, research knowledge will also help you become a more informed citizen on issues of public policy and planning. For example, the emerging debate on a national day care policy is based on both developmental and family research. Implementation of handicapped persons' access and service delivery requires an understanding of the special health, physical, social, and psychological needs of the handicapped. Information about these needs is provided through research.

OBJECTIVES OF THE SCIENTIFIC APPROACH

Four major goals of scientific research can be identified:

1. To describe behavior
2. To identify causes and explanations for behavior
3. To predict behavior
4. To apply scientific findings

Many researchers who study families and human development are concerned with how behavior changes and how to explain these changes. Others are concerned with studying how factors associated with the family, such as maternal employment, marital status, or friendship patterns, affect the behavior of family members. Some family specialists may be more involved in predicting future outcomes such as the placement of children in foster families or predicting recovery from physical illness. Application of findings includes dissemination of nontechnical reports and development of programs to help children, adults, or families.

Description of behavior

A basic goal of science is to provide a complete description of behavior. For example, a researcher interested in children's play would use research methods to provide a complete picture of the play activities studied. Whether the researcher selects a single isolated behavior or a spectrum of representative behaviors to study, an accurate and reliable description is required. In human development, one focus is on describing behavior that is systematically related to age. Thus, the researcher might study how social play changes between three and five years of age. Or, another researcher might study how play behavior differs among children from single-parent homes in contrast to traditional homes.

Causes of behavior

What are the factors that cause or affect behavior? The study of families and human development uncovers many behavioral changes that appear related to age. For example, we may observe that young adults express more self-confidence in new locations than children or elderly adults. However, is age per se responsible for the developmental and aging differences? What other age-related factors might be involved? Research studies could be conducted to identify the factors that are directly responsible for the differences in self-confidence. Some family variables that might affect degree of self-confidence include family size, birth order, marital status, education, income level, and social support.

Explanations of behavior

In addition to description and identifying causes of behavior, research seeks to explain *why* the behavior we study occurs. For example, we might discover that young adults learn faster than children and older adults because they use special learning techniques or strategies. But why do they use these strategies? Do younger children know about these strategies? Do elderly adults forget to use these strategies? Can the use of these strategies be taught?

As you can see, the activities of identifying causes of behavior and advancing explanations are closely related. Because research consists of a series of analytical steps, causes identified in early phases of research may suggest explanations that later prove inadequate as new and additional causes are identified. Part of the excitement of conducting research is knowing that you are involved in the discovery of knowledge; with each new finding, additional opportunities for inquiry are created.

Prediction of behavior

Descriptions of behavior provided in early phases of research will indicate whether some events are systematically related to one another. For example, different kinds of play occur more frequently at different age levels (see Rubin, Fein, & Vandenberg, 1983). Whether or not we have identified the causes of this developmental change in play, the descriptive information allows us to anticipate developmental progressions in children's behavior. In other words, we can predict that older children will engage in play that is different from younger children. In this regard, our ability to predict often helps us make better decisions. For example, information regarding the kinds of play activities associated with children of different ages can be used to help us select more toys that are age appropriate or design more play activities that are especially suited to children of different ages.

As noted, research is exciting because you can be involved in the discovery of knowledge. Research is also gratifying when you begin to see the link between research findings and the potential for improving the quality of human life. Research that allows prediction of behavior takes us one step closer to helping people. For example, knowing the characteristics of fall-prone older adults allows the identification of individuals at risk for injuries and provides the basis for helping them.

Application of scientific knowledge

A final activity of the scientific enterprise is the application of research findings. For example, a researcher discovers that listening to certain kinds of music facilitates relaxation with older adults. The scientist subsequently designs a music program for audio cassette tapes based on the research findings. Another researcher may write articles for the popular press that discuss scientific findings in lay terms. These articles might suggest the best kinds of listening music for relaxation.

Another example is provided by activities sponsored by the Johnson and Johnson Baby Products Company. This company sponsors scientific conferences concerning human development. Scientists gather to discuss their most recent discoveries. Publications and brochures based on these conferences are produced that provide nontechnical reports (e.g., Gunzenhauser & Caldwell, 1986). Such items are available in bookstores, and the brochures are distributed by human development specialists. Also, the basic research findings discussed at these meetings may, in turn, have an impact on the development of products designed to promote healthy infant and child development.

Scientific research consists of different activities: Description, identification of causes and explanations, and prediction are closely intertwined. These activities are cumulative; each study builds on past findings, and each finding suggests new understandings and questions for study.

ADVANTAGES OF THE SCIENTIFIC APPROACH

Scientists seek to describe, explain, understand, and predict behavior. To achieve these goals, they use an approach called the *scientific method*. What makes this approach different from other ways of learning and thinking about human development or families? People have always been fascinated by behavioral changes that occur with age and that are influenced by family dynamics. Explanations are sought by various means. When the scientific method is used, reliable and valid information can be provided. Unfortunately, many people base their views of development and the family solely on authority and intuition, instead of on the scientific method.

Authority and intuition

The philosopher Aristotle was concerned with the factors that determine persuasion and attitude change. In his *Rhetoric*, Aristotle describes credibility: "Persuasion is achieved by the speaker's personal character when the speech is so spoken as to make us think him credible. We believe good men more fully and readily than others." Thus, Aristotle would argue that we are persuaded by a speaker who seems prestigious, trustworthy, and respectable rather than by one who seems ordinary, dishonest, and disreputable.

Many of us might accept Aristotle's arguments simply because he, himself, is considered an authority. Similarly, many people are all too ready to accept anything they learn from the news media, a book, government officials, or a religious figure. They believe that the statements of such authorities must be true. However, this situation is not necessarily the case. In addition, authorities sometimes offer conflicting opinions. As we shall see in this text, the scientific approach rejects the notion that you can accept on faith the statement of any authority, and it provides us with the means for selecting among alternative views.

As a way of knowing something, intuition is in many ways the opposite of authority. When you believe in an authority, you accept unquestioningly what he or she tells you about the world. In contrast, when you rely on intuition, you accept unquestioningly what your own personal judgment tells you about the world. The intuitive approach takes many forms. Often it involves finding an explanation for our own behaviors or the behaviors of someone else. One problem with this approach is that there are numerous biases that affect our perceptions, and also we often cannot accurately identify the true causes of our behavior (see Nisbett & Wilson, 1977; Nisbett & Ross, 1980). Indeed, we are often unaware of our bias because we are so close to it.

Skepticism and science

The scientific approach recognizes that both authority and intuition are sources of ideas about behavior. However, the scientist does not accept on faith the pronouncements of anyone, regardless of that person's prestige or authority. Nor does a scientist unquestioningly accept his or her own intuitions—the scientist recognizes that his or her ideas are just as likely to be wrong as are anyone's. Scientists are skeptical people. They insist that scientific methods be used to evaluate assertions about the nature of behavior, and they refuse to trust either authority or intuition.

The essence of the scientific method is the insistence that all propositions be subjected to evaluation. This method embodies a number of rules for testing ideas through research, and these are explored throughout this book. The important point here is that systematic tests of ideas allow the scientist to investigate a supposition under conditions in which the idea may be either supported or refuted. Further, the test is performed in a manner that can be observed, evaluated, and replicated by others. Thus, the scientific method, in contrast to the use of authority or intuition, does not rely on accepting assertions generated by someone else or on your own personal, unsystematic perceptions of the world.

Conclusion

The advantage of the scientific approach over other methods of learning about the world is that it provides an objective set of rules for gathering and evaluating information. However, some qualifications are necessary. First, there is nothing wrong with accepting the assertions of an authority as long as we don't accept them as scientific evidence. Often scientific evidence isn't obtainable; for example, when religions ask us to accept certain beliefs on faith. In general, there is nothing wrong with having opinions or beliefs as long as they are presented simply as opinions or beliefs. However, it is a good idea to ask whether an opinion can be tested scientifically. For example, opinions on whether exposure to violence on television is harmful are only opinions until scientific evidence on the question is gathered and evaluated; however, certain beliefs such as whether God exists cannot be tested and thus are beyond the realm of science. Scientific ideas must be testable and thus able to be shown to be false.

Finally, you should be aware that scientists often become authorities when they express their ideas. When someone claims to be a scientist, should we be more willing to accept what he or she has to say? The answer: It depends on whether the scientist has scientific data that support the assertions being made. If there is no such evidence, the scientist is no different from any other authority. Even if scientific evidence is presented, you will want to evaluate the methods used to gather the evidence. Also, many "pseudoscientists" use scientific jargon to substantiate their claims (e.g., astrologists). A general rule: Be highly skeptical whenever someone who is labeled as a "scientist" makes assertions that are supported only by vague or improbable evidence. Skepticism in general is always useful to a specialist in human development and family relations. This book will help you learn how to translate your skepticism of assertions and findings into a useful appraisal of their underlying assumptions and data.

BASIC AND APPLIED RESEARCH

Human development and family relations research falls into three general categories:

Basic research
Applied research
Evaluation research

Basic research

Basic research is designed to uncover evidence about fundamental behavioral processes. Such studies may examine theoretical issues or may be prompted by chance observations of interesting behavioral events. The following citations provide examples of journal articles that illustrate some basic research questions:

> Brody, G. H., Pellegrini, A. D., & Sigel, I. E. (1986). Marital quality and mother-child and father-child interactions with school-aged children. *Developmental Psychology, 22*, 291–298.
>
> Conger, R. D., McCarthy, J. A., Yang, R. K., Lahey, B. B., & Burgers, R. L. (1984). Mother's age as a predictor of observed maternal behavior in three independent samples of families. *Journal of Marriage and the Family, 46*, 403–411.
>
> Stevenson, H. W., & Newman, R. S. (1986). Long-term prediction of achievement and attitudes in mathematics and reading. *Child Development, 57*, 646–659.

Applied research

The preceding research articles are not concerned with any immediate practical application or the solution of a specific problem. In contrast, *applied research* addresses practical problems and suggests specific solutions. To illustrate, examine the following citations:

> Gottfried, A. W., Guerin, D., Spencer, J. E., & Meyer, C. (1984). Validity of Minnesota Child Development Inventory in screening young children's developmental status. *Journal of Pediatric Psychology, 9*, 219–229.
>
> Morse, J. M., Tylko, S. J., & Dixon, H. A. (1987). Characteristics of the fall-prone patient. *The Gerontologist, 27*, 516–522.
>
> Wolfe, D. A., Mendes, M. G., & Factor, D. (1984). A parent-administered program to reduce children's television viewing. *Journal of Applied Behavior Analysis, 17*, 267–272.

Much applied research in human development is conducted by governmental agencies such as state or local departments of education. Reports of this research are often published in technical reports and news bulletins rather than in scientific journals. Such research is often used for public policy decisions or to support requests for legislative funding. A major example is "Nation at Risk: A Report to the Nation and the Secretary of Education," the 1983 report published by the National Commission on Excellence in Education, United States Department of Education.

Comparing basic and applied research

Both basic and applied research are important, and neither should be considered superior to the other; they each address different objectives. Basic research enhances our knowledge of fundamental processes, whereas applied research provides solutions to contemporary problems. Success in applied research can often be attributed to advances in basic research. For example, Psychologist B. F. Skinner's basic research on operant conditioning conducted in the 1930s provided the basis for more recent applied work in behavior modification therapy techniques. The following vignette illustrates how basic research findings provided the foundation for applied research, which in turn led to practical applications:

> During the 1970s, basic research was conducted to identify techniques for enhancing learning proficiency in children (see Rohwer, 1973). The research used standard laboratory learning tasks such as the method of paired associates, which required children to learn experimentally constructed lists of unrelated word pairs. Different instructional methods and presentation media were evaluated to identify optimal learning conditions. Evidence from the basic research showed that if children used a mental imagery learning strategy, substantial gains were observed. This strategy identified in the basic research was adapted in applied research to evaluate its effectiveness for the learning of school-relevant information such as foreign language vocabularies (see Pressley, Levin, & Delaney, 1982). This applied research found that the mental imagery strategy, called the *keyword method* was indeed successful for learning school information. Figure 1.1 provides a schematic illustration of the use of the keyword method for acquiring Spanish vocabulary items. Additional applied research has extended our knowledge about the effectiveness of the imagery learning strategy across different kinds of school materials including simple matching activities (e.g., states and capitals, cities and products) and memory for story ideas (e.g., Levin, Morrison, McGivern, Mastropieri, & Scruggs, 1986). Finally, instructional material for classroom application has been developed based on outcomes from the applied research.

Program evaluation research

A final type of research is *program evaluation*. Such studies relevant to human development evaluate programs, innovations, and social reforms that occur in education, mental health institutions, and governmental programs. The following citations illustrate program evaluation research:

**Figure 1.1
Illustration of the keyword method for learning a Spanish vocabulary**

The *keyword method* can be used to learn the English translations for Spanish words. The procedure consists of the three steps illustrated:

Step 1. List to-be-learned Spanish words with English translations (e.g., Spanish **perro** = English **dog**).

Step 2. Identify an English word that sounds like each Spanish word. This new word is called a *keyword* (a good keyword for **perro** is the English word **pear**).

Step 3. Generate a sentence and/or a visual image that links the referents of the keyword and the English word in an interaction (e.g., The **dog** eats the **pear**).

Perro = Dog
Perro   Pear
The dog eats the pear.

Perro = Dog

Honig, A. S. (1983). Evaluation of infant/toddler intervention programs. *Studies in Educational Evaluation, 8,* 305–316.

Mov, V., Sherwood, S. S., & Gutkin, C. (1986). A national study of residential care for the aged. *The Gerontologist, 26,* 405–417.

Weikart, T. (1982). Preschool education for disadvantaged children. In J. Travers & R. Light (Eds.), *Learning from experience: Evaluating early childhood demonstration programs.* Washington, D.C.: National Academy Press, 1982.

Programs can be viewed as experiments designed to achieve certain outcomes (Campbell, 1969). One example is the Head Start Program that is targeted at children from low-income families. Program evaluation is necessary to determine if the programs are having their intended effects. If not, program modification is required or alternate programs should be tried.

A major focus of program evaluation research has been on *outcome evaluations:* Did the program have the intended positive impact? Such evaluations may also include analysis of cost effectiveness and consideration of unintended side-effects. Advances in the field now call for evaluation in initial phases of program planning and execution (see Rossi, Freeman, & Wright, 1979).

Conclusion

<u>Distinctions between basic, applied, and evaluation research</u> have been considered. Different goals are addressed by researchers who conduct the different kinds of research. However, the use of scientific methods characterizes the approach to understanding in each research area. The remainder of this book provides detailed consideration of the various methods, tactics, and strategies available for the scientific study of human development and family relations.

SUMMARY

Scientific research provides the tools that help us understand human development and family relations. The four major goals of scientific research are (1) to describe behavior, (2) to identify causes and explanations for behavior, (3) to predict behavior, and (4) to apply scientific findings. The advantage of the scientific approach over other ways of knowing about the world (e.g., authority and intuition) is that it provides an objective set of rules for gathering and evaluating information. Furthermore, the scientific method encourages us to be skeptical of claims until we carefully evaluate the merits of the underlying scientific data. Finally, the three categories of research in human development and family relations are (1) basic research, (2) applied research, and (3) evaluation research.

STUDY QUESTIONS

1. Why is it important for someone in human development and family relations to have knowledge of research methods?
2. Distinguish between the following objectives of the scientific approach: description, determination of causes and explanations, prediction, and application.
3. How is the scientific approach different from other ways of gaining knowledge about human development and family relations?
4. Provide examples of basic, applied, and program evaluation research.

CHAPTER 2

The Origins of Scientific Inquiry

CAREER PROFILE

Linda P. Acredolo/Journal Editor

Linda holds a B.A. in Psychology from Bucknell University and a Ph.D. in Child Development from the Institute of Child Development, University of Minnesota. She is a Professor of Developmental Psychology at the University of California, Davis. Her professional activities fall into three categories: teaching, research, and her work as an Associate Editor of the journal of *Child Development*.

"As a teacher I provide students with an exciting overview of the major theories and research in the field. As a researcher, my primary interests are in the development of spatial orientation in very young children and the development of communication skills. This latter interest stemmed from my discovery in my own infant of a tendency to spontaneously develop gestures to represent objects symbolically. Finally, as an editor I bear responsibility for deciding which papers from my colleagues will be published in the journal. I read each manuscript carefully and solicit evaluations from authorities in the field. The challenge is to be sure that the review process is fair and constructive. I enjoy my role a great deal. Not only do I learn about the new and exciting discoveries being made in my field, but I also get to know many of the researchers themselves on a personal level."

Linda offers the following recommendations for students in human development and family relations: (1) "Develop a strong knowledge of and appreciation for statistics and good experimental design. This background will greatly enhance your ability to evaluate both research findings of others and individual observations of your own." (2) "Be observant. Even though you think you know everything there is to know, you may be surprised. That's what happened to me as I watched my daughter Katie begin to communicate: I gained insight into a fascinating and previously unexplored facet of early communicative behavior."

Suppose you wanted to conduct a research project. Where would you begin? Where do scientists come up with their ideas? How can you find out about other people's ideas and research on human development? In this chapter, we explore some sources of scientific ideas.

SOURCES OF IDEAS

Scientific researchers study an enormous variety of questions about human development and family relations. Where do these questions come from? As we will see, the process does not necessarily begin with a trip to the university library: Idea sources are all around us.

Common sense, clichés, and adages

One body of knowledge that can yield testable ideas is your own common sense. Such "logical" areas to delve into for ideas include the things we all believe to be true or that our grandmothers may have told us. Researchers often prefer to work with ideas that run *counter* to what is deemed as common sense. However, testing a "common sense" adage can be valuable, because such clichéd notions don't always prove to be correct. An entire line of research on the effects of physical punishment has been inspired by the Victorian warning "Spare the rod and spoil the child!" Another saying has prompted a tremendous amount of debate and research on the effects of early experience in child development: "As the twig is bent, so grows the tree."

Educational researchers might wonder whether it is really true that "A picture is worth 1,000 words." Jean Mandler and her associates (Mandler & Johnson, 1976; Mandler & Ritchey, 1977; Mandler & Robinson, 1978) found that the accuracy with which we remember pictures depends greatly on the type of information we are trying to remember and the nature of the test. A *recognition test*, in which several pictures are shown and we must pick out the original, can be easy or difficult depending on the similarity between the target picture and the new pictures (called *distractors*). Under some conditions, our memory for certain kinds of pictorial information can be quite poor, and we are heavily influenced by the familiarity of the scene. Extending these counterintuitive findings to the field of education, you might wonder whether it is always a good idea to add pictures to textbooks. This question has engendered a great deal of research: Sometimes pictures are helpful; sometimes they are not (see review by Levin, 1983). These examples show how entire research paths have been inspired by "common sense" notions.

Curiosity and serendipity

Sometimes the best research ideas come from our own experiences. For example, we can become intensely curious about something important in our own lives, and we can begin to study it. Or sometimes a serendipitous (lucky or fortuitous) event occurs that provides an opportunity for a research project.

One example of research that stems from personal experience is a study of the families of older women who are returning to college (Ballmer & Cozby, 1981). Ballmer was a returning student. Her own experiences in terms of changing roles within her family and new interactions and interests at the university inspired her to study other women who returned to college. Her curiosity led her to the library to find out what others had said about this topic, to conduct interview and questionnaire studies, and to investigate the family environments of women who returned to college.

Serendipity was responsible for a study on moral judgments and attitudes toward the pardon of former President Richard Nixon (Woll & Cozby, 1976). The authors shared an office and taught the same course. As luck would have it, former President Gerald Ford pardoned Nixon for his role in the Watergate cover-up, just as the researchers were about to discuss theories of moral thinking in their classes. They decided to "connect" these two events by giving a moral judgment scale and an attitude measure to their classes (as well as to a broader sample of students). The results were used to help illustrate several concepts and issues in the course; they also provided some important insights into the meaning of the moral judgment scale, which was ultimately reported in a journal.

Observation of the world around us

Current events reported in the news media typically cover political and economic news, world affairs, and local events. However, there is almost always a current event issue related to human development. In recent years, people have been concerned about the effects of day care on child development, whether aluminum causes Alzheimer's disease, the causes and prevention of family violence and child abuse, whether exceptional intellectual growth can be produced via infant-enrichment programs, and so forth. All of these issues can be approached empirically, that is, with research designed to address specific questions. In the 1980s, for example, demographers observed a trend for some women to delay starting their families until their mid-thirties. A natural research question concerns the effects of early versus later parenthood on both child development and on the parents themselves.

Popular periodicals frequently feature such human development issues. To take a rather sensational and controversial example, in 1986 *People* magazine reported on a campaign launched by the Parents Music Resource Center (PMRC), a group organized by several legislators' wives in Washington, D.C. PMRC wished to ban radio broadcast of rock music songs that the group considered objectionable. Their concern was that the messages contained in the lyrics could harm impressionable teenagers by encouraging sex, drug use, and violence. A relevant research question is whether adolescents actually attend to and remember such lyrics. Two criminologists, Lorraine Prinsky and Jill Rosenbaum (1987) conducted a survey to study how well the lyrics were understood and remembered by teenagers. They asked honors students, private school students, public school students, and remedial students to name their three favorite songs and to explain in three or four sentences what the song was about. Only 7 percent of the students said that their favorite songs had anything to do with sex, violence, drugs, or Satan. Most had difficulty explaining the songs they liked, or they gave superficial explanations. The authors concluded that even for songs that adolescents listen to repeatedly, the messages in the lyrics are not automatically picked up. Their results suggested that the musical beat or overall sound of a recording is of greater interest to teenagers. Such data cast doubt on the theory that teenagers are adversely influenced by the lyrics in rock music. Such a theory would have to explain exactly how the lyrics make their impact, if they are so poorly attended, understood, and remembered. This example illustrates how empirical research is sometimes motivated by current controversies. It also illustrates how research data can cause us to reexamine our theories.

Theories

<u>Theories organize and explain a variety of specific facts.</u> Specific facts about behavior are not meaningful by themselves; thus, theories are needed to impose a framework on them. This framework makes the world more compre-

hensible by providing a few abstract concepts around which we can organize and explain a variety of behaviors. As an example, Erik Erikson's theory provides a general framework for understanding some of the major changes that occur during the life span. Another example is Jean Piaget's theory of equilibration that helps us understand the interaction between a baby's inborn maturational programs and his or her experiences with the external environment. Both Erikson's and Piaget's theories are examples of stage theories, which are especially relevant to developmental research. *Stage theories* propose that development follows a sequence of stages, each qualitatively different from the others.

Theories generate knowledge by focusing our thinking so that we notice new aspects of behavior—theories guide our observations of the world. Piaget's famous observations of his own infant children were thoroughly guided by his theoretical notions. Knowledge is generated by research that tests theories: A theory generates hypotheses about behavior, and the researcher conducts research to see if these hypotheses are correct. If the studies confirm the hypotheses, the theory is supported. A theory is never proven, though; research can provide support for the correctness of a theory, but it also reveals weaknesses in a theory and forces researchers to modify the theory or develop a better one. For example, even though Piaget has been the major theoretician on children's cognitive development, not all of Piaget's theories are supported by solid evidence. Researchers who use such discrepant findings to modify Piaget's original theories are sometimes known as "neo-Piagetians." Erikson's theories have been reexamined as well, and some theoreticians have proposed additional developmental stages to account for issues that become particularly important in mid-adulthood. New or revised theories generate their own set of research questions, and so forth.

Past research

Perhaps the most important ingredient in the process of idea generation is to have a certain amount of already established knowledge about a problem. Knowing the background of a given issue can save us from "reinventing the wheel," in case someone has already found the answer to our question. Previous knowledge about scientific techniques and tactics can suggest new approaches to specific problems. For example, signal-detection theory was first used to investigate how people perceive signals in noisy backgrounds (e.g., air traffic controllers). This approach was later adapted to the study of recognition memory by asking people to distinguish between events they've actually witnessed (signals) and similar events they have not (noise). In addition to suggesting approaches and technologies, a good base of knowledge can influence the kinds of questions asked: Knowing good questions about one issue can lead us to ask similar questions about a related issue. For example, many of the early studies of memory changes during the later adult years were conducted by people who had previously researched the question of how memory works in young adults.

In summary, there are many sources of ideas for research, ranging from formal scientific theories to hunches and ordinary observations. Now, let's examine how professionals communicate their ideas and findings, both to each other and to the public at large.

HOW SCIENTISTS COMMUNICATE

Professional societies

Researchers have established professional societies for purposes of communicating scientific knowledge and recognizing important accomplishments. Members of such organizations are professionals (and students) who share common interests and backgrounds. Holding conventions is perhaps the most important function of professional societies. Conventions enable researchers and practitioners from all over the world to exchange ideas face-to-face, to plan collaborative research, and to keep informed about the latest ideas and techniques. Another important function of professional societies is the publication of scholarly journals. Finally, some large and powerful organizations engage in political advocacy, attempting to influence the public or the government about a specific issue of concern such as educational reform, programs for health care of the elderly, the effects of unemployment on the mental health of family members, and so on.

The Society of Research in Child Development (SRCD) illustrates a professional organization in action. SRCD is the major organization for researchers in child development from a variety of related disciplines, including anthropology, ethology, medicine, sociology, psychiatry, nursing, audiology, nutrition, special education, behavioral pediatrics, psychology, and other allied fields. Its members include the leading child researchers in the world. To give you an idea of the breadth of interests of SRCD members, Table 2.1 lists the various panels of a recent SRCD convention. Note that the panels cover issues in infancy, early childhood, adolescence, families, and various applied topics.

Educators can join the American Educational Research Association (AERA). The American Sociological Association (ASA) is the major U.S. organization for sociologists, the American Anthropological Association (AAA) serves anthropologists, and the American Psychological Association (APA) serves both researchers and practitioners in all areas of psychology. In addition to these large, broadly based organizations, a number of smaller, more specific societies exist, including the Society for the Experimental Analysis of Behavior, the Behavior Genetics Association, the Cognitive Science Society, the Jean Piaget Society, and the International Conference on Infant Studies. Researchers who are interested in life-span issues can join the American Geriatrics Society or the Gerontological Society; and those interested in family studies can join the National Council on Family Relations.

It is often the case that ideas discussed at conventions are preliminary,

Table 2.1
Topics represented at a recent SRCD convention

Panel	1:	Infancy: Social and Emotional Processes
Panel	2:	Infancy: Perception, Cognition, Communication
Panel	3:	Sensory, Perceptual, and Motor Processes; Physiological and Biological Bases of Development
Panel	4:	Infants and Children at Risk
Panel	5:	Adolescence, Life Course Development
Panel	6:	Language and Development
		A: Phonology, syntax, semantics, and pragmatics
		B: Bilingualism, language disorder, exceptional language, assessment
Panel	7:	Cognition 1: Concepts, Space, Reasoning, Problem Solving
Panel	8:	Cognition 2: Attention, Learning, Memory
Panel	9:	Educational Issues: Intelligence, Learning or Language Disabilities, Reading, Writing, Mathematics
Panel	10:	Social Development and Behavior: Prosocial Behavior, Aggression, Play, Affective Development
Panel	11:	Social Cognition
Panel	12:	Family and Kinship
Panel	13:	Sociocultural and Ecological Contexts: Culture, Schools, Peers, Media
Panel	14:	Developmental Correlates of Gender, Ethnic Group
Panel	15:	Atypical Development: Psychopathology, Sensory or Motor Handicaps, Giftedness, Mental Retardation
Panel	16:	Methods, History, Theory
Panel	17:	Child Development Research and Social Policy
Panel	18:	Interdisciplinary and Other

tentative, or "in progress." When scientists wish to set down the results of their work in more permanent form, they communicate their ideas in books, journals, and other scientific publications.

Publishing

Books An important source for research knowledge consists of books that feature research reviews. These books are published roughly every few years, and they present a comprehensive review of the topics most important in the area, written by recognized leaders in their respective fields. The following are some examples of serial publications that publish research reviews:

Mussen's Handbook of Child Psychology

The Minnesota Symposia on Child Psychology

The Review of Child Development Research

New Directions for Child Development

Advances in Developmental Psychology

Advances in Child Development and Behavior

Life-Span Development and Behavior

Handbook of the Psychology of Aging

Journals on human development Of the dozens of journals in the human development field, you should know about a few leading publications

Table 2.2 Leading journals in human development and family relations

Adolescence	Journal of Child Language
American Journal of Community Psychology	Journal of Clinical Child Neuropsychology
American Journal of Orthopsychiatry	Journal of Clinical Psychology
Child Development	Journal of Divorce
Child Welfare	Journal of Early Adolescence
Cognition	Journal of Educational Psychology
Cognitive Development	Journal of Experimental Child Psychology
Contemporary Educational Psychology	Journal of Experimental Education
Developmental Psychobiology	Journal of Genetic Psychology
Developmental Psychology	Journal of Gerontology
Developmental Review	Journal of Learning Disabilities
Exceptional Children	Journal of Marriage and the Family
Experimental Aging Research	Journal of Mental Deficiency Research
Family & Child Mental Health Journal	Journal of Pediatric Psychology
Family Planning Perspectives	Journal of Psycholinguistic Research
Family Process	Merrill–Palmer Quarterly
Family Relations	Monographs of the Society for Research in Child Development
Genetic Psychology Monographs	Pediatrics
Gifted Child Quarterly	Psychology and Aging
Infant Behavior and Development	Psychology in the Schools
Intelligence	Reading Research Quarterly
International Journal of Aging and Human Development	Review of Educational Research
International Journal of Behavioral Development	Sex Roles
Human Development	Social Casework
Journal of Abnormal Child Psychology	Social Psychology Quarterly
Journal of Applied Behavior Analysis	Studies in Educational Evaluation
Journal of Applied Developmental Psychology	The Gerontologist
Journal of Autism and Developmental Disorders	Young Children

(Table 2.2). *Child Development* is published by the SRCD and it features both research reports and theoretical reviews of research with children. *Developmental Psychology* is published by the APA, and it covers the entire life span, including research with animals. *The Journal of Experimental Child Psychology* publishes articles that feature technically sophisticated experimental procedures and designs; most of the studies involve laboratory investigations rather than field observations. *Developmental Review* is a relatively new journal that publishes reviews of research on a wide variety of topics; some articles present new research along with reviews of previous studies. The *Journal of Educational Psychology* concentrates on topics relevant to learning, whether in the formal educational setting or not. The *Journal of Marriage and the Family* is published by the National Council on Family Relations. The *Journal of Gerontology* presents research on aging.

The peer review system in scientific publishing Have you ever wondered who decides what gets published? In high-quality books and journals, manuscripts are selected or rejected by the people most qualified to judge them—

other researchers in the same field. Linda Acredolo, presented in this chapter's career profile, has served as an editor of a major journal. Each journal has an editorial board of scientists who are active in their field of scholarship. These reviewers volunteer their time to read and evaluate drafts of their colleagues' work that is submitted for publication. Each manuscript is reviewed by an average of three experts who put in long hours considering the merits of the ideas, procedures, conclusions, and composition of the paper. Most good journals use a "blind" review process, wherein the author is not identified, so that this knowledge cannot influence the reviewers' judgments. It is extremely unusual for a manuscript to be accepted for publication exactly as is. In fact, high-quality journals routinely reject the majority of manuscripts because of various methodological and conceptual flaws. For many journals, a rejection rate exceeding 80 percent is common. Most of the manuscripts that are not rejected outright are returned to the author for revisions based on the reviewers' suggestions. Suggestions can range from minor revisions to clarify writing, to major reanalysis of the results, to the execution of additional research to bolster a weak case. Only after the revised manuscript satisfies the reviewers' concerns is it published.

The peer review system has several important consequences. First and foremost, it is designed as a quality-control system. Because the findings generated by research are meant to become part of the cumulative store of knowledge in the scientific community, it is essential that what is published passes rigorous tests of quality, validity, and clarity of communication. However, the review system also contributes to a major problem in information flow—*publication lag*. Major research projects may take a minimum of several months to carry out and write up. The review process can easily add another half a year or more before the manuscript is accepted for publication. Finally, the article is scheduled to appear in a future edition of the journal. Because of publication lag, scientists maintain active networks of colleagues for purposes of sharing early reports of noteworthy findings. National and regional conventions are a source of preliminary research reports to provide a preview of ongoing projects. At conventions, researchers share drafts of their manuscripts with others in their field. The most successful researchers have good contacts to help beat the publication lag.

Literature searching

Abstracts of scientific publications Because of the sheer volume of published scientific work, a person who wishes to locate information about a specific topic is faced with a staggering task. Fortunately, scientists have worked out systems for organizing and retrieving information, which are known as *abstracts* (brief summaries).

Psychological Abstracts publishes "nonevaluative summaries of the world's literature in psychology and related disciplines." It is published monthly by the APA, and each volume contains approximately 12,000 abstracts of published articles. To find articles on a specific topic, you must use the index at the end of each volume.

The summaries of the articles are brief descriptions of the research findings. On the basis of this information, you can determine the relevance of an article for your purposes. The reference section of the library has abstracts for many disciplines:

Child Development Abstracts and Bibliography
ERIC, Resources in Education
Gerontology Abstracts
Sociological Abstracts
Family Studies Abstracts
Criminal Justice Abstracts
Women Studies Abstracts

The following example illustrates how to use *Psychological Abstracts:* First, locate the index that accompanies each volume. The index is organized by subject category. Some categories, such as "Preschool Age Children," "Memory," or "Aged," are quite large; other categories, such as "Runaway Behavior" or "Heterozygotic Twins," contain only a few references. The more general the category, the greater the number of references. As a general rule, the most efficient search is achieved when the category has been narrowed to be as specific as possible.

Suppose you are interested in sex roles and how they are presented in children's reading materials. You locate an index for *Psychological Abstracts*, say Volume 62. In the index, you find a category labeled "Sex Role Attitudes," in which many articles are listed alphabetically by description. Each listing describes the content of the study and gives an abstract number. Usually not all the articles listed are of interest. From the larger set, you select listings that seem relevant to you, for example:

1. high vs. low stereotyped TV cartoons, sex role stereotyping, 5–6 yr old females, 13208
2. occupational sex role orientation, sex differences in educational & career orientation, high school students, 14933
3. male vs. female stereotypic vs. reversed sex role content in reading materials, choice & recognition of sex traits, 5th graders, 3398
4. self-esteem & sex identity feelings, negative vs. positive attitudes toward opposite sex, 3rd & 4th graders, 11396

The third description seems most relevant to your topic, so you can locate it in the appropriate volume of abstracts (in this case, Volume 62). The abstracts are listed in numerical order. Article 3398 is a typical abstract:

3398. Koblinsky, Sally G.; Cruse, Donna F. & Sugawara, Alan I. (Oregon State U) Sex role stereotypes and children's memory for story content. *Child Development*, 1978(Jun), Vol 49(2), 452–458. —Examined children's memory for stereotypic and reversed stereotypic sex role content in their reading materials. In Exp I, lists of traits and behaviors deemed typical of boys and girls were obtained from 29 male and 25 female 5th graders. Four experimental stories were developed from these lists of stereotypic items, each depicting a male and female character who exhibited an equal number of masculine and feminine characteristics. In Exp II, 24 5th graders of each sex read 2 stories and were administered a choice-recognition test. Both sexes remembered more of the masculine sex-typed characteristics of male characters and more of the feminine sex-typed characteristics of female characters. Ss were less proficient in remembering trait than behavioral descriptions and were particularly unlikely to remember the feminine traits of male characters. It is speculated that children use the sex role stereotype as an organizational framework in reading comprehension. Implications for children's reading programs are discussed. —*Journal abstract*

If the abstract suggests that the article is relevant to your topic of interest, the next step is to find the original article:

1. Check to see if your library subscribes to the journal; if so, read it in the library and take notes or make a photocopy, especially of the references.
2. Many libraries have an interlibrary loan policy so that a copy of the article from another library can be ordered.
3. Write to the researcher requesting a reprint of the article and copies of any related material; many researchers are happy to provide free reprints as long as their supplies last.

The key article approach to literature searching Abstracts are useful if you are preparing a comprehensive review and wish to cover the field exhaustively. However, for specific research problems, a more efficient strategy is often to seek only those articles that are most relevant to your specific issue. Figure 2.1 diagrams this process. The best way to start such a search is to find a recent *key article* in an area, which is an article that people would say makes a substantial contribution to the field. Such articles are commonly cited in book chapters, review articles, or in research reports. Another way to find a classic study is to ask an expert. Researchers commonly ask one another "What's a good reference?" in a given area. They are looking for a key article to help them search forward and backward in time to survey the literature in the most efficient manner.

Looking backward in time can easily be accomplished by using references cited in the key article. Those articles contain other references, and so forth. But, how do you search forward in time? How do you find out what has happened *since* the key article was published? To accomplish this trick, you use the *Social Science Citation Index (SSCI)*. This publication references articles published in all areas of social science. Its primary function is to list articles that have cited a specific key article as a reference. For example, the 1985 edition lists nearly 1,000 citations to dozens of books and articles by Jean Piaget. More typically, each article receives a small number of citations during the period covered. For example, the Koblinsky, Cruse, and Sugawara article we looked up in *Psychological Abstracts* was published in 1978. To find a list of articles published since that time that cite the Koblinsky article,

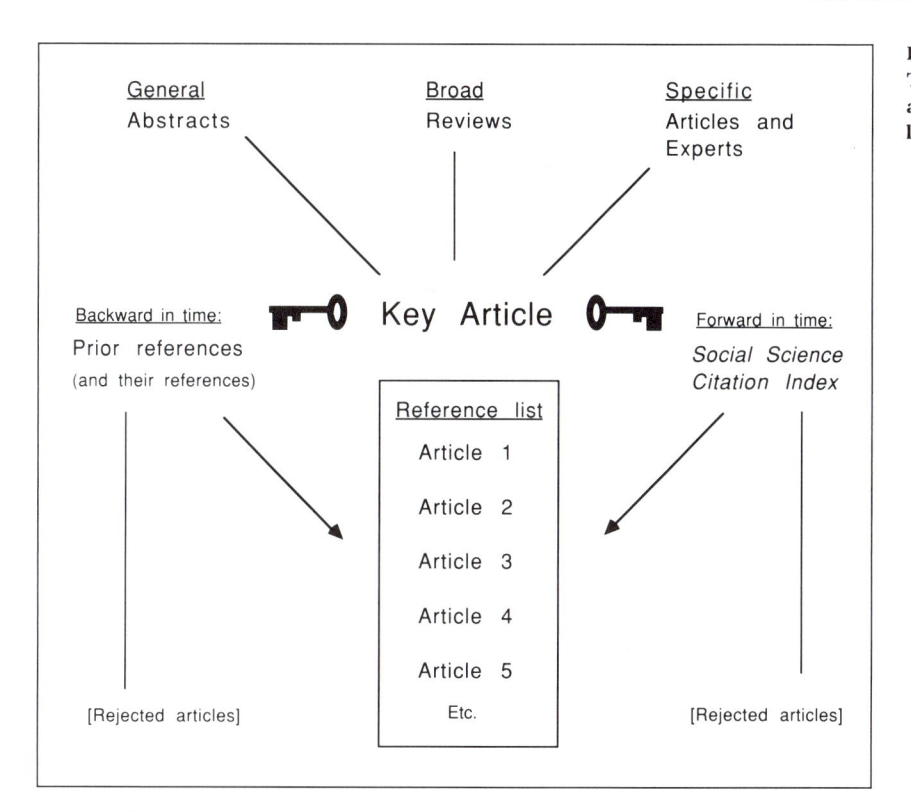

Figure 2.1
The key article approach to literature search

```
General            Broad              Specific
Abstracts          Reviews            Articles and
                                      Experts
       \              |              /
        \             |             /
         \            |            /
Backward in time:   🔑 Key Article 🔑   Forward in time:
Prior references                         Social Science
(and their references)                   Citation Index
         |          Reference list       |
         |          Article 1            |
         |          Article 2            |
         ↓          Article 3            ↓
                    Article 4
                    Article 5
[Rejected articles]   Etc.        [Rejected articles]
```

you must select a *SSCI* volume that is more recent than 1978, say 1985. *SSCI* citations are listed alphabetically by author. Looking under Koblinsky, we find:

KOBLINSKY SG
    78 CHILD DEV 49 452

Auth.	Journal	Vol.	Pg.	Yr.
FISK WR	DEVEL PSYCH	21	481	85
HALPERN DF	SEX ROLES	12	363	85
NEWMAN J	CHILD ST J	15	107	85
ZARBATAN L	DEVEL PSYCH	21	97	85

    Each entry gives the first author, journal, volume, first page, and year of an article that cites the Koblinsky study. It should provide enough information for you to be able to locate the new articles. In this fashion, you can discover research that is tangential to, inspired by, or critical of the key article. Moreover, each of *these* articles has references that can be investigated. One or more of these recent articles may become a new key article, and so the process continues. At first a literature search may seem discouragingly limitless, but sooner or later (depending on the scope of the topic), the researcher begins to find fewer and fewer new citations on the topic. At some point, you may feel fairly confident that you have located all the relevant and most of the tangential articles on your topic. You are now an expert on your topic.

Anatomy of a research article

Now that you have selected a research article, what can you expect to find in it? As you can see by referring to the article presented in Appendix A, journal articles usually have six sections:

1. An abstract similar to the ones found in *Psychological Abstracts*
2. An introduction that explains the problem under investigation and the specific hypothesis being tested
3. A method section that describes in detail the exact procedures used to test the hypothesis
4. A results section in which the findings are presented, usually with statistical analysis
5. A discussion section in which the researchers may speculate on the broader implications of the results, propose alternative explanations for the results, discuss reasons why a specific hypothesis was not supported, or suggest directions for future research on the problem
6. A list of references

Let's discuss each of these sections.

Abstract The *abstract* is a summary of the research report and is usually no more than 150 words in length. The abstract should contain basic information about each of the major sections of the article, the background (introduction), method, results, and implications of the study. The abstract is meant to be fully self-contained in that you should be able to understand the gist of the study without having to refer to the article itself. This is important because, as we have seen, abstracts are often published separately from their articles. Finally, the abstract should feature what is most important and interesting about the article, so that readers will be enticed to take a look at the article itself.

Introduction In the *introduction*, the researcher describes the problem that has been investigated. Past research and theories relevant to the problem are described in detail. The specific expectations of the researcher are given, often as formal hypotheses. In other words, the investigator introduces the research in a logical format that shows how past research and theory are connected to the research problem and to the expected results.

Method The *method section* is divided into subsections; the number of subsections is determined by the author and depends on the complexity of the research design. Sometimes the first subsection presents an overview of the study's design, to prepare the reader for the material that follows. The next subsection describes the characteristics of the subjects: Were they male, female, or were both sexes included? What was the average age? How many subjects participated? Did these subjects have any unusual characteristics?

For example, if alcoholics and nonalcoholics are being compared, what criteria were used to identify subjects in the two groups? The next subsection details the procedure used in the study. In this section, the author describes exactly what the subjects experienced when they participated in the study—the instructions they were given, the situation they were exposed to, the questionnaires they filled out, the amount of time allotted for the task, and so on. Readers need to know every detail necessary to carry out the procedure exactly as in the original research. Information about the procedure is often required to make sense of the results; indeed, there have been occasions when different results from two similar studies could be explained on the basis of a seemingly minor procedural point. The remaining subsections describe other important aspects of the study such as the apparatus or testing materials used. The number and type of subsections depend on the research topic and the journal's specifications.

Results In the *results section*, the author presents the findings, usually in three ways. First there is a description in narrative form. For example: "It was found that children who watched Mr. Rogers' Neighborhood showed an increase in prosocial behavior." Second, the results are usually presented in statistical language. Third, the material is often depicted in tables and/or graphs, which summarize the data in visual form.

The statistical terminology of the results section may seem incomprehensible at first. However, lack of knowledge about the calculations is not really a deterrent to understanding the article or the logic behind the statistics. The researcher merely uses statistics as a tool for evaluating the outcome of the study.

Discussion In the *discussion section*, the author talks about the research from various perspectives. Did the results support the hypothesis? If they did, the author should give all of the possible explanations for the results and should discuss why one explanation is superior to another. If the hypothesis has not been supported, the author should offer suggestions to explain this outcome. What might have been wrong with the methodology, the hypothesis, or both? The author may discuss how the results fit in with past research on the topic. This section may also include suggestions for possible practical applications of the research and for future studies on the topic.

References Scientists make a practice of giving credit to their colleagues for previous work, products, and even ideas when they are especially noteworthy. These *references* set each new study into the context of the work from which it derives and gives the scientific method its continuity.

How to read an article Research papers are written according to a highly constrained, formal pattern. The style is deliberate, enabling rapid and efficient scientific communication. As you become more experienced in reading research articles, you will become more familiar with the pattern and will be able to use it rapidly to extract the content you are looking for. For a first reading, experts rarely read journal articles straight through from start to finish: They usually read the abstract first, then skim the article to decide whether they can use the information provided; if so, they review the article in detail. Because they are familiar with the format, they can concentrate on only the sections of most interest to them. For instance, if they are interested in a procedural point, they might read the method section first; if they are interested in the statistical treatment, they may skip directly to the results section. Finally, articles should be read with a critical eye. Even though most articles have passed through the peer review process, research projects are rarely perfect in every respect. Students often generate the most useful criticisms.

SUMMARY

Researchers select variables to study from a variety of sources. Common sense, clichés, and adages have provided numerous interesting questions for social scientists to test. Curiosity and serendipity have also led to a number of surprising or fortuitous findings. Observation of the world around us sometimes reveals interesting trends that inspire further investigation. Finally, and more formally, theories and past research provide a structured, programmatic foundation for many of the research questions pursued. Theories guide future research with a proposed framework by which we can organize and explain a variety of behaviors. By examining past research, we can identify questions that remain to be answered.

Researchers communicate in a variety of ways, ranging from presentations of work in progress at professional conventions, to research reports on specific projects published in books and journals, to broad reviews of entire research areas published in resource books. Publication of scientific materials is governed by a system of peer review, in which manuscripts are judged by researchers in the same field (often "blind" to the author's identity).

Published research in the area of human development and family relations can be located in a variety of ways: by consulting specialized books or journals, by consulting abstract resources, or by asking experts. One of the most efficient ways to begin a literature review is to find a key article and search backward in time (using its references) and forward in time (using the *Social Science Citation Index*).

Since journal articles represent a major means of disseminating research findings, most articles follow a prescribed format. An abstract presents a brief summary of the study. The introduction explains the problem under investigation and the specific hypothesis being tested. A method section describes the exact procedures used to test the hypothesis. A results section presents the findings, usually with statistical analysis. A discussion section presents the researchers' speculations about the broader implications of the results. The references guide the reader to other research in the same area. This traditional article format enables rapid and efficient communication of ideas, methods, and findings. In Chapter 3 we turn to a more specific discussion of how relationships between variables are studied.

STUDY QUESTIONS

1. Describe five sources of ideas for research. Do you think any one source is better than the others or that one source is used more frequently than the others? Why?
2. Describe the two functions of a theory.
3. Name three professional organizations that someone with your interests might wish to join.
4. What is the "key article" approach to literature searching? Describe how it is possible to search forward in time from a key article.
5. What are the six major sections in a research article in a journal?

CHAPTER 3

Studying Relationships Between Variables

CAREER PROFILE

David K. Slay / Child Guidance Center Clinical Director

David holds B.A. and M.A. degrees in General/Experimental Psychology from California State University, Long Beach, and a Ph.D. in Clinical Psychology from the California School of Professional Psychology. He is Clinical Program Director of Child Guidance Centers, Inc., in Fullerton, California.

"One of the more challenging aspects of my work is the range of ages and developmental stages I encounter while helping children, adolescents, parents, and families resolve emotional and behavioral problems. Treatment plans require consideration of patients' psychological characteristics, such as cognitive development, emotional maturity, and personality, and psychosocial variables, such as family relations and social/interpersonal skills. My job includes a range of activities, such as direct clinical work (e.g., psychological testing), clinical case supervision and training of psychology interns, program development, administration, evaluation, and some research. Because the agency is funded by community support and tax dollars, we need to demonstrate our effectiveness. We do so by conducting studies that utilize operational definitions, explicit procedures, analysis and interpretation of actual data, and communication to others about what we are doing and why it works. Our agency is also a consumer of research findings. This information is provided through continuing education programs, monthly in-service training, and workshops.

"It seems to me that most of the major fields leading to careers in human development or family relations are a mixture of 'science' and 'practice.' In psychology, for example, many people are engaged in and think entirely in terms of scientific investigation—doing research, generating results, and advancing knowledge for others to learn from and apply. Others work entirely as practitioners—practicing the 'art' of psychotherapy or applying the scientific results of psychology in a range of settings. Appreciation of this continuum from science to practice allows you to place yourself in terms of your own personality and interests."

As noted in Chapter 1, scientists seek to describe, explain, and predict behavior. To achieve these goals, scientists conduct research investigations in which they study the behaviors that interest them. Most often, their research focuses on the relationships between variables. Examples include the relationships among age and play behavior, mental imagery and learning, viewing television violence and aggression, and health status and life satisfaction among the elderly. This chapter explores such relationships and the fundamental procedures for studying them. First, however, we must define what we mean by a "variable."

SCIENTIFIC VARIABLES

In the career profile, David Slay noted that he must consider various factors such as emotional maturity and social/interpersonal skills when he develops treatment plans. These factors are variables David has identified and found to be important in his clinical work. A *variable* is a general class or category of objects, events, situations, responses, or characteristics of a person. It is easy to think of characteristics of a person such as age, socioeconomic status, gender, marital status, health, or personality characteristics such as extraversion or self-esteem. Situations may include conditions under which learning occurs, and responses may include a person's recall of material that has been presented earlier.

Within the general category, specific instances will vary (hence the term "variable"). Thus for each variable, there are levels or values: For example, for gender, the values are male and female. For any variable that is a characteristic of people, people will vary. Sometimes, there are a limited number of values or levels—such as gender or marital status. Sometimes there are many values—self-esteem can range from very low to moderate to very high, and income level can have even more values. The main point is that a variable refers to the general class, and there are specific instances that characterize each variable one might study.

An example illustrates situation and response variables. Foellinger and Trabasso (1977) wondered whether children would recall commands better in a situation in which they are shown what to do as opposed to a situation in which they are told what to do. The *situational variable* is the method of giving the command—telling versus showing (note that there are two levels in this case). The *response variable* is recall of the commands. In a study designed to test whether the variables are related, the researchers gave eight commands either verbally or through an overt demonstration. The results showed that the children recalled more commands when they were provided with a demonstration.

OPERATIONAL DEFINITIONS

In actual research, the investigator must decide on a method to study the variables. Since a variable is an abstract concept, it must be translated into concrete forms of observation or manipulation. Thus, variables such as learning condition, life satisfaction, self-esteem, intelligence, marital satisfaction, or recall must be defined in terms of the specific method used to measure or manipulate the variable. Scientists refer to the *operational definition* of a variable, which is a definition of the variable in terms of the concrete operational techniques the researcher uses in measuring or manipulating it.

Operational definitions of variables are necessary to study them scientifically. Note that there is often no single, exclusive operational definition for a given variable. Even a simple variable, such as gender, may be operationally defined in terms of a person's report of being male or female, or it can be defined in terms of the results of a complex medical test of chromosomal material (recall some of the controversies that have occurred in recent international sporting events!).

To illustrate the issue of operational definitions further, consider a manager of a children's museum who wants to know which exhibits children find most interesting. Children might be asked to rate the exhibits. In this case, "interest" could be defined as a score on a rating scale in which "1" equals no interest and "5" equals extreme interest. A less direct measure of interest would be to keep track of how fast the floor tiles wear out next to the various exhibits. This indirect measure was actually applied at the Chicago Museum of Science and Industry (Webb, Campbell, Schwartz, Sechrest, & Grove, 1981). The tiles next to the chick-hatching exhibit had to be replaced every six weeks; elsewhere the tiles lasted for years! Even though one could argue about which measure of "interest" is better, it is still the case that the interest variable was measured adequately, although differently, in both cases. The operations of recording responses on a rating scale and counting worn floor tiles are both perfectly well specified. Anyone can record the results and arrive at an accurate measurement. Researchers must always translate their variables into specific operations, so that the variables can be studied by the researcher and the procedures can be understood and replicated by other researchers.

The task of operationally defining a variable forces the scientist to discuss abstract concepts in concrete terms. The process sometimes results in the realization that the chosen variable is too vague to study. Vagueness does not mean that the concept is meaningless, rather, it means that systematic research is not possible until the concept can be operationally defined. Sometimes the scientific study of a concept depends on the development of something else that makes an operational definition possible. For instance, the scientific study of hearing in infants was made possible by the electroencephalogram, which shows changes in brain wave patterns when a stimulus such as a sound is presented to the infant.

Operational definitions also facilitate communication of our ideas to others. For example, if someone wishes to tell you about aggression, you need to know what the person means. *Aggression* could be operationally defined in such ways as (1) the number and duration of shocks delivered to another person, (2) the number of times a child punches an inflated toy clown, (3) frequency of crimes committed according to recent social statistics, (4) spousal abuse, or (5) scores on a personality measure of aggression, among other possibilities. Communication with another person and scientific progress are facilitated when we agree on exactly what we mean when we use the term aggression in the context of research on the variable.

There is rarely a single, infallible method for operationally defining a variable; a variety of methods may be available, each of which has advantages and disadvantages. Researchers must decide which method is best for studying a specific problem. Since no one method is perfect, it is clear that complete understanding of any variable involves studying the variable using a variety of operational definitions.

TYPES OF RELATIONSHIPS

When a researcher tries to discover whether there is a relationship between two variables, he or she wants to know whether the levels of the two variables vary systematically together. As age increases, does the amount of co-

CHAPTER 3 STUDYING RELATIONSHIPS BETWEEN VARIABLES

operative play increase as well? Does viewing television result in greater aggressiveness? Does poor health result in lower life satisfaction among the elderly? The most common relationships found in research are

The linear positive
The linear negative
The curvilinear relationship
The situation in which there is no relationship between the variables

These relationships are best illustrated by line graphs that show the way changes in one variable are accompanied by changes in a second variable. The four graphs in Figure 3.1 show these four types of relationships.

Figure 3.1 Four common types of relationships found in research: (a) a positive linear relationship, (b) a negative linear relationship, (c) a curvilinear relationship, and (d) no relationship

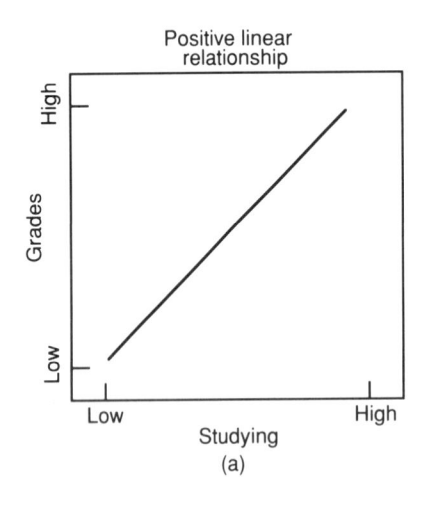

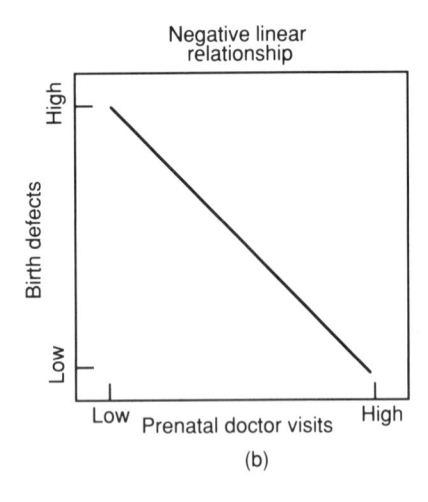

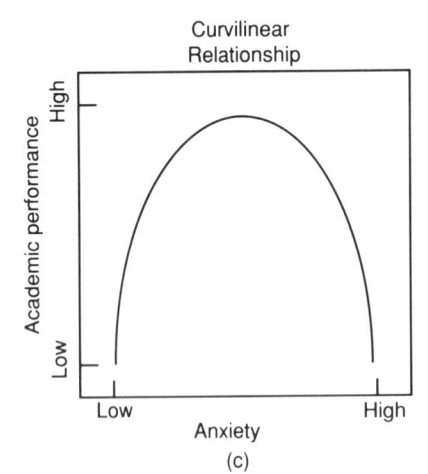

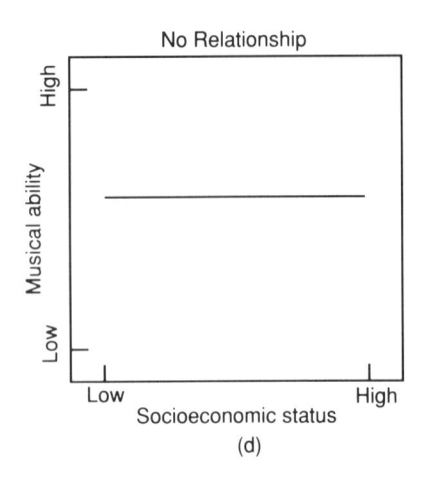

32

Positive linear relationship

In a *positive linear relationship*, increases in the values of one variable are accompanied by increases in the values of the second variable. Figure 3.1a illustrates the positive relationship between studying and grades. In such a graph, there is a horizontal axis and a vertical axis. Values of the first variable are placed on the horizontal axis, labeled from low to high. Values of the second variable are placed on the vertical axis. The figure shows that greater amounts of studying are associated with higher grades. You might try to think about other possible positive relationships: Do you think there is a positive relationship between health and life satisfaction? Between frequency of sexual intercourse and marital satisfaction?

Negative linear relationship

Variables can also be negatively related. In a *negative linear relationship*, increases in the values of one variable are accompanied by *decreases* in the values of the other variable. Figure 3.1b illustrates a negative relationship between prenatal doctor visits and birth defects. As the number of doctor visits increase, the incidence of birth defects decreases. The two variables are systematically related, just as in a positive relationship; only the direction of the relationship is reversed.

Curvilinear relationship

In a *curvilinear relationship*, increases in the values of one variable are accompanied by both increases and decreases in the values of the other variable. In other words, there is a positive relationship when you look at a portion of the values of one variable, and there is a negative relationship for the other values of the variable. Figure 3.1c shows a curvilinear relationship between anxiety and academic performance. This particular relationship is called an *inverted-U relationship*. Increases in anxiety are accompanied by increases in performance, but only up to a point (i.e., a little bit of anxiety helps). The relationship then becomes negative; further increases in anxiety are accompanied by *decreases* in academic performance.

No relationship

When there is no relationship between the two variables, the graph is simply a flat line. Figure 3.1d illustrates the relationship between socioeconomic status of one's parents and one's musical ability. Unrelated variables vary independently of one another. As we look at families with increasing socioeconomic status, we do not find any specific increase in the musical talent of the children.

These graphs illustrate several kinds of "shapes"; almost any shape can describe the relationship between two variables. Other relationships are described by more complicated shapes than those depicted in Figure 3.1. Remember, these are general patterns of relationships: Even if, in general, there is a positive linear relationship, that does not necessarily mean that everyone who scores high on one variable will also score high on the second variable. Individual deviations may stray from the general pattern.

There are two ways of studying the relationship between variables: the correlational method and the experimental method. The remainder of this chapter explores the differences between these two approaches.

THE CORRELATIONAL METHOD

When the *correlational method* is used, the researcher observes (or measures)[1] the variable or variables of interest. That is, behavior is observed as it occurs naturally. This method is "nonexperimental" in nature, because observation is the sole basis for obtaining data. Such observation may be achieved by asking people to describe their behavior, by directly observing behavior, or even by examining various public records such as census data. In a correlational study of the relationship between two variables, the researcher would operationally define the two variables and measure people on those variables. Thus, in a study of the relationship between viewing television violence and aggression, a researcher might (1) ask children to list their favorite television programs and (2) have teachers rate the children on their aggressiveness at school. The researcher would then use some index of violence in various television programs to yield a score for each child on preference for watching violence on television. Finally, the researcher would ask whether there is a relationship between the two variables: Is it the case that children whose favorite programs are more violent are in fact more aggressive?

Suppose such a study is conducted and it is found that there is a positive relationship between television violence preference and aggressiveness. You might be tempted at this point to conclude that watching violent television *causes* aggressiveness. However, such a conclusion would be premature because of two problems that are associated with the correlational method: direction of cause and effect and extraneous "third" variables (Figure 3.2).

Direction of cause and effect

One potential problem in any investigation of the relationship between two variables is determining which variable caused the other. In studying the relationship between television violence and aggression, did watching television cause the aggressive behavior, or is it possible that aggressive people like to watch violent programs? In the study of these two variables using the

---

1. The terms *observation* and *measurement* are used interchangeably throughout the text.

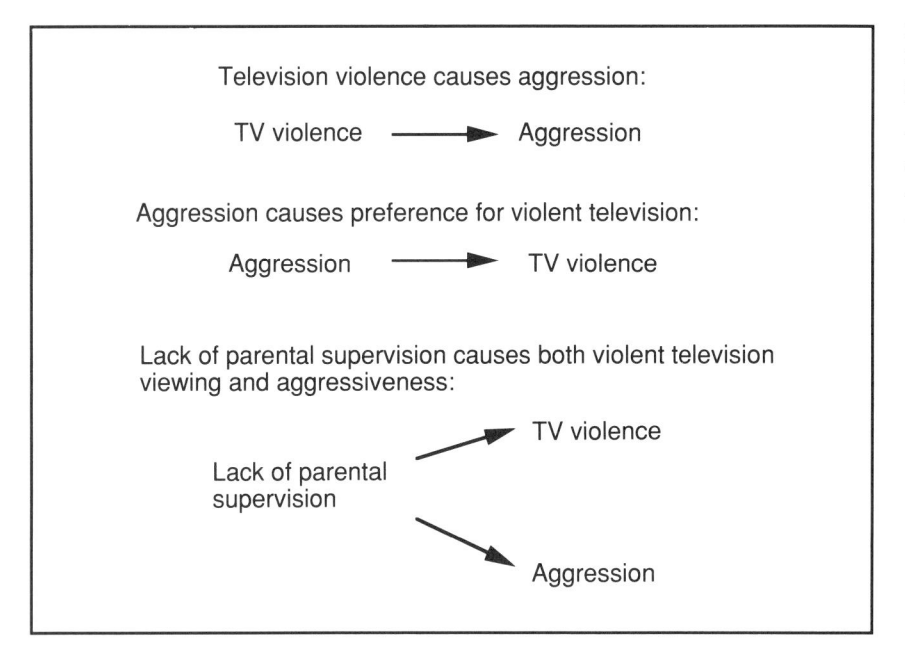

Figure 3.2 Possible reasons for a relationship between television violence viewing and aggression in a correlational study

Television violence causes aggression:

TV violence ⟶ Aggression

Aggression causes preference for violent television:

Aggression ⟶ TV violence

Lack of parental supervision causes both violent television viewing and aggressiveness:

Lack of parental supervision ⟶ TV violence
Lack of parental supervision ⟶ Aggression

correlational method, it is impossible to determine which variable caused the other: Because both variables were measured at a single point in time, you cannot say whether it was the violence that produced the aggressiveness or whether aggressiveness determines television violence preferences. This problem is a general one of the correlational method. If you measured health and life satisfaction among a group of elderly individuals and found that poor health is associated with low satisfaction, the direction of cause and effect would be ambiguous. Does poor health lead to low life satisfaction, or does dissatisfaction with life cause people to be more susceptible to health problems?

The "third-variable" problem

The second problem with the correlational method is the possibility that some other "third" extraneous variable could be responsible for an observed relationship between the variables. In a correlational study, it is possible that the two variables are not directly related at all. For example, in a correlational study on television violence and aggression, an observed relationship between the variables might be due to extraneous variables such as amount of parental supervision (e.g., children with little parental supervision watch more violent television *and* are more aggressive). Thus, lack of parental supervision could lead to all sorts of "undesirable" behaviors including watching violent television and aggression. The viewing of violent television and aggressiveness may not be directly related.

Again, it should be emphasized that the third-variable problem is a general one of the correlational method. In a study of health and life satisfaction, it is possible that a third variable such as marital status is responsible for the results—perhaps being married is responsible for both better health and higher life satisfaction.

THE EXPERIMENTAL METHOD

The second approach to the study of relationships between variables is called the *experimental method.* In contrast to the correlational method, the experimental method involves manipulation of variables: The researcher directly manipulates one or more variables by establishing the conditions for studying behavior. The behavior is then observed under the different conditions. Using the experimental method, a researcher interested in the effects of television violence on aggression might expose one group of children to a violent program condition and another group of children to a nonviolent program condition. The researcher would then measure the amount of aggressive behavior in the two conditions to determine whether watching television violence did in fact affect their aggressive behavior. With the experimental method, it is easier to infer that one variable caused the other, because of the sequence of events in time and control over extraneous "third" variables.

Sequence of events

The experimental method makes it easier to infer direction of cause and effect because the researcher determines the sequence of events. Subjects first encounter one variable, watching either a violent or nonviolent program. The second variable, aggression, is then measured. If the two groups differ in their aggression, the researcher may conclude that the violent program caused the aggression and may reject the notion that aggression caused viewing of television violence.

Control of extraneous variables

Another characteristic of the experimental method is that it attempts to eliminate the influence of all extraneous variables (variables other than the primary variables that are the objects of the investigation). This feature is called *control of extraneous variables,* and it is usually achieved by ensuring that every feature of the environment except the manipulated variable is held constant. Any variable that cannot be held constant is controlled by making sure that the effects of the variable are random. Through randomization, the influence of any extraneous variable is equal in the experimental conditions. The procedures used ensure that any differences observed on the measured variable can be attributed to the influence of the variable that was manipulated.

Experimental control   Through experimental control, extraneous variables are kept constant. If a variable is kept constant, it cannot influence the results. For example, variables to be controlled in an experiment on aggression might include room temperature, noise, the attractiveness of the rooms where the experiment is conducted, the sex of the experimenter, and the method of recruiting subjects. If any such variable systematically differed in the two conditions, it could affect the results of the experiment.

Randomization   Sometimes it is difficult to keep a variable constant. The most obvious such variable is any characteristic of the subjects. If in a study using the experimental method, the subjects in the violent program condition were students at one elementary school whereas subjects in the nonviolent condition were students from a different elementary school, the subjects in the two conditions might be different on some variable, such as socioeconomic status. This difference could cause an apparent relationship between television violence and aggression. In other words, students from the one school might watch more television violence *and* be more aggressive than students from the other school. If so, television violence viewing and aggression would be related to one another, but there would be no direct causal connection between the two variables.

The experimental method eliminates the influence of such variables by *randomization*, which assures that the extraneous variable is equally as likely to affect one experimental group as it is to affect the other group. To eliminate the influence of subject characteristics, the researcher assigns subjects to the two groups in a random fashion. Randomization assures that the subject characteristic composition of the two groups will be almost identical. Thus, the subjects in the groups will be equivalent in terms of intelligence, height, weight, socioeconomic status, and so on.

Any other variable that cannot be held constant is also controlled by randomization. For instance, an experiment can be conducted over a period of several days or weeks. Because all subjects in both conditions cannot be tested simultaneously, the researcher uses a random order of testing subjects. This procedure prevents a situation in which only the nonviolent condition is studied during the first few days and only the violent condition is studied during the last few days. Similarly, the nonviolent condition is not studied only during the morning, and the violent condition is not studied only in the afternoon.

Time of day is an especially interesting extraneous variable in studies of small children. Usually such studies are conducted only in the morning, when the children are most active—illustrating experimental control of the variable. Through randomly determining the order of the conditions each morning, there is further assurance that one condition is not run in the early morning hours whereas the other is run in the late morning.

INDEPENDENT AND DEPENDENT VARIABLES

When researchers study the relationship between variables, the variables are usually conceptualized as having a cause-and-effect connection: That is, one variable is considered to be the "cause" and the other is the "effect." Thus, television violence is generally considered to be the variable that has an effect on aggression. Viewing the variables in this fashion occurs in both experimental and correlational research, even though as we have seen there is less ambiguity about direction of cause and effect when the experimental method is applied. Researchers use the terms *independent variable* and *dependent variable* when they refer to the variables being studied. The variable that is considered to be the "cause" is the independent variable, whereas the variable that is the "effect" is the dependent variable.

In an experiment, the manipulated variable is the independent variable. One way to remember the difference is to relate the two terms to what happens to a subject in an experiment. The researcher devises a situation to which subjects are exposed, such as watching a violent (or nonviolent) television program. This situation is the independent (manipulated) variable, because the subject has nothing to do with its occurrence. In the next step of the experiment, the researcher measures the subject's response to the manipulated variable. The subject is responding to what happened to him or her; therefore, the researcher assumes that what the subject does or says is caused by the independent variable. The independent variable, then, is the variable that is manipulated by the experimenter. The dependent variable is the measured behavior of the subject that is assumed to be caused by the independent variable.

To make this distinction more concrete, consider a study of the effect of "action" in a television program on attention paid to the program (Potts, Huston, & Wright, 1986). Preschool boys watched television programs that were either high or low in the amount of action contained in the programs. Their attention was measured by recording how long each boy watched the television screen. The independent variable is the "program action," and the dependent variable is the duration of attention. The results of this study showed that program action did affect attention; rapid action programs were watched longer.

CHOOSING A METHOD

Thus far, the advantages of the experimental method have been stressed. However, it also has its disadvantages; and, there are also good reasons to select the correlational method. When researchers choose a methodology to study a problem, they must weigh the advantages and disadvantages in the context of the overall goals of the research. In the following section, some of the drawbacks of the experimental method and advantages of the correlational method are discussed.

Artificiality of experiments

Most experiments are conducted in laboratory environments. In a laboratory experiment, the independent variable is manipulated within the carefully controlled confines of a laboratory. This procedure permits relatively unambiguous inferences concerning cause and effect and reduces the possibility that extraneous variables could influence the results. Such experimentation is an extremely valuable way to study many problems. However, the high degree of control and the laboratory setting may sometimes create an artificial atmosphere that limits either the questions that can be addressed or the generality of the results. For this reason, researchers may decide that the correlational method is preferable.

Some researchers have attempted to conduct experiments in field settings to counter the problem of artificiality. In a field experiment, the independent variable is manipulated in a natural setting. As in any experiment, the researcher attempts to control all extraneous variables via either randomization or experimental control.

As an example of a field experiment, consider an experiment by Langer and Rodin (1976) on the effects of giving elderly nursing home residents greater control over decisions that affect their lives. One group of residents was given a great deal of responsibility to make choices concerning the operation of the nursing home; a second group was made to feel that the staff would be responsible for their care and needs. The experimenters measured dependent variables such as activity level and happiness of the residents. The results showed that the people in the group that was given responsibility were more active and happy. In a follow-up study, this group also showed greater improvements in physical health (Rodin & Langer, 1977).

The great advantage of the field experiment is that the independent variable is investigated in a natural context. The great disadvantage is that the researcher loses the ability to directly control many aspects of the situation. The laboratory experiment permits researchers to keep extraneous variables constant more easily, thereby eliminating their influence on the outcome of the experiment. Of course, it is exactly this control that leads to the artificiality of the laboratory investigation.

Ethical and practical considerations

Many of the most important variables in human development and family relations are studied using the correlational method because it would be unethical or impractical to use the experimental method. For example, child-rearing practices are impractical to manipulate with the experimental method. Even if it were possible to assign parents randomly to two child-rearing conditions, such as using withdrawal of love versus physical types of punishment, the manipulation would be unethical. Instead of manipulating variables such as child-rearing techniques, researchers usually study them as they occur in natural settings. Many important research areas present similar problems: for example, studies of the effects of alcoholism in a family unit, divorce and its consequences, and the impact of maternal employment on children. Such problems must be studied, and generally the only techniques possible are nonexperimental. Finally, many variables cannot be manipulated at all. These variables are *subject variables*, which are characteristics of persons such as marital status, gender, or personality.

Successful prediction of future behavior

In many "real-life" situations, a major concern is to make a successful prediction about a person's future behavior—for example, success in school, ability to learn a new job, and probable interest in various major fields in college. In such circumstances, it is possible to design measures that increase the accuracy of predicting future behavior. School counselors may give tests to decide whether students should be in "enriched" classroom programs; employers may use a test to help determine whether or not to hire an applicant, and college students can take tests that can help them decide on a major. There are even tests that couples can take to help them decide whether they are suited for marriage. These types of measures can lead to better decisions for many people.

CONCLUSION

In this chapter, we have focused on the experimental method versus the correlational method as ways of studying relationships between variables. In Chapter 4, we examine the fundamental issue of the measurement of variables. We then look much more closely at both experimental and nonexperimental methods: Chapters 5, 6, and 7 discuss procedures and considerations when performing experiments, and Chapter 8 explores the methods used when conducting nonexperimental research such as surveys, field observation, and case studies.

You are probably wondering how researchers select a methodology to study a problem. A variety of methods are available, and researchers select the method that best enables them to address the questions posed. No method is inherently superior to another. Rather, a researcher chooses a method after considering the problem that is being studied, the goals of the research, and the cost and time constraints that exist. This chapter has emphasized many of the advantages of the experimental method in terms of inferences of cause and effect although you should note that nonexperimental methods, in which observation rather than manipulation of the variables is the primary focus, are often most desirable to study important questions about human development and the family. Moreover, such methods are not inherently "easier" than the experimental method. In fact, the careful observational strategies often required in nonexperimental research makes this approach especially difficult for researchers. The main point, though, is that use of both experimental and nonexperimental methods is necessary to understand the wide variety of behaviors that are of interest to students of human development and family relations. Complete understanding of any problem or issue requires study using a variety of methodological approaches.

SUMMARY

Researchers in human development and family relations study behavioral variables. A variable is a general class or category of events, situations, responses, or characteristics of individuals. For each variable, specific instances will vary. Every variable has two or more values or levels: For example, gender has two values; income has many values.

Researchers must operationally define variables to study them. The operational definition of a variable is the method that is used to measure or manipulate the variable. An operational definition translates an abstract concept into concrete terms for studying the variable.

There are four general types of relationships between variables. In a positive relationship, increases in the values of one variable are accompanied by increases in the other variable. In a negative relationship, increases in the values of one variable are accompanied by decreases in the values of the other variable. In a curvilinear relationship, increases in one variable are accompanied by both increases and decreases in the other variable. When there is no relationship, increases in one variable are not accompanied by any changes in the other variable.

There are two general ways of studying relationships between variables. With the correlational method, variables are observed or measured to see if there is a relationship. Two major problems with the correlational method are (1) determining the direction of cause and effect and (2) the possibility that extraneous "third" variables influenced the results. With the experimental method, one variable is manipulated and its effect on the other variable is observed. There is less ambiguity about direction of cause and effect because the sequence of events is determined by the researcher. Also, extraneous variables are controlled by either (1) experimental control (keeping a variable constant) or (2) randomization (using randomization procedures to ensure that other variables affect each group equally in the experiment).

When studying relationships between variables, the causal variable is called the independent variable. Independent variables have effects on dependent variables. In experiments, the independent variable is the variable that is manipulated, and the dependent variable is the variable that is observed.

A major drawback of experimental studies is their artificiality. However, experiments can be conducted in field settings. The experimental method also cannot address many important questions in which it would be unethical or impractical to manipulate variables. Using tests to predict future behavior is an important research area in which experimental techniques are not appropriate. There is no single, best method for studying behavior: Sometimes an experiment is the best approach; often, however, a nonexperimental approach is preferable.

STUDY QUESTIONS

1. What is a variable? Give examples of variables that are characteristics of persons, situations, and responses.
2. What is an operational definition of a variable? Try to think of three ways to define operationally (a) family discord and (b) stranger anxiety in eight-month-old infants.
3. Describe the four general types of relationships between variables. Draw graphs that depict these relationships.
4. What is the difference between the correlational method and experimental method?
5. What is the difference between an independent variable and a dependent variable?
6. Distinguish between laboratory and field experiments.
7. What is meant by the problem of direction of cause and effect and the third-variable problem?
8. How does direct experimental control reduce the possible effects of extraneous variables?
9. Describe how randomization deals with the problem of extraneous variables.
10. What are some reasons for using the correlational method to study relationships between variables?

CHAPTER 4

Measurement

CAREER
PROFILE

Camilla Freitag / Social Worker

Camilla received her undergraduate degree in Social Work from the University of Oklahoma, Norman, and a Master of Social Work at the University of Texas, Austin. She is a Child Welfare Social Worker in San Diego County, California.

"My caseloads consist of all ages of children who are under the jurisdiction of the San Diego County Juvenile Court. Much of my work deals directly with the Juvenile Court. My work with attorneys, probation officers, and the police revolves around placements that are in the best interests of the child. As a Child Welfare Social Worker, I am considered an officer of the Court. Part of my job consists of the necessity of taking children into custody. Making recommendations to the Court as to a child's best interests is a large part of my job. Working with natural parents and foster parents, in responsible planning for a child, is supposed to be done with an unbiased view. In these cases in which a minor has been removed from his or her parents, the Court orders me to provide child welfare services to the family.

"Many of the clients I see are ordered by the Court to get psychological evaluations. I refer them to psychologists whose testing and interpretation skills I am confident in. An awareness of reliability and validity of the tests influences my impressions of the psychologist's report and the psychologist I use." Camilla often uses results from research reports " . . . to assess and identify high-risk situations or environments." She also keeps up to date with current research and reads the *Harvard Medical Letter* and *Journal of Social Work Monthly*. "Attending workshops also keeps me apprised of current findings, which I then use to help and understand dysfunctional families I work with."

Measurement is fundamental to the research enterprise. Noting a person's age is in actuality a measurement of a variable. Similarly, observing aggressive behavior on a school playground, testing for memory, giving a personality scale to married couples, or asking elderly citizens to rank order their housing preferences are all examples of measurement. In the career profile, you read about Camilla Freitag's use of the results of various tests to make decisions about placement of children in the juvenile justice system. In experimental research, the dependent variable is a measure of behavior; that is, it is the response to the independent variable. In correlational research, investigators study the relationship between two or more measures of behavior. Table 4.1 lists some commonly used measures in human development and family relations. In this chapter, we explore some of the fundamental concepts of measurement, a variety of techniques that are used when measuring variables, and important criteria that are used to assess the quality of measures such as the ones listed in the table. Generally, measures are of four types:

Self-report measures
Behavioral measures
Physiological measures
Projective measures

SELF-REPORT MEASURES

A *self-report measure* is simply a subject's own response to a question posed by a researcher. You have probably been asked to fill out a questionnaire for one purpose or another. Or, you may have been interviewed in a survey over

**Table 4.1
Some widely used measures in developmental and family research**

Infancy

Brazelton Neonatal Behavioral Assessment Scale (Brazelton, 1973)
HOME Inventory—assesses intellectual stimulation provided by a child's home environment (Bradley & Caldwell, 1980)

Intelligence

Bayley Scales of Infant Development (Bayley, 1969)
Stanford–Binet IQ Test (Terman & Merrill, 1973)
Wechsler Intelligence Scales (Wechsler, 1967, 1974, 1981)
   WPPSI (preschoolers)
   WISC–R (children)
   WAIS–R (adults)

Behavioral control

Matching Familiar Figures Test (Kagan, Rosman, Day, Albert, & Phillips, 1964)
Draw-A-Line, Walk-A-Line (Toner, Holstein, & Hetherington, 1977)

Self-concept

Coopersmith Self-Esteem Inventory (Coopersmith, 1967)
Harter Self-Concept Scale (Harter, 1982)
Piers–Harris Self-Concept Scale (Piers & Harris, 1969)

Achievement motivation

Intellectual Achievement Responsibility Questionnaire (Crandall & Battle, 1970)

Empathy

Affective Situation Test for Empathy (Feshbach & Roe, 1968)
Empathy Test for Children and Adolescents (Bryant, 1982)

Moral development

Defining Issues Test (Rest, 1979)
Sociomoral Reflection Measure (Gibbs, Widaman, & Colby, 1982)

Sex roles

Bem Sex-Role Inventory (Bem, 1974)
Personal Attributes Questionnaire (Spence & Helmreich, 1978)
Children's Personal Attributes Questionnaire (Hall & Halberstadt, 1980)

Marital and family satisfaction

Dyadic Adjustment Scale (Spanier, 1976)
Family Environment Scale (Moos & Moos, 1981)
Locke–Wallace Marital Adjustment Scale (Locke & Wallace, 1959)

Life satisfaction and life stress

Life Satisfaction Index (Neugarten, Havighurst, & Tobin, 1961)
Social Readjustment Rating Scale (Holmes & Rahe, 1967)

Table 4.1
(*continued*)

Adult development

Research Instruments in Social Gerontology, Vol. 1—Clinical and Social Gerontology (Mangen & Peterson, 1982a)
Research Instruments in Social Gerontology, Vol. 2—Social Roles and Social Participation (Mangen & Peterson, 1982b)

General references for sources of measures

Mental Measurements Yearbook (Buros, 1978)
Measures of Social Psychological Attitudes (Robinson & Shaver, 1973)

---

the telephone or at a shopping mall. The primary feature of a self-report measure is that the subjects tell the researcher something about their behaviors, thoughts, emotions, or memories. The report may be a paper-and-pencil questionnaire, a test, or an attitude survey. Or, the researcher may directly ask questions in a face-to-face interview or over the telephone. The questions may even be posed at a computer terminal with answers recorded when the subject presses keys on the computer. Because of their ease of use and directness, self-reports are the most commonly used methods of measuring behavior.

Self-report measures can be used to ask people about their child-rearing practices, sexual behaviors, attitudes, personality, or memory. Indeed, the exams that you take in your classes are self-reports of your learning of the facts and concepts presented in the class. Although you probably have a good idea of what constitutes a self-report measure, there are several important issues to consider. These issues are discussed in the following sections and in Chapter 8 when we review survey research techniques.

Devising your own test or using an existing measure

Sometimes the nature of the research question demands that a unique measure be devised. However, most of the time a previously developed measure is available. Thus, you would probably not devise your own intelligence test or marital satisfaction measure, because such measures have already been developed by others and used in previous studies. Most important, the existing measures have proven to be useful in other studies, more is known about the meaning of these measures, and the results of any new study can be easily compared to previous research findings.

Closed versus open-ended questions

One issue when asking people to answer questions about themselves is whether to ask closed or open-ended questions. With *closed questions*, there are a limited number of fixed response alternatives given to subjects. With *open-ended questions*, subjects are free to respond in any way they like. Thus, you may ask a child "Did you like the toy because of its color or the noise it makes?" or "What did you like about the toy?"

Closed questions are easier to score, and the range of responses is consistent for all subjects. The range of alternatives must be adequate for the subjects, however, or they will not be able to provide an accurate response to the question. In other words, the number of response alternatives to the question must be appropriate for the question. For some questions, two or three alternatives may work (e.g., yes, no, undecided), whereas for other questions, a scale with five or more alternatives may be needed (e.g., a five-point scale ranging from "disagree strongly" to "agree strongly"). Open-ended questions require time to categorize and score the responses, and they are therefore more costly. Sometimes a subject's response cannot be coded at all, because the response doesn't make sense or the person couldn't think of an answer. Still, an open-ended question can yield valuable insights into what the subjects are thinking.

Open-ended questions are most useful when the researcher needs to know what people are thinking and how they naturally understand their world. Closed-ended questions are more likely to be used when relevant variables and their dimensions have been defined through previous research or theoretical considerations.

BEHAVIORAL MEASURES

Behavioral measures use direct observation of behavior rather than self-reports. To illustrate, in a self-report, a child can be asked to point to the most preferred toy in a set of eight. In contrast, the child can also be left alone in a room with the eight toys while an observer records the amount of time that the child actually plays with each one—a behavioral measure. In fact, a similar behavioral measure was used in the classic studies of infant pattern perception by Fantz (1961, 1963). Babies were placed on their backs in a "looking chamber"—a table-sized structure from which various objects and patterns could be suspended above the infants. An observer watched the babies' eye fixations through a peephole in the roof of the looking chamber. If the infant looked at both patterns the same length of time, it could mean that the patterns looked the same or that the baby didn't have a preference. However, if the infant looked longer at one pattern than at the other, it was assumed both that the difference in the patterns could be perceived *and* that there is a preferred pattern. By employing this *preferential-looking technique*, Fantz found that young infants preferred viewing more complex patterns than simple ones and that they especially preferred human, facelike stimuli.

Behavioral measures in experiments are often relatively straightforward observations of distinct behaviors. These observations include artificial laboratory tasks such as naming colors and copying figures (cf. Anyan & Quillian, 1971), reaction time to visual stimuli (Cantor, 1968), and response and movement time in a lever-pull task (Kubose, 1972). Some research settings are less artificial, and they are designed to simulate more "real-life" situations. For example, after viewing violence on television, researchers may observe how many of the violent acts are acted out (Bandura, Grusec, & Menlove, 1966). Other researchers observe behavior in the home (cf. Clarke-Stewart, 1973; Baumrind, 1971), and others observe the behavior of teachers and students in classrooms (Serbin, O'Leary, Kent, & Tonick, 1973) to study the ways adults respond to children's behaviors (and vice-versa). We discuss considerations involved in the observation of behavior in more detail in Chapter 8.

PHYSIOLOGICAL MEASURES

Physiological measures are recordings of the physiological responses of the body. Several are commonly used. The galvanic skin response (GSR) is used as a measure of general emotional arousal and anxiety. The GSR is a measure of the electrical conductance of the skin, which changes when sweating occurs. Another physiological measure is the electromyograph (EMG), which measures muscle tension. The EMG is frequently used as a measure of tension and stress. Other physiological measures include heartrate changes, skin temperature, and even elements taken from urine samples. These measures have been used in a number of research investigations. As an example, an increase in body temperature in the genital area is an indicator of sexual arousal. It isn't necessary to place a thermometer on a person's skin to take this measurement, though; a camera with heat-sensitive film can record changes in body temperature with no invasion of a subject's privacy (Seeley, Abramson, Perry, Rothblatt, & Seeley, 1980).

An important physiological measure is the electroencephalogram (EEG), which is a measure of the electrical activity of brain cells. The EEG is generally used as a measure of cortical arousal and can be used to investigate activity in different parts of the brain when subjects are performing different tasks (cf. Dawson, Finley, Phillips, & Galpert, 1986). For example, activity is greater in the brain's left hemisphere when subjects are working on a verbal task; right hemisphere activity is greater when subjects are working on a drawing task.

PROJECTIVE MEASURES

Instead of directly asking subjects about themselves, *projective measures* attempt to assess subjects' psychological states indirectly. A projective measure is a relatively ambiguous stimulus that is shown to a subject. When the subject is asked questions about the stimulus, it is assumed that the responses reflect the person's underlying personality, attitudes, and values. You have probably heard of the Rorschach Inkblot Test that is used in clinical diagnosis in psychology. The test consists of 10 "inkblot" cards that a person describes in terms of content, color, and location of objects in the ambiguous figure.

Clinicians are trained to interpret the psychological meaning of the responses to the inkblots.

Projective tests have been developed for children, including the Children's Apperception Test (Bellak & Bellak, 1949, 1965), the Michigan Picture Test (Andrew, Hartwell, Hutt, & Walton, 1953), the School Apperception Method (Solomon & Starr, 1968), and the Make-a-Picture Story Test (Shneidman, 1952). In some tests, the child is shown a picture and asked to make up a story about it. During testing, the child is questioned about what the characters in the story are thinking, feeling, and doing. In other tests, children are asked to draw a person or their family. The child's responses in such tests are considered to be indicators of the child's psychological states (e.g., self-esteem). Projective tests are useful in many instances because children may not be able to verbalize or understand questions about their feelings.

Projective tests are not widely used as measures in research investigations. When they are used, they usually provide the basis for dividing subjects into personality categories such as low versus high self-esteem. A major problem with the use of projective measures is that their reliability and validity are not as well established as other types of measures are. Reliability and validity are important dimensions that researchers use to evaluate measures of behavior, and these topics are discussed in the next section.

EVALUATING MEASURES OF BEHAVIOR

Each of the specific techniques for measuring or observing people has unique qualities that make it preferable for a specific project. However, some general considerations are important in evaluating any measurement technique. These considerations include reactivity, reliability, and validity of measures.

Reactivity and unobtrusive measures

A measure is said to be *reactive* if awareness of being measured changes the behavior of the subject. A reactive measure tells what subjects are like when they are aware of being observed, but it doesn't tell how the subjects would behave under natural circumstances.

Reactivity is most likely to be a problem in self-report measures. Subjects may attempt to "look good" to the researcher by giving socially desirable responses, for example, a problem we return to in Chapter 8. Reactivity can also be a problem in behavioral observation unless the observer is completely concealed. Otherwise, the observer's mere presence or the personality or characteristics of the observer can affect the subjects' behavior. Similarly, physiological measures may be reactive, since attaching electrodes and other recording devices to the body can affect the way the individual responds.

Fortunately, there are ways to minimize or eliminate reactivity. The reactivity of self-report measures can be reduced by honesty between the researcher and subject. Also, when people know they are being observed—as in physiological recording or behavioral observation—the researcher can allow enough time for the subjects to adapt to the presence of the observer or the apparatus. After a period of time, subjects become used to the recording equipment or the observer, and it is expected that their behavior will be natural.

The use of *unobtrusive measures* is another way to eliminate reactivity. A measure is unobtrusive when subjects are completely unaware that their behavior is being studied. The use of heat-sensitive film to record changes in body temperature qualifies as an unobtrusive measure. Much observation of behavior in public places is unobtrusive: For example, Rosenblatt and Cleaves (1981) noted interaction rates (touching, talking, and smiling) of different sized family groups in shopping malls. Public records are unobtrusive, since such measures have usually been collected as a part of normal record-keeping. Thus, various public health statistics; birth, marriage, and divorce records; census data; crime statistics; and so forth can be sources of nonreactive data.

A number of examples of unobtrusive measurement techniques are described by Webb and his colleagues (1981). Some of their examples are quite humorous. For instance, in 1872 Sir Francis Galton used public records to examine the efficacy of prayer in producing long life. Galton wondered whether British royalty, who are frequently the recipients of prayers by the populace, live longer than other people do. He checked death records and found that members of royal families actually led shorter lives than other people. The book by Webb and his colleagues is a rich source of such unobtrusive measures and has influenced researchers to seek alternatives to traditional self-reports.

Reliability

Reliability refers to the consistency, or stability, of a measure. For example, a reliable measure of length yields the same measurement of a table every time the table is measured. A measuring device that says that a table is 4 feet long today will yield an identical measure tomorrow. If it doesn't, the device lacks perfect reliability and contains some "measurement error." Similarly, a measure of intelligence is unreliable if it measures the same person as "average" one week, "dull" the next, and "bright" during the next week. Put simply, a reliable measure does not fluctuate randomly.

Any measure can be thought of as being made up of two components: a *true score*, which is the person's "real" score on the variable being measured, and *measurement error*, which is random error in the measure. An unreliable measure of intelligence, then, contains measurement error, and it thus does not provide an accurate indicator of intelligence. In contrast, a reliable measure of intelligence—one that contains little measurement error—yields an identical (or nearly identical) intelligence score each time the same individual is measured.

The importance of reliability is obvious. An unreliable measure of length (say, a ruler made of elastic) is useless in building a table; an unreliable measure of a variable such as intelligence is useless in studying that variable. Researchers cannot use unreliable measures to discover relationships between variables. When the measure of the variable lacks reliability, the variable will usually be unrelated to other variables.

The reliability of a measure can be assessed in several ways, all of which are based on *correlation coefficients* (symbolized as *r*). A correlation coefficient can range from −1.00 to +1.00. A correlation of 0.00 indicates no relationship. A common way to assess reliability is called *test-retest reliability*. To assess reliability, the same individuals are measured at two points in time, usually not more than a few weeks apart. A correlation coefficient is then computed to see whether scores at time 1 are strongly related to the scores at time 2; the result is referred to as a *reliability coefficient.* If the measure is reliable (i.e., consistent), a reliability coefficient approaching +1.00 will be obtained. A high correlation (over +.80 or so) tells us that each individual's score on the first measure is quite similar to that individual's score on the same measure taken later. Thus, with test-retest reliability, the measure shows consistency over time. (Correlation coefficients are discussed more fully in Chapter 11.)

You should note that reliability is increased when several questions are used to measure the variable of interest. For example, a single item measure of marital satisfaction is less reliable than a measure that contains a number of items asking about satisfaction in different ways. Many tests or questionnaires you have filled out have probably included a number of similar questions to increase their reliability.

When it is impractical to take measures at two points in time, or if the measure isn't expected to be consistent over time (e.g., a measure of temporary moods), an alternative to test-retest reliability is *split-half reliability.* Here, a correlation is computed between scores on the first half of a measure and scores on the second half. Again, if the measure is reliable, a high correlation is expected: That is, the persons taking the test scored similarly on both the first and the second halves of a measure.

Another approach is to correlate scores on each item of a test with the total score on the test—which is called *internal consistency reliability.* Internal consistency is high when all the individual items correlate highly with the total, indicating that all the items measure the same variable.

Studies in which an observer must record the behaviors of subjects present a special problem of reliability. How do you know that the data recorded by the observer are in fact reliable? This problem may not be serious if the behavior observed is relatively simple (e.g., observing whether a child does or does not pick up a specific toy). However, observers must often code more complex behaviors, such as the degree of intimacy in a conversation between a married couple. Here, the solution is to use at least two observers; reliability can then be determined by correlating the ratings of the observers—called *interrater* or *interobserver reliability.* Reliability is indicated when there is high agreement among the observers. If the observers are using a rating scale (e.g., intimacy of the conversation), the ratings of the observers are usually averaged before performing statistical analyses.

Validity

In addition to having high reliability, a measure should have *validity*, which is defined as the extent to which a measure actually measures what it is intended to measure. That is, a valid measurement device measures what it is supposed to measure. For example, a measure of scholastic aptitude such as the Scholastic Aptitude Test (SAT) is supposed to measure the ability to succeed in college. The validity of such a test is determined by whether it does, in fact, measure this ability.

Face validity The simplest type of validity is *face validity*, which tells whether the measure "appears" (on its face) to measure what it is supposed to measure. A measure of marital satisfaction with face validity is likely to ask questions about time spent together, perceived commitment toward a spouse, and perceived rewards in the relationship. Face validity is not very sophisticated, because it is based only on the appearance of the measure. However, it is useful as a first approximation of validity, and most researchers prefer to use measures that have face validity.

Criterion validity A second type of validity is *criterion validity*. Criterion validity is crucial when the purpose of the measure is to predict how individuals will behave on some future behavior or criterion. Thus, the purpose of an "English Usage Test" may be to predict whether or not a student will succeed in an English honors course. In this case, the criterion is success in the course, and the test is called a *predictor measure*. The validity of the English Usage Test is dependent on showing that scores on the test are in fact related to grades in the class; a high correlation between test scores and class grades is evidence for the criterion validity of the measure. Once criterion validity is demonstrated, the test can be used as a selection device to decide whether a student should be admitted to the class. You can see that criterion validity is quite important when tests must be used to evaluate applicants for a job, a training program, or a school. To be useful, scores on the measure must be related to the criterion.

Construct validity *Construct validity* is most important in basic, theoretical research, but it is important in applied research as well. A measurement device that actually measures the theoretical variable, or construct, that it is supposed to measure is said to have construct validity. Such theoretical constructs include self-esteem, marital satisfaction, romantic love, or intelligence. These variables cannot be directly observed; they differ from variables such as age, length of marriage, or frequency of sexual intercourse. It is relatively simple to measure length of marriage, but how would you devise a measure to indicate the amount of romantic love felt toward a dating partner? This task is difficult because love is a theoretical variable that is assumed to exist but must be inferred in some way in order to measure it.

Psychologist Zick Rubin (1970, 1973) decided to devise a self-report measure of romantic love. He began by searching through the writings of poets, psychologists, novelists, and philosophers to find definitions and examples of love. His search led him to a large number of items that were worded so that subjects could indicate their degree of agreement. For example, the item, "When _____ and I are together, we are almost always in the same mood," can be responded to on a scale ranging from "no agreement" to "complete agreement." Many college students responded to these items, and after analyzing their responses (using a technique called *item analysis*), Rubin created a 13-item measure of romantic love.

After determining that the measure was reliable, Rubin needed to assess the construct validity of the scale. Construct validity is never demonstrated in a simple, infallible way. Instead, the researcher must ask whether the measure is in fact related to other measures that are theoretically related. Thus, persons who score high on a scale of love, in contrast with persons who score low on the measure, should be more likely to say they are "in love," give higher estimates of their probability of marriage, and still be together when contacted six months later. In fact, Rubin reported these findings when he studied dating couples, and so he gathered evidence for the construct validity of his scale. He even found that couples who score high on the scale look into each other's eyes more when conversing with one another!

Construct validity is rarely shown conclusively. In the case of Rubin's research, other indicators of love still need to be studied, and the scale must be given to a broader range of subjects including married couples and persons from different ethnic groups. As further research is conducted, the measure may be modified or better measures of the construct may emerge. Note, though, that even though the "perfect" measure of romantic love may never be devised, Rubin's "imperfect" scale can be used to study many questions about the meaning of romantic love. It can even be used by marriage counselors to assess couples.

A final word about measurement: This chapter, especially this section on construct validity, should convince you that measurement is both important and complex. It is easy to come up with a measure of something or another, and you will encounter many measures of personality, learning readiness, or parental competence in magazines, journals, or at professional meetings. It is difficult, though, to devise a *good* measure that is accurate and useful. You should be prepared to ask questions about validity, reliability, and reactivity.

SCALES OF MEASUREMENT

We conclude the chapter with a discussion of the concept of scales of measurement. Whenever a variable is measured, the measure represents one of four kinds of measurement scales:

Nominal scales   Interval scales
Ordinal scales   Ratio scales

The scale that is used determines the type of statistical test that is appropriate when the results of the study are analyzed (see Appendix B). Also, the conclusions that can be drawn about the meaning of a specific score on a variable are dependent on which type of scale is used for measuring the variable.

Nominal scales

Nominal scales have no numeric or quantitative properties. An obvious example is sex or gender. A person is classified as either male or female. Being female does not imply a greater amount of "gender" than being male; the two levels of the sex variable are merely different. This scale is called a *nominal scale* because we simply assign *names* to different categories. Another example is the classification of adults into categories of marital status (e.g., single, married, divorced, widowed). A single person is not entitled to a higher number than a married person; these are simply different classifications. Even if you were to assign numbers to the different categories, the numbers would be meaningless, except for identification purposes.

Ordinal scales

Ordinal scales are a bit more complex than nominal scales because they involve quantitative distinctions. *Ordinal scales* allow us to rank order people or events on the variable being measured. For example, you may have children rank order their preferences among a set of toys. Or, you may ask adults to rank order the most important qualities they look for in a date or potential marriage partner. Such qualities may include attractiveness, personality, income, religious beliefs, and similarity of interests. The results of this measure indicate which quality is ranked first, second, and so on. The rating system here is not a nominal scale because the ranking is meaningful in terms of a numeric continuum.

A measure asking people to indicate the qualities they look for in a marriage partner is an ordinal scale because it only provides information about the rank order of the categories. When a person ranks personality first, similarity second, and attractiveness third, we are provided with quantitative distinctions on a continuum of importance. However, we do not know whether the difference in importance between personality and similarity is the same as the difference between similarity and attractiveness. Thus, with an ordinal scale, we know that one category is "greater than" or "less than" another category, but there is no information about the size of the intervals between the categories or numbers on the scale.

Interval scales

In an *interval scale*, the difference between the numbers on the scale is meaningful. The intervals between the numbers must be equal in size, therefore the difference between 1 and 2 on the scale, for example, is the same as the difference between 2 and 3.

A household thermometer measures temperature on an interval scale: The difference between 50° and 60° Fahrenheit is equal to the difference between 60° and 70°. However, there is no absolute zero on the scale to indicate the absence of temperature. The zero point on any interval scale is only an arbitrary reference point. The implication of the property of interval scales is that we cannot form ratios of the numbers; that is, we cannot say that one number on the scale represents twice as much (or three times as much, etc.) as another number. You cannot say that 90° Fahrenheit is three times warmer than 30° and that 60° is two times warmer.

A measure of marital satisfaction may qualify as an interval scale. The difference between a scores of 30 and 40 on such a scale may be psychologically the same as the difference between scores of 50 and 60. However, we cannot say that the person who scores 60 is twice as satisfied as the person who scores 30, because there is no absolute zero point to indicate the absence of the variable of marital satisfaction.

In the social sciences, it is often difficult to know whether an ordinal or interval scale is being used. However, it is often useful to assume that the variable is being measured on an interval scale, because interval scales allow for more sophisticated statistical analyses than are allowed with ordinal scales. Thus, a measure of marital satisfaction is assumed to be an interval scale; in contrast, an obvious ordinal measurement such as teachers' rank ordering of students on the basis of popularity can only be considered as an ordinal scale.

Ratio scales

Ratio scales have an absolute zero point that indicates the absence of the variable being measured. Examples include many physical measures such as length, weight, time, or age. With a ratio scale, it is possible to make such statements as "a person who weighs 100 kilograms (220 pounds) weighs twice as much as a person who weighs 50 kilograms (110 pounds)." Similarly, a person who answers a question in 1 second is responding twice as fast as a person who answers in 2 seconds; and, a 1,000 square foot classroom is twice as large as a 500 square foot classroom and can accommodate twice as many students. Because so much research on developmental and family issues investigates less precise variables—such as intelligence, marital satisfaction, and attitude similarity—you are more likely to read about nominal, ordinal, and interval scales than ratio scales.

SUMMARY

Measurement of variables occurs in every research study: Variables are measured in both experimental and nonexperimental research.

Self-report measures are subjects' responses to questions that are posed either on a questionnaire or by an interviewer. One issue in self-report measures is whether to use closed or open-ended questions. Behavioral measures are direct measures of behavior. Physiological measures allow researchers to examine responses of the body; such measures include the GSR, EMG, EEG, and body temperature. With projective measures, an ambiguous stimulus such as a picture is shown to a person: The response is assumed to reflect the projection of psychological states such as motives or emotions.

A measure is reactive if awareness of being measured changes a person's behavior. Reactivity can be reduced by being honest with subjects, allowing time for subjects to adapt to the measuring device, and using unobtrusive measures in which subjects are unaware of being measured.

Measures of behavior must be reliable. Reliability refers to the consistency, or stability, of a measure. In more precise terms, a reliable measure is an indicator of a person's true score rather than measurement error. Reliability is assessed in a variety of ways: test-retest, split-half, internal consistency, and interrater reliability.

Validity is the extent to which a measure actually measures what it is intended to measure. Face validity refers to whether the measure "appears" to be a good indicator of the variable being measured. Criterion validity is the extent to which a measure relates to some behavioral criterion, which is quite important when a test is used to predict future behavior. Construct validity is the extent to which a measure of a variable relates to other variables that are theoretically expected to be related.

Whenever a variable is measured, the measure represents one of four measurement scales. Nominal scales have no quantitative properties; they simply allow names to be assigned to different categories. With ordinal scales, the measure allows for rank order distinctions along a numeric continuum, but there is no information about the size of the intervals between the numbers or categories on the scale. With interval scales, the intervals between the numbers are equal in size. There is more information than a rank ordering; however, there is no zero point on the scale. With ratio scales, there is an absolute zero point. Ratio scales are most likely to be physical measures such as age, weight, or time. The type of scale that is used in a study is important in terms of interpreting scores and determining the appropriate statistical analysis.

STUDY QUESTIONS

1. What is a self-report measure? Distinguish between questionnaire and interview techniques.
2. Why would a researcher use an existing self-report measure?
3. When would a researcher use an open-ended or a closed question?
4. Define behavioral measures.
5. Describe the physiological measures discussed in the text.
6. What are projective measures?
7. What is a reactive measure? What methods are available to reduce the problems of reactivity?
8. What is meant by reliability of a measure? Distinguish between true score and measurement error.
9. Describe the types of reliability discussed in the text.
10. What is meant by validity of a measure? Distinguish between face validity, criterion validity, and construct validity.
11. Distinguish between nominal, ordinal, interval, and ratio scales.

CHAPTER 5

Designing Experiments

CAREER PROFILE

Donna Chafe / Elementary School Teacher

Donna received her B.A. in Psychology from Whittier College and a M.A. in Education from Pepperdine University. She teaches kindergarten at McGaugh Elementary School in Seal Beach, California. In addition, she serves on school district committees concerned with educational philosophy and curriculum. Her committee activities include review of educational material, selection of resource and in-service teachers, and follow-up evaluations of classroom programs.

"The children I teach are chronologically four, five, and six, but within each age category there are different developmental ages. Thus within the classroom, there is a tremendous range of entering behaviors and a challenging span of social, emotional, and intellectual needs for the teacher to meet. Skill development and self-esteem enhancement are at the heart of my classroom environment. The results of a Title IV–C Project called Early Success were responsible for this emphasis. The study showed that academic scores increased significantly when children engaged in both thinking skill activities and activities that enhanced self-esteem."

Donna is one of the many consumers of research in human development and family relations. Her familiarity with research results influences the instructional methods selected and enhances her ability to communicate effectively with parents about their children's education. About her career, Donna comments that " . . . it is a career requiring high energy, a love and respect for the individuality of children, and opportunities to display flexibility and creativity. I look forward to each day knowing some of the givens and anticipating some surprises."

In the experimental method, extraneous variables are controlled. To test the hypothesis that crowding impairs academic performance, for example, you would put one group of students in a crowded room and another group in an uncrowded room. The students in each of the groups would then study the same material and take identical tests. Now suppose that the students in the crowded group do not perform as well as those in the uncrowded condition. Can the difference in test scores be attributed to the difference in crowding? Yes, *if* there is no other difference between the groups. But what if the room in which the crowded group was placed had no windows and the room with the uncrowded group did have windows (e.g., two different rooms in a high school)? In such a case, it would be impossible to know whether the poorer scores of the students in the crowded group were due to the crowding or to the lack of windows.

This chapter discusses the fundamental procedures of experimental design. Recall from Chapter 3 that the experimental method has the advantage of allowing for a relatively unambiguous interpretation of results. The researcher manipulates the independent variable to create groups that differ in the levels of the variable (e.g., a crowded versus uncrowded classroom). He or she then compares the groups in terms of their scores on the dependent variable. All other variables are kept constant, either through direct experimental control or through randomization. If the scores of the groups are different, the researcher can conclude that the independent variable caused the results, because the only difference between the groups is the manipulated variable. When experiments are well designed, the results yield valuable information that advances research and application. You can see how experimental results are applied in Donna Chafe's classroom: Donna incorporates classroom teaching methods that research showed were effective in increasing academic success.

Although the task of designing an experiment seems simple, researchers sometimes make mistakes and use designs that look perfectly acceptable but actually contain serious flaws. A detailed look at the flaws in such designs will lead to a better understanding of good experimental designs. This chapter first considers the concepts of internal validity and external validity. We then examine three poorly designed experiments with all their flaws. Two "true" experimental designs are described. We conclude by briefly considering quasi-experimental designs—experimental designs that have some flaws but are extremely useful in many applied settings.

CONFOUNDING AND INTERNAL VALIDITY

In the hypothetical crowding experiment, the variables of crowding and window presence are confounded. *Confounding* occurs when the researcher fails to control some extraneous variable. A variable other than the manipulated variable has been allowed to exert a differential effect in the two conditions. If the window variable were held constant, the presence or absence of windows might have affected subject performance, but the effect of the windows would be identical in both conditions. In this case, the presence of windows would not be a factor requiring consideration when interpreting the difference between the crowded and uncrowded groups. When the variables of crowding and windows are confounded, the effect of the window variable is different in the crowded and the uncrowded conditions.

In the crowding experiment, both rooms should have had windows or both should have been windowless. Because one room had windows and one room did not, any difference in the dependent variable (test scores) cannot be attributed solely to the independent variable (crowding). An alternative explanation can be offered—the difference in test scores may have been caused, at least in part, by the window variable.

Good experimental design involves eliminating possible confounds that result in alternative explanations. A researcher can claim that the independent variable caused the results only when there are no competing explanations. When the results of an experiment can confidently be attributed to the effect of the independent variable, the experiment is said to have *internal validity*. To achieve internal validity, the researcher must design and conduct the experiment so that only the independent variable can be the cause of the results.

When you design an experiment or read about someone else's research, it is important to consider internal validity. Several different experimental designs that have been described by Campbell and Stanley (1966) illustrate the internal validity problem. These designs are considered shortly after we examine the issue of external validity, which is the extent to which the results of a study can be generalized to other settings, other subject populations, and so on.

EXTERNAL VALIDITY

External validity refers to the generalizability of a study (cf. Cook & Campbell, 1971). If a study uses college students, can the results be generalized to other adults? Are the results applicable to only a certain cultural context? In the hypothetical study of classroom crowding and test performance, you might want to know if the same results would be obtained in different schools with different student populations, or whether the results are the same with different types of material being learned in the class (e.g., math versus history). If our study tested students in only one school on one type of material, the study would have relatively low external validity. If the study included several schools and used several types of material, it would have a relatively high degree of external validity.

Even if a single study has little external validity, the findings may prove to be highly generalizable when researchers conduct replications using different subjects and different ways of operationally defining the variables. Such replications are extremely important in increasing our confidence about the generalizability of research findings.

In Chapter 3, a distinction was made between laboratory and field experiments. Field experiments may appear to have greater external validity than laboratory experiments simply because they are less artificial. This situation is not necessarily the case, however. A field experiment in a nursing home may be limited in generalizability—for example, the results could apply only to nursing home residents of a specific health and financial status. In contrast, consider B. F. Skinner's work on reinforcement, which studied the behavior of pigeons under highly controlled and artificial conditions (cf. Skinner, 1953). Skinner's work proved to have high generalizability—to children and adult humans in a variety of settings. His work with pigeons thus has had important applications to education and clinical psychology.

POORLY DESIGNED EXPERIMENTS

The following poorly designed experiments illustrate the internal validity problems that arise when there is a failure to control for extraneous, confounding variables.

The missing control group

Suppose you want to test the hypothesis that married couples who participate in a marriage enrichment seminar are more satisfied with their marriage as a result of the seminar experience. The independent variable here is the marriage enrichment program; the dependent variable is marital satisfaction. Now suppose that you identified such a program—a seminar that meets once each week for six weeks—and gained permission to administer a marital satisfaction scale at the end of the last meeting. Your design would look like this:

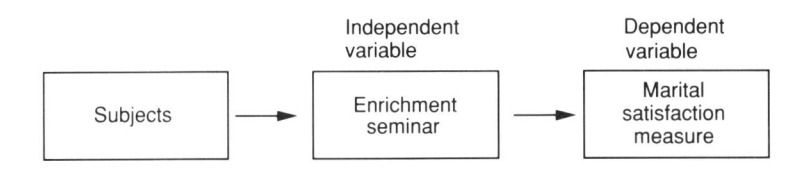

Subjects → Enrichment seminar (Independent variable) → Marital satisfaction measure (Dependent variable)

Now suppose that the overall average satisfaction score of the participants is 5 on a 1–7 scale (5 corresponds to "moderately satisfied"). Unfortunately, this finding is not interpretable: You don't know whether couples who do not participate in the seminar are less satisfied with their marriages than the couples you tested are. Couples who did not participate might be equally satisfied or show even greater marital satisfaction than the participants.

This design, formally called a *one-shot case study* by Campbell and Stanley (1966), lacks a crucial element: a control or comparison group. A well-designed experiment must include some sort of comparison condition to enable you to interpret your results.[1]

One way to obtain a comparison is to administer the marital satisfaction scale to a group of couples who did not participate in the seminar program. An alternative way to provide comparison is to measure subjects before the manipulation (a pretest) and again afterward (a posttest). An index of change from the pretest to the posttest could then be computed. Although this *one-group, pretest-posttest design* sounds fine, it has some major problems.

The one-group, pretest-posttest design

Using a one-group, pretest-posttest design, you would administer the measure of marital satisfaction both before and after couples had participated in the seminar. You would hope to find that the average score on the satisfaction measure was higher the second time. Your design would look like this:

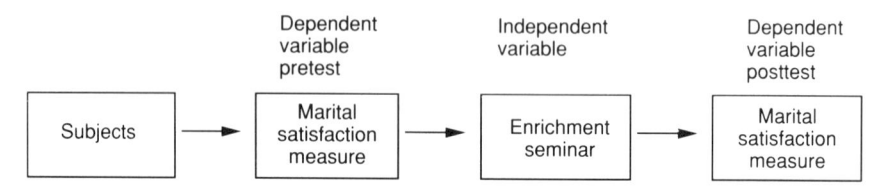

```
                    Dependent          Independent         Dependent
                    variable           variable            variable
                    pretest                                posttest

                    Marital                                Marital
   Subjects    →    satisfaction  →    Enrichment    →    satisfaction
                    measure            seminar             measure
```

If you did find an increase in satisfaction, you would *not* be able to assume that the result was due to the marriage enrichment program. This design has failed to take into account several competing alternative explanations:

History	Instrument decay
Maturation	Statistical regression
Testing	

---

[1]. The one-shot case study with its missing comparison group has serious deficiencies in the context of designing an experiment to measure precisely the effect of an independent variable on a dependent variable. However, case studies are valuable in other contexts. For example, a researcher who becomes a participant observer in a marriage enrichment seminar can provide a rich account of the dynamics of the seminar experience, why people participate, and the possible effects of participation. Such approaches to scientific inquiry are described in Chapter 8.

History *History* refers to any event that occurs between the first and second measurements but is not part of the manipulation. For example, a widely publicized television movie dealing with family issues might be shown between the two measurements that could stimulate communication and improve satisfaction among couples. Or, perhaps the seminar ended just before Christmas when family "togetherness" is at a yearly peak. Any such event is a potentially confounding variable that would invalidate the results.

Maturation of subjects People change over time. In a brief period they become bored, fatigued, perhaps wiser, and certainly hungrier. Over a longer period of time, children become more coordinated and analytical. Any changes that occur systematically over time are called *maturation effects.* Maturation could be a problem in the marriage enrichment example if couples are more satisfied with increasing length of marriage. Such changes would result in an increase in scores from the pretest to the posttest that might be mistakenly attributed to the effect of the program rather than to maturation.

Testing *Testing* becomes a problem if simply taking the pretest changes the subject's behavior. For example, taking a marital satisfaction test might be enough to stimulate a couple to change their perceptions of each other and perhaps their patterns of interaction. Thus, the increased scores on the posttest could be the result of taking the pretest rather than the program itself. In other contexts, taking a pretest may sensitize people to the purpose of the experiment, or it may make them more adept at a skill being tested. Again, the experiment would lack internal validity.

Instrument decay Sometimes the basic characteristics of the measuring instrument change over time. This problem, termed *instrument decay*, is especially likely when human observers are used to measure behavior. An observer may gain skill, lose energy, or change the standards on which the observations are based. In the one-group, pretest-posttest design, any such change over time would be confounded with manipulation of the independent variable.

Statistical regression *Statistical regression* is sometimes called *regression toward the mean*. It is likely to occur whenever subjects are selected because they score extremely high or low on some characteristic. When they are retested, their scores tend to change in the direction of the mean: Extremely high scores are likely to become lower; extremely low scores are likely to become higher.

Statistical regression would be a problem in the marriage enrichment program if participants were selected because they scored especially low on the marital satisfaction measure. If the average score in the population were, say, 5 (on our 1–7 scale), and the selected couples scored between 1 and 3, the chances are that the posttest scores would show an apparent increase in interaction quality. Such a change could be due to statistical regression—not to the program itself.

Statistical regression also occurs when we try to explain "real-world" events. Sports columnists often refer to the hex that awaits an athlete who appears on the cover of *Sports Illustrated:* The performances of a number of athletes have dropped considerably after they were the subjects of *Sports Illustrated* cover stories. Although it is possible that cover stories cause the lower performance (e.g., the notoriety could result in nervousness and low concentration), statistical regression is also a likely explanation. An athlete is selected for the cover of the magazine because he or she is performing at an exceptionally high level. The principle of statistical regression says that high performance is likely to deteriorate. We could verify that regression toward the mean is responsible for this hex if *Sports Illustrated* also did cover stories about athletes who were in a slump and being on the cover at such a time in an athlete's career became a good omen for them!

All these problems can be eliminated through use of an appropriate control group. Such a group that does not receive the experimental treatment provides an adequate control for the effects of history, statistical regression, and so on. For example, outside historical events would have the same effect on both the experimental and control groups. If the experimental group differs from the control group on the dependent measure administered after the manipulation, the difference between the two groups can be attributed to the effect of the experimental manipulation.

In forming a control group, the subjects in the experimental condition and the control condition must be equivalent. If subjects in the two groups are different *before* the manipulation, they will probably be different *after* the manipulation as well. The design discussed in the next section illustrates this problem.

The nonequivalent control group design

The *nonequivalent control group design* employs a separate control group, but the subjects in the two groups—the experimental group and the control group—are not equivalent. The differences become a confounding variable that provides an alternative explanation for the results. This problem, which is called *selection differences*, usually occurs when subjects who form the two groups in the experiment are chosen from existing natural groups. If the marriage enrichment program is studied with the nonequivalent control group design, the design would look like this:

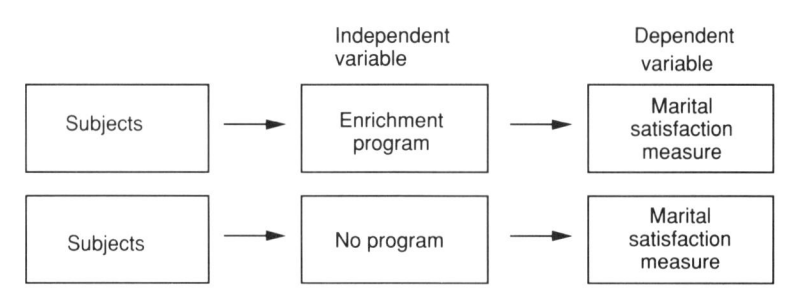

```
                    Independent              Dependent
                     variable                 variable

  ┌──────────┐     ┌──────────┐            ┌──────────┐
  │          │     │Enrichment│            │  Marital │
  │ Subjects │ ──▶ │ program  │ ─────────▶ │satisfaction│
  │          │     │          │            │ measure  │
  └──────────┘     └──────────┘            └──────────┘

  ┌──────────┐     ┌──────────┐            ┌──────────┐
  │          │     │          │            │  Marital │
  │ Subjects │ ──▶ │No program│ ─────────▶ │satisfaction│
  │          │     │          │            │ measure  │
  └──────────┘     └──────────┘            └──────────┘
```

The subjects in the first group are given the marital satisfaction measure after completing the enrichment seminar; the subjects in the second group do not participate in any program. In this design, the researcher does not have any control over which subjects are in each group. Thus, it is likely that subjects in the first group chose to participate in the enrichment seminar program, and the subjects in the second group are simply couples who for whatever reasons did not sign up for the seminar. For example, the control group subjects might be couples who attended a PTA meeting or who are married students at a college. The problem of selection differences arises because couples who choose to participate may be different from couples who do not. Perhaps people who participate have especially distressed marriages; alternatively, you might think of reasons why couples who have especially good marriages might participate. In either case, the preexisting differences make it difficult to interpret any results obtained in the experiment.

It is important to note that the problem of selection differences arises in this design even when it appears that the researcher has successfully manipulated the independent variable using two similar groups. For example, a researcher might have a group of teachers from one school participate in a prejudice reduction program whereas teachers from another school serve as a control group. The problem here, of course, is that the teachers in the two schools may have differed in prejudice *prior* to the prejudice reduction program.

For the prejudice reduction experiment, we could use a pretest to tell us whether the groups were equivalent before the manipulation. Such a pretest would improve this design, but it wouldn't completely solve the selection differences problem because the two groups could still differ on other, unmeasured, variables. At the conclusion of this chapter, we discuss such a design—a "quasi-experimental" design—that can be used when there is no possibility of using a true experimental design.

WELL-DESIGNED EXPERIMENTS

Now that you understand how an experiment is designed and some problems to be avoided, let's look at a well-designed experiment, a "true" experimental design.

The simplest possible experimental design has two variables—the independent variable and the dependent variable—and two groups—an experimental group and a control group. Researchers must make every effort to ensure that the only difference between the two groups is the manipulated variable. Remember, the experimental method involves control over extraneous variables, either through keeping such variables constant (experimental control) or using randomization to make sure that any extraneous variables affect both groups equally. The simple experimental design can take one of two forms. The first is a posttest-only design. The second is a pretest-posttest design.

Posttest-only design

A researcher who uses the *posttest-only design* must

1. Obtain two equivalent groups of subjects
2. Introduce the independent variable
3. Measure the effect of the independent variable on the dependent variable

The design looks like this:

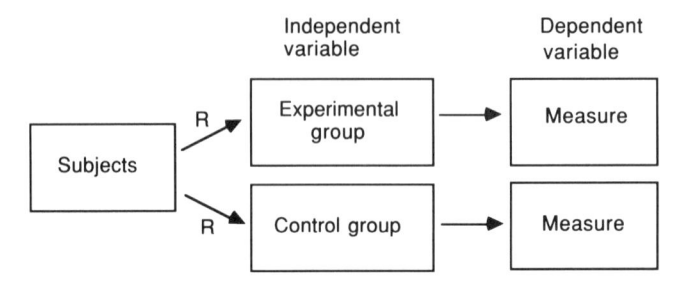

```
                           Independent         Dependent
                           variable            variable
                        ┌──────────────┐    ┌──────────┐
                     R→ │ Experimental │ →  │ Measure  │
┌──────────┐            │    group     │    │          │
│ Subjects │            └──────────────┘    └──────────┘
└──────────┘            ┌──────────────┐    ┌──────────┐
                     R→ │ Control group│ →  │ Measure  │
                        └──────────────┘    └──────────┘
```

Thus, the first step is to choose the subjects and assign them to the two groups. The procedures used must achieve equivalent groups to ensure elimination of the problem of selection differences. Groups can be made equivalent by randomly assigning subjects to the two conditions or by having the same subjects participate in both conditions. The "R" in the diagram means that subjects were randomly assigned to the two groups.

Next, the researcher must choose two levels of the independent variable such as an experimental group that receives a treatment and a control group that does not. Thus, a researcher might study the effect of reward on motivation by rewarding one group of children after they played a game and by giving no reward to children in the control group. A study that tests the effect of a treatment for dating anxiety could compare one group that receives the treatment with a control group that does not. Another approach would be to use two different amounts of the independent variable—to use more reward in one group than the other, or to compare the effects of a six-week marital enrichment program with a one-week program. Either of these approaches provides a basis for comparison of the two groups.

Finally, the effect of the independent variable is measured. The same measurement procedure is used for both groups, so that comparison of the two groups is possible. Since the groups were equivalent to begin with, various factors—such as history or maturation—should affect both groups equally. Thus, any difference between the groups on the dependent variable must be attributed to the effect of the independent variable. The result is an experimental design that has internal validity. In actuality, a statistical significance test would be used to assess the difference between the groups. However, we don't need to be concerned with statistics at this point. An experiment must be well designed and confounding variables eliminated. If not, the results are useless and statistics will be of no help.

Pretest-posttest design

The only difference between the posttest-only design and the *pretest-posttest design* is that in the latter a pretest is given before the experimental manipulation is introduced. This design makes it possible to ascertain that the groups were, in fact, equivalent at the beginning of the experiment. However, this precaution is usually not necessary if subjects have been randomly assigned to the two groups. With a sufficiently large sample of subjects, random assignment will produce groups that are virtually identical in all respects. Although there are no clear-cut rules for specifying a "sufficiently large" sample, a minimum of 10 subjects per group is a good rule of thumb. The larger the sample, the less likelihood there is that the groups will differ in any systematic way.

Advantages and disadvantages of the two designs

Each design has advantages and disadvantages that affect the decision of whether to include or omit a pretest. The first decision factor concerns the equivalence of the groups in the experiment. Although randomization is likely to produce equivalent groups, it is possible that, with small sample sizes, the groups will not be equal. Thus, with a pretest it is possible to assess whether the groups were in fact equivalent at the outset of the experiment.

Sometimes a pretest is necessary to select a specific type of subject. In a program designed to increase math ability, a mathematics test might be given as a pretest, with the lowest scorers selected to be assigned to the experimental and control groups. Also, the researcher who uses a pretest can measure the extent of change in each subject. If the math program appears to increase some subjects' scores more than others, attempts can be made to find out why.

A pretest is also necessary whenever there is the possibility that subjects may drop out of the experiment. For example, if a program lasts over a long period of time, some people may drop out of the program. The dropout factor in experiments is called *mortality*. People may drop out for reasons unrelated to the experimental manipulation, such as illness; but sometimes mortality is related to the experimental manipulation. Even if the groups are equivalent to begin with, different mortality rates can make them nonequivalent. How might mortality affect a program designed to enhance marital satisfaction? The least "adjusted" couples in the experimental group might wind up leaving the program, which would cause scores on the posttest to be higher in the experimental group than in the control group. Use of a pretest makes it possible to assess the effects of mortality—you can look at the pretest scores of the dropouts and know whether mortality affected the final results. Mortality is likely to be a problem when the experimental manipulation extends over a long period of time. In such a situation, a pretest is a good idea.

One disadvantage of a pretest is that it may be time-consuming and awkward to administer in the context of the experimental procedures being used. Perhaps most important, a pretest can sensitize subjects to what you are studying, enabling them to figure out your hypothesis. The subjects may then react differently to the manipulation than they would have without the pretest. When a pretest affects the way subjects react to the manipulation, it is difficult to generalize the results to people who have not received a pretest. That is, the independent variable may not have an effect in the real world, where pretests are rarely given.

When such a problem seems likely, it is sometimes possible to disguise the pretest. One approach is to measure subjects so that they are not aware that they are being tested. Concealed observation of behavior is one way to do this. Sometimes the pretest can be disguised by conducting it in a completely different situation with a different experimenter. Another approach is to embed the pretest in a set of irrelevant measures so that it is not obvious that the researcher is interested in a specific topic. When reading about an experiment in which a pretest-posttest design was used, you should try to determine whether such precautions were taken.

QUASI-EXPERIMENTAL DESIGNS

Sometimes a research problem requires an approach that doesn't allow all the niceties of a true, well-designed, experiment. In such situations, it is best to approximate a true experiment by trying to eliminate alternative explanations. Campbell (1968) has advocated using *quasi-experimental designs* when real-world problems make true experiments impossible.

Earlier in this chapter, we mentioned that the nonequivalent control group design could be improved by including a pretest. When this modification is made, we have a *nonequivalent control group, pretest-posttest design*. The design is one of several quasi-experimental designs described by Campbell (cf. Campbell, 1968, 1969; Cook & Campbell, 1979; Campbell & Stanley, 1966). This design is one of the most useful quasi-experimental designs; it can be diagrammed as follows:

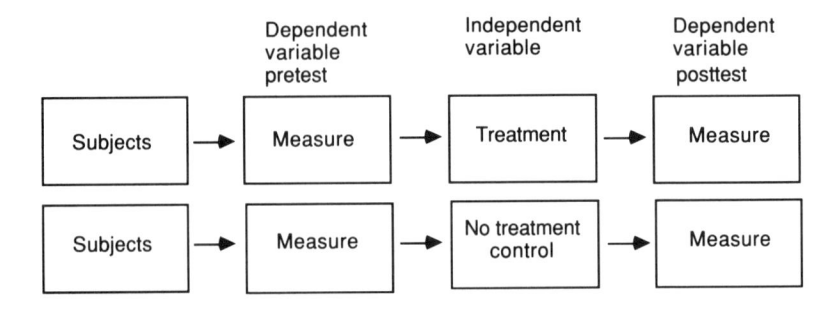

```
                    Dependent           Independent         Dependent
                    variable            variable            variable
                    pretest                                 posttest

  [Subjects]  →    [Measure]   →       [Treatment]    →   [Measure]

  [Subjects]  →    [Measure]   →       [No treatment  →   [Measure]
                                        control]
```

It is not a true experimental design because assignment to groups is not random; thus, it is possible that the two groups are not equivalent. However, we have the advantage of knowing the pretest scores, and we can see whether the groups scored the same on the pretest. Even if the groups are not equiv-

Table 5.1 Summary of designs

Design type	Problem(s)
One-shot case study	No comparison group
One-group pretest-posttest	History
	Maturation
	Testing
	Instrument decay
	Statistical regression
	Mortality
Nonequivalent control group	Selection differences
	Mortality
Posttest-only true experiment	None; possibly mortality
Pretest-posttest true experiment	None; possibly mortality, but can assess with pretest information. Sensitizing subjects to hypothesis is a potential problem.
Nonequivalent control group, pretest-posttest	A quasi-experimental design used to offset problems of nonequivalent control group design when random assignment to groups is not possible. Selection differences are possible, but change scores allow assessment of independent variable effect.

alent, we can look at *changes* in scores from the pretest to the posttest. If the independent variable has an effect, the experimental group should show a greater change than the control group does (Kenny, 1975).

Such a quasi-experimental design could be useful in a variety of settings. For example, attitudes and behaviors of pediatric nurses in a neonatal intensive care unit of a hospital could be assessed before and after a new training program were administered. A control hospital of similar size could be chosen in which staff would be measured on the same variables without the new program. Even though the pretests may reveal initial differences between the two hospitals, change scores should indicate whether the program was effective. Similarly, this design could be used to assess the impact of an independent variable manipulation among residents of two different nursing homes or among students in two different schools.

SUMMARY

Good experimental design requires control of all extraneous variables so that only the independent variable can be responsible for subjects' responses on the dependent variable. Confounding occurs when an extraneous variable is allowed to co-vary along with the independent variable. An experiment is said to have internal validity when any difference between groups on the dependent variable is due to the effect of the independent variable and not to some extraneous variable.

In contrast to internal validity, external validity is the extent to which the results of an experiment can be generalized to other types of subjects, other settings, and other ways of operationally defining the variables.

The one-shot case study design lacks a crucial element of an experiment: a comparison or control condition. The one-group, pretest-posttest design allows comparison of change from the pretest to the posttest, but several confounding variables may stem from (1) history, (2) maturation, (3) testing, (4) instrument decay, and (5) statistical regression. The nonequivalent control group design addresses these problems, but it has the problem of selection differences, which occurs when scores on the dependent variable in the two groups could be due to preexisting differences in the groups.

In well-designed experiments, there is an experimental group and a control group. The groups are equivalent because subjects are randomly assigned to groups. Such true experiments may be either pretest-only or pretest-posttest designs.

Quasi-experimental designs are close approximations to true experimental designs. A common quasi-experimental design is the nonequivalent control group, pretest-posttest design in which nonequivalent experimental and control groups receive both a pretest and a posttest. Although the groups may not be equivalent, change scores allow for meaningful comparisons between groups.

The various designs described in this chapter are shown in Table 5.1 in summary form. You should familiarize yourself with the designs, the threats to internal validity, and the reasons why true experimental designs eliminate these threats.

STUDY QUESTIONS

1. What is meant by confounding?
2. What is meant by the internal validity of an experiment?
3. What is meant by external validity of an experiment?
4. Describe the threats to internal validity discussed in the text: history, maturation, testing, instrument decay, statistical regression, selection differences, and mortality.
5. Why does having a control group eliminate the problems associated with the one-group, pretest-posttest design?
6. How do "true" experimental designs eliminate the problem of selection differences?
7. Distinguish between the posttest-only design and the pretest-posttest design. What are the advantages and disadvantages of each?
8. What is a quasi-experimental design? Why is the nonequivalent control group, pretest-posttest design a quasi-experimental design rather than a true experimental design?

CHAPTER 6

Types of Experimental Designs

CAREER PROFILE

Jerriann M. Wilson / Child Life Specialist

Jerriann has a bachelor's degree in Education and Child Development, and a master's in Education. She is an Assistant Professor in the Johns Hopkins University School of Medicine and is President of the Association for the Care of Children in Hospitals (ACCH).

"A Child Life Specialist, specially trained in child development, uses play and other forms of communication to help children and parents cope with and maximize a hospital experience. We provide familiar activities to create a sense of normalcy and to emphasize a child's wellness. In addition, through the use of medical play and other related activities we help prepare children for planned procedures and assist them in dealing with medical events that they have already experienced. Parents are a very important part of a child's hospital stay and so are thus often present 24 hours a day to provide support and comfort to their child. I have the rare opportunity, compared to most child development situations, to work with families, too."

Jerriann provides two examples of the impact of research on her activities. (1) "Past research tells us that parents' attitudes and feelings toward hospitalization and caregivers can influence the reactions their children have to medical care, and there is much we can do to influence parents' attitudes to help their children and thus help us." (2) "Research underway at this time helps us choose the most 'at risk' children in a hospital setting and tailor the best kind of therapeutic play program to meet their needs most effectively."

Jerriann Wilson, the Child Life Specialist in our profile, described how research has revealed the relationship between parents' attitudes and children's reactions to medical care. A key ingredient in such research is the experimental design used. In Chapter 5, the logic of experimental design was presented. The importance of having equivalent groups of subjects in the different experimental conditions was stressed. This chapter focuses on the fundamental procedures of experimental design, primarily the way that subjects are assigned to groups in an experiment. There are two basic ways of assigning subjects to groups. One way—an *independent groups design*—is to assign subjects randomly to the various conditions, and each subject participates in only one group. In the second procedure—a *repeated measures design*—subjects participate in more than one group. In the simplest experiment, each subject would be assigned to both levels of the independent variable. This procedure is called a repeated measures design, because each subject is measured after receiving each level of the independent variable.

INDEPENDENT GROUPS DESIGNS

In this section, we discuss the independent groups design. Two procedures may be used to assign different subjects to each of the groups:

Simple random assignment

Matched random assignment

Simple random assignment

The simplest method for assigning subjects to different groups is *simple random assignment*. If there are two groups in the experiment, a possible randomization procedure would be to flip a coin to assign subjects to one or the other group. Even better, and when there are more than two groups, the researcher can use a table of random numbers to assign subjects. A table of random numbers and instructions for using it are shown in Appendix C. The researcher can use the arrangement of the numbers in the table to determine the assignment of each subject to his or her group. Random assignment is assumed to prevent any biases, because the groups should end up equivalent in terms of subject characteristics such as social class, intelligence, age, or political attitudes. If the two groups happen to be selected on the basis of one subject characteristic such as age, random assignment will equate the groups on the other subject characteristics. An important consideration is sample size, because the assumption that random assignment procedures produce equivalent groups becomes more reasonable as the number of subjects increases.

Matched random assignment

A somewhat more complicated method of assigning subjects to different groups is called *matched random assignment*. Matching procedures can be used when the researcher wants to ensure that the groups are equivalent on a specific subject characteristic, especially when small samples are involved. Typically, the matching variable is a subject characteristic that is strongly related to the dependent variable. For example, in many experiments comparing children with learning disabilities with nondisabled children, subjects are matched on the basis of IQ (intelligence quotient) scores, so that the specific learning disability, not overall intelligence, is the critical variable. However, if intelligence is not related to the dependent measure (say, ability to walk on a balance beam), matching on the basis of intelligence is not useful.

When matched random assignment procedures are used, the first step is to obtain a measure of the matching variable from each subject. The subjects are then rank ordered from highest to lowest on the basis of their scores on the matching variable. Now, the researcher can form subject pairs that are approximately equal on the characteristic (the highest two subjects form the first pair, the next two form the second pair, etc.). Finally, the members of each pair are randomly assigned to the conditions in the experiment.

Matching can make it possible to account for some of the individual differences in response to the independent variable. Suppose you conduct an experiment in which the independent variable is written versus audio presentation of educational materials, and the dependent variable is students' ability to recall facts from the material. When you examine the results, you may find that the average ability to recall is different in the two groups. You may also find that, within each group, subjects' recall scores vary; children do not respond with the exact same score even though they were in the same group. With simple random assignment, we don't know why this variability exists; it is merely called "error" or unexplained variance in the scores. With matched random assignment to groups, it is possible by using appropriate statistical procedures to account for much of the variability within each group. For instance, if IQ is related to the ability to remember material, we can statistically identify the extent to which individual differences in reactions to the independent variable are due to IQ. The ability to explain the variability in scores on the dependent variable reduces the amount of "error"; when error or unexplained variability is reduced, we are more likely to find that the differences in the means are statistically significant.

These issues of variability and statistical significance are discussed further in Chapter 10 and in Appendix B. The main point here is that matching on a variable makes it more likely that statistically significant differences between groups will be found in an experiment. That is, matching can make our research more sensitive and precise.

However, matching procedures can be costly and time-consuming. They require that subjects be tested on the matching variable prior to the experiment. Care must be taken that such testing does not inadvertently bias the subjects' behavior on the experimental test. For example, suppose we give adolescents a pretest that assesses level of moral reasoning and then place the subjects in a situation in which it is either easy or difficult to cheat on a test (the independent variable in this case is "risk of being caught"). If the adolescents take the pretest as a cue that we are interested in measuring moral behavior, they may be less likely to cheat than they would in a real-world situation. In addition to the problem that a pretest can contaminate the actual experiment, it may not be worth the effort if the sample size is large enough. If we have a large enough sample, a simple randomization procedure should result in adequately matched groups without the bother of pretesting. Such efforts are worthwhile only when the matching variable is strongly related to the dependent measure.

In both simple and matched random assignment procedures, each subject participates in only one of the groups in the experiment, which is also known as a *between-subjects design.* An alternative procedure is to have the same subjects participate in all of the groups—the repeated measures design mentioned earlier in the chapter, also called a *within-subjects design.*

REPEATED MEASURES DESIGNS

Consider an experiment that investigates whether early readers are better at reading uppercase or lowercase letters. In an independent groups design, one group of subjects would be given uppercase text to read, and another group would receive lowercase text. In a repeated measures design, the same subjects are used in both conditions. Thus, subjects first read the uppercase material, and the experimenter then assesses reading proficiency by recording the amount of time taken to read the passage or perhaps the number of errors. The same subjects next read the same passage printed in lowercase letters. You can see why this design is called a repeated measures design—subjects are repeatedly measured on the dependent variable after being in each condition of the experiment.

The problem of order effects

There is an immediate problem associated with the repeated measures experiment. Suppose that reading is better (faster, more error-free) in the lowercase condition. Such a result could be caused by the manipulation of the case variable. However, the result could also simply be an *order effect*, in which the order of presenting the treatments affects the dependent variable. Thus, more proficient reading in the lowercase condition could be attributed to the fact that the lowercase passage came second in the order of presentation of the conditions. Performance on the second task might increase simply because of the practice developed on the first task or familiarity with the passage. Order effects are common any time there might be a "warm-up" effect (e.g., nursery school children become more responsive as they shed their initial shyness when meeting an unfamiliar experimenter). Warm-up effects produce better performance in conditions conducted later in the sequence. The opposite effect can be produced by fatigue; for example, children may perform more poorly in later conditions because they are tired or become less cooperative for reasons such as boredom or wandering attention.

Counterbalancing in repeated measures designs

In a repeated measures design, order effects are controlled by *counterbalancing*. With complete counterbalancing, all possible orders of presentation are included in the experiment. In the reading-test example, one-half of the children would be randomly assigned to the lowercase/uppercase order (A–B), and the other half would be assigned to the uppercase/lowercase order (B–A) (Figure 6.1).

Counterbalancing principles can be extended to experiments with three or more groups: with three groups, there are six possible orders (A–B–C, B–C–A, C–A–B, C–B–A, B–A–C, and A–C–B); with four conditions, there are twenty-four possible orders. In practice, with four or more groups, the order of presentation is either randomized across subjects or a partially counterbalanced design is used. Otherwise, it wouldn't be feasible to conduct all the potential orders. The object is to design the experiment in such a way that any potential effects of order are distributed evenly across the subjects in the various conditions.

Advantages and disadvantages of repeated measures designs

The repeated measures design has several advantages. Using this design, some experiments can be conducted with fewer subjects, because each subject participates in all conditions. When subjects are scarce or when it is costly to use subjects, a repeated measures design may be preferred. For instance, in much research on adult perception, extensive training of subjects

CHAPTER 6 TYPES OF EXPERIMENTAL DESIGNS

Figure 6.1
Example of counterbalancing

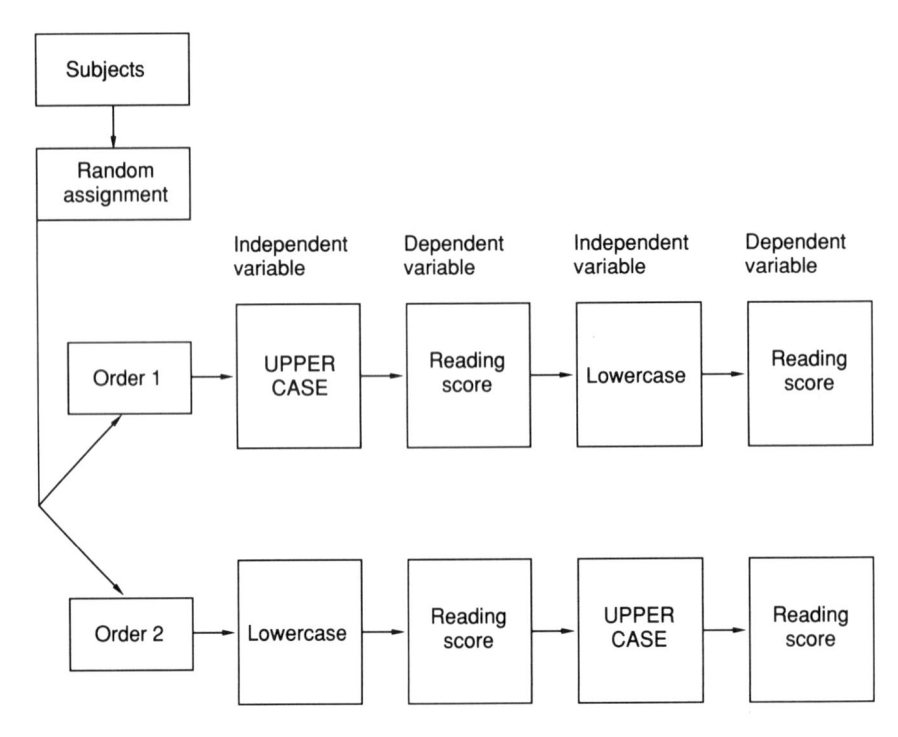

```
Subjects
   │
   ▼
Random
assignment
   │
   ├──► Order 1 ──► UPPER CASE ──► Reading score ──► Lowercase ──► Reading score
   │                (Independent    (Dependent       (Independent   (Dependent
   │                 variable)       variable)        variable)      variable)
   │
   └──► Order 2 ──► Lowercase ──► Reading score ──► UPPER CASE ──► Reading score
```

is necessary before the actual experiment is begun. Such research often involves only a few subjects who participate in all conditions of the experiment.

An additional advantage of repeated measures (or within-subjects) designs is that they are extremely sensitive to finding differences produced by the independent variable. Because subjects in the various conditions are identical in every respect (they are the same people), error variability due to subject differences (e.g., IQ, personality, past history) is minimized. The principle of these designs is the same as the matching designs, but subjects are not just matched on a single characteristic—they are identical on all characteristics. The result is that we are much more likely to detect an effect of the independent variable if a repeated measures design is used. Despite these advantages, repeated measures designs have limitations.

Carry-over effects A major drawback to repeated measures designs is the possibility of *carry-over effects*, which occur if the effects of one treatment are still present when the next treatment is given. That is, because of their nature, the effects of certain manipulations tend to persist. For example, consider an experiment in which condition A is physical exercise and condition B is listening to soothing music; the dependent variable is a measure of subsequent stress reduction in employed, single parents. Counterbalancing would not necessarily remedy the carry-over problem in this example, because the procedure assumes that the carry-over effect from condition A to condition B is the same as from B to A. If condition A is quite fatiguing, its very nature could affect condition B (if subjects are still tired from the exercise) more than the carry-over effect of listening to soothing music first in the B–A order. A possible remedy is to arrange a long enough interval between conditions for the effects of the first condition to erode. For instance, the participants could be tested on two different days. Another alternative, of course, is to use an independent groups design.

Demand characteristics Another problem in a repeated measures design is that the subjects have knowledge of all the conditions. When subjects participate in all of the groups, they may quickly figure out the true purpose of the experiment. Thus, subjects may behave differently than they would if they were unaware of the hypothesis. It is usually more difficult for subjects to discern the true purpose of the experiment in an independent groups design. This problem is one of *demand characteristics*, in which various aspects of the experiment provide cues that enable the subject to discover the researcher's hypothesis.

In sum, repeated measures designs have advantages and disadvantages. The advantages are the following:

1. Possible savings in the number of subjects required to run the experiment
2. Greater control over subject differences and thus greater ability to detect an effect of the independent variable.

The disadvantages are the following:

1. Carry-over effects
2. Demand characteristics

Obviously, the advantages are worthwhile only if the disadvantages seem minimal.

LONGITUDINAL VERSUS CROSS-SECTIONAL DESIGNS

Special issues concerning independent groups versus repeated measures designs arise when researchers study how a variable changes as a function of age. We may be interested in testing a theory that concerns changes in ability to reason as children grow older, the age at which self-awareness develops in infants, or the global values people have as they move from adolescence through old age. In all cases, the major variable is age. Whereas age, strictly speaking, is not a true experimental variable (we cannot manipulate it directly), developmental researchers study the age variable by selecting subjects at different ages or studying the same individuals at different points in their lives.

Two general methods are used to study the age variable:

The longitudinal method
The cross-sectional method

Using the *longitudinal method*, the same subjects are observed repeatedly as they grow older. This method is conceptually similar to a repeated measures design. For example, a longitudinal study may follow a group of children from age 5 to age 13 at two-year intervals.

Using the more common *cross-sectional method*, persons of different ages are studied at only one point in time. For example, a researcher using a cross-sectional design might study five different groups of children, grouped by age (say, 5, 7, 9, 11, and 13), to compare how a specific behavior differs as a function of age.

Measuring developmental difference: cross-sectional studies

Suppose an educational researcher wants to determine the optimal age for use of the keyword "mental imagery strategy" discussed in Chapter 1. The most efficient kind of design is a cross-sectional one, in which the length of the study is determined by how quickly the researcher can test the different age groups; the experimenter does not have to wait while the children age. Not only does this type of design save the experimenter time, but the results will also be available to educators in a timely fashion. Thus, economy and timeliness are two major advantages of the cross-sectional approach.

However, there are also a number of disadvantages to cross-sectional studies. For one example, they do not directly tell us about developmental trends. For instance, the preceding study does not tell us about the changes in children's understanding of the keyword method as they grow cognitively. The comparison of different children at different ages provides only an indirect picture of performance at different points on the developmental ladder. Because a group of older children performs better than a different group of younger children, we are able to infer that ability to use an imagery strategy improves with age, but we haven't observed this improvement directly.

Another problem with the cross-sectional approach concerns the equivalence of the groups studied. In dealing with the practical problem of finding subjects, researchers draw different aged subjects from different pools: hospital records, newspaper solicitations, university nursery schools, public schools, churches, colleges, senior citizens' clubs, and so on. Such methods of subject selection do not tell us whether the subjects selected are equivalent on the matching variables of interest. For example, consider college students who presumably represent a high level of academic ability versus elementary school children who span the entire range of academic skills. If we are interested in matching these groups on intellectual ability, are they really comparable?

Whenever we compare groups with substantially different characteristics, the different groups are called *cohorts*. K. Warner Schaie (1986) pointed out that cohorts may be based on various classification systems such as biological age, societal age, historical experiences, or other defining conditions. For example, a societally defined cohort may include people entering retirement or beginning their second marriage; a history-based cohort may consist of the initial staff of a new hospital or corporation. In developmental research, the term "cohort" is usually assumed to refer to groups that are defined on the basis of biological age, unless another definition is explicitly given.

Alternate sources of cohort differences (other than biological age) are especially interesting to consider whenever we compare groups with wide age differences. Suppose we want to compare intelligence of 20-year-olds with that of 80-year-olds. Our research question is whether intelligence declines with age. If we find that the 80-year-old cohort scores lower on our IQ test than the 20-year-olds, we may conclude that intelligence does indeed decline with age, but there are a surprising number of differences between the two age groups that have nothing to do with age per se (i.e., the biological differences in body chemistry and function associated with aging). Table 6.1 lists some possible cohort differences between these two hypothetical groups. Note that many of the cohort differences, such as level of education and standard of living, seem to favor the younger cohort. However, some of

Table 6.1 Hypothetical cohort differences between 80-year-olds and 20-year-olds

Birth order

More later-born individuals in older cohort because of larger average family size; it has been proposed that intelligence is negatively related to birth order position and family size

Communications

Younger cohort has experienced information explosion because of global communications capability; the world of influence was smaller when older cohort was growing up

Diet

Younger cohort has grown up with more synthetic food

Education (amount)

Older cohort may not have had as much education as younger cohort

Education (type)

Different trends in pedagogy have existed throughout the decades; style of education may have been different for different cohorts

Gender

Because of differential life spans of men and women, more females in older cohort

Life experiences

Older cohort has experienced Great Depression, major wars; younger cohort has experienced relative global political and economic stability

Standard of living

Younger cohort has probably experienced higher average standard of living

Table 6.1
(*continued*)

Technology

Younger cohort has grown up in technologically advanced environment

Television

Younger cohort grew up with TV

Urbanization

Older cohort grew up in more agrarian society

Values and mores

Younger cohort has experienced erosion of family and traditional community values

Women's roles

Older cohort had fewer acceptable roles to which women could aspire.

---

the variables do not yield easy predictions. For example, there have been major dietary changes over this century. Which cohort do you think has had the most nutritious diet? The younger cohort has grown up with television. Is this an advantage or a disadvantage? On average, there are more women in the older cohort. How does this make-up affect the group's intellectual performance? Can you think of any other cohort differences that may influence performance on an intelligence test?

The point: Cohort differences can obscure the developmental changes we are seeking. In technical terms, cross-sectional designs confound age and cohort differences. It can be that the 80-year-olds have not actually experienced any age-related (i.e., physical, biological) declines in intelligence; they score lower than 20-year-olds because they have less education on average. The only way to determine conclusively whether we lose intellectual ability as we age is to conduct a longitudinal study.

Measuring developmental change: longitudinal studies

The primary advantage of the longitudinal design is that the researcher can observe actual changes occurring in the subject. To use this approach, we select a group of young adults and follow them over the course of several decades. Because such a design is in effect a repeated measures design, we do not have to worry about the irrelevant sources of variability that characterize between-groups comparisons. In this study, there are no cohort effects because we are always studying the same cohort.

The main disadvantage of the longitudinal method is that it is expensive and time-consuming to track people over long periods of time. For example, it would take 60 years to conduct our hypothetical intelligence study. The experimenters would probably not live to see the results of the study! Imagine the cost of tracking a large group of people over 60 years: Some would invariably be lost; some would die. If there is some relationship between mortality and the variable of interest, this relationship would bias the data gathered in the later stages of the study. In other words, if more intelligent people live longer, our measurement of IQ as the subjects aged would be too high, relative to the intelligence of the entire original group.

If you are thinking that these problems would only occur in the extreme example under discussion, think further. For example, research with infants and preschool children is especially affected by the problem of untestable subjects. In a major longitudinal study in which children were tested several times between the ages of 12 and 72 months, Allen Gottfried and his colleagues noted that on some occasions children were unresponsive or uncooperative and could not be tested. Rather than eliminating them from the study, Gottfried and his associate Kay Bathurst were able to test them on subsequent occasions and found that these children were significantly lower on a wide range of abilities (Bathurst & Gottfried, 1987). If uncooperative subjects had been thrown out of the study, especially if they were untestable at an early session, their elimination would have biased the results. You can see why subject attrition is a major concern in longitudinal research—not simply because the sample shrinks, but also because the validity of the results is threatened.

Finally, the sheer amount of time it takes to perform a longitudinal study is a major disadvantage. The research team can lose its funding in the middle of the project. The development of a new measurement technique (e.g., a new revision of a standardized test) can make the early results obsolete or at least difficult to compare to the later measurements. By the time the results are available, the original research questions may seem trivial or no longer appropriate. These are some of the reasons why longitudinal studies are conducted infrequently.

Nevertheless, good longitudinal studies provide us with some highly valuable insights. For example, Ross and his colleagues (1985) conducted a 40-year study of 160 mentally retarded individuals who were placed in special classes in school based on childhood IQs of less than 80. Extensive data were gathered on their education, intelligence, personality, work, marriage and family, and social milieu across the 40-year span studied. The following paragraph summarizes some of the intriguing conclusions drawn as a result of this massive study.

> The subjects of our study, classified as retarded in school but functioning as reasonably competent citizens in adulthood, seem to have owed their success in life to (1) stable, supportive family relationships during the formative years of development and throughout childhood, (2) special attention to their educational needs and learning problems in the schools and to some extent in their homes, (3) conditions of high employment when they were ready to enter the labor market, and (4) marriage to spouses of higher ability, who helped to enhance and stabilize family life (Ross, Begab, Dondis, Giampiccolo, & Myers, 1985, p. 148).

Sequential designs

Fortunately, there are various ways of compromising between the longitudinal and cross-sectional approaches. For example, when groups of overlapping ages are tested longitudinally, it is known as a *sequential design*. One group of children can be studied at ages 5, 7, and 9; another group can be studied at ages 9, 11, and 13. This method requires 5 years of data gathering, as opposed to 9 years for a complete longitudinal study. Using a sequential approach, the researcher is provided with immediate rewards because useful data on differences in age groups are available even in the first year of the study.

Consider a hypothetical study of how preschoolers learn the alphabet. We could devise a simple test of alphabet knowledge and administer it to two cohorts, say, children ages 3–4 and 5–6. We could assess their alphabet knowledge three times over the course of a year. This study combines the longitudinal and cross-sectional approaches in that it tests individual subjects repeatedly over a period of time, plus it compares two age groups. This design would enable us to determine the difference in alphabet knowledge between the two ages and to assess the development of alphabet knowledge in the individual children we were studying.

TIME-SERIES EXPERIMENTS

Another approach to the manipulation of variables is typically used by researchers in behavior modification. This research tradition can be traced to the work of B. F. Skinner (1953) on reinforcement schedules, and it is often seen in applied and clinical settings when behavior modification techniques are used. However, the techniques and logic of *time-series* procedures can be readily applied to other research areas. The basic procedure is accomplished by systematically presenting and withdrawing the independent variable and observing changes in the dependent variable. Often this procedure is used with individual subjects, and it is thus called a *single-subject experiment*.

Reversal designs

The basic issue in single-subject experiments is how to determine that the manipulation of the independent variable has had an effect. One method is to demonstrate the reversibility of the manipulation. A *single-subject, reversal design* takes the following form:

>A *(control condition)*
>B *(experimental manipulation)*
>A *(control condition)*

This design, frequently called an *ABA design*, involves measuring the subject to obtain a baseline of behavior during a control period, introducing the manipulation and measuring behavior during this period, and finally, measuring the subject during a second control period. For example, an adolescent's studying behavior can be observed during the first control period (the baseline phase). The researcher then records the number of minutes of studying per day. Next, the experimental manipulation is introduced—the subject may be reinforced for studying by earning the right to watch a certain amount of television for every half hour of schoolwork. The amount of studying during the experimental period (the treatment phase) is recorded. Finally, the reinforcement is removed, and studying is again observed (the reversal, or withdrawal phase). If the experimental manipulation is effective, we may expect to see the amount of time studying increase during the experimental period and then decrease, a reversal, in the final control period. For instance, the ABA sequence of studying behavior may be 20 min, 60 min, and 30 min during each of the three phases of the experiment. Such results indicate the effectiveness of the manipulation by demonstrating a reversal of the behavior.

The ABA design can be greatly improved by extending it to an *ABAB design*, in which the experimental manipulation is introduced a second time. When an ABA design is used, it is possible to argue that various other factors are responsible for the reversal. For example, outside events that happen to coincide with the experimental manipulation can cause the results. If there were to be a major test in one of the student's classes during the treatment phase, the test might have motivated the student to study more during that period. Or, the manipulation might have coincided with a reading assignment that the student happened to find especially interesting and enjoyable. It is also possible that any observed changes reflect a normal cyclical pattern of behavior. If an ABAB design is used, such arguments could be rejected more easily: It seems unlikely that coincidental factors could be responsible for two reversals in behavior. Thus, evidence from an ABAB design experiment is especially convincing.

Let's consider an experiment in which researchers used a single-subject, reversal design to raise the rate of social interaction exhibited by a 4-year-old girl in a preschool classroom (Allen, Hart, Buell, Harris, & Wolf, 1964). The girl was isolated and withdrawn and primarily interacted with her teachers rather than with the other children. The goal of the study was for the child to achieve and maintain more play relationships with her peers. Baseline measurements were taken by two observers who sampled her proximity and interaction behaviors in 10-sec intervals. The baseline period covered 5 days. During the intervention phase, her teachers rewarded her by smiling, touching, talking, and giving assistance to her only when she was interacting with other children. Their praise markedly increased her contact with children during this period. During the reversal phase, the girl resumed her interactions solely with adults. Reinstatement of the intervention restored

Figure 6.2 Percentages of time spent in social interaction with adults and with children (after Allen, Hart, Buell, Harris, & Wolf, 1964)

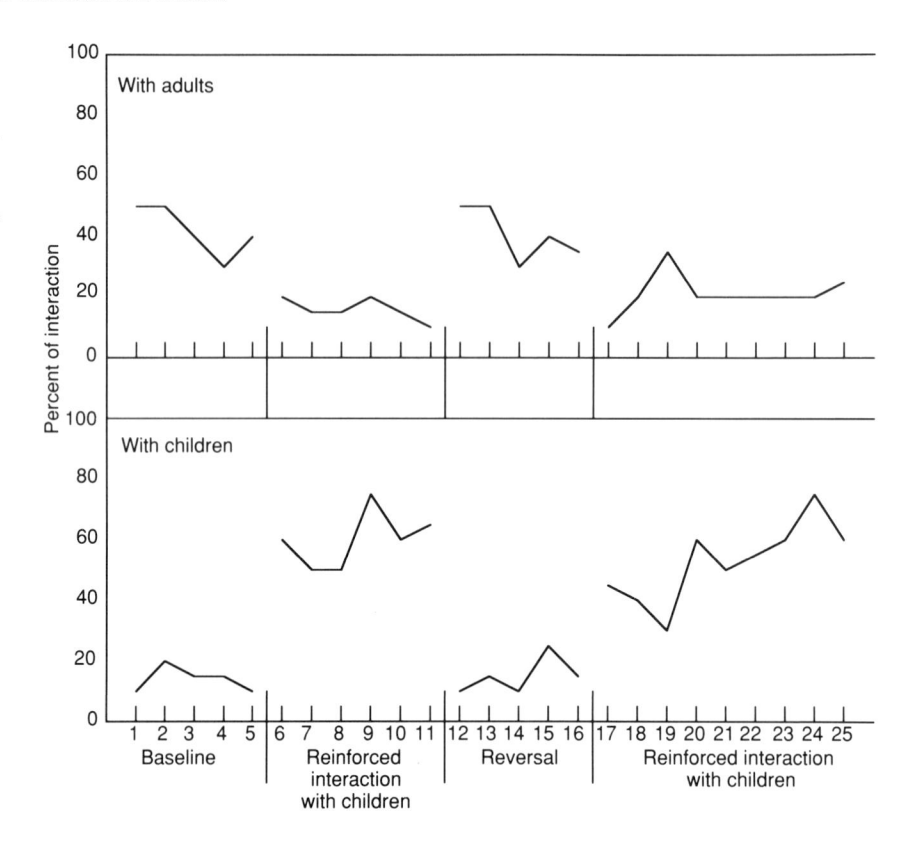

peer interaction. Once this social behavior with peers became firmly established, the teachers presented the reinforcement on an increasingly intermittent schedule until the child was exhibiting a normal pattern of peer socialization on her own. Figure 6.2 shows an approximation of what the results looked like in this study. You can observe the child's level of interaction with adults and with children rise and fall depending on the presence of reinforcement.

Multiple baseline design

It may have occurred to you that a reversal of some behaviors may be impossible or unethical. For example, it is unethical to reverse a treatment that reduces undesirable or illegal behavior, such as drug abuse, eating disorders, or self-injurious behaviors. In such cases, multiple measures over time can be made before and after the manipulation. If the manipulation is effective, a change in behavior will be immediately observed, and the change will continue to be reflected in further measures of the behavior. In a *multiple baseline design*, the effectiveness of the manipulation is demonstrated if a behavior changes only when the manipulation is introduced.

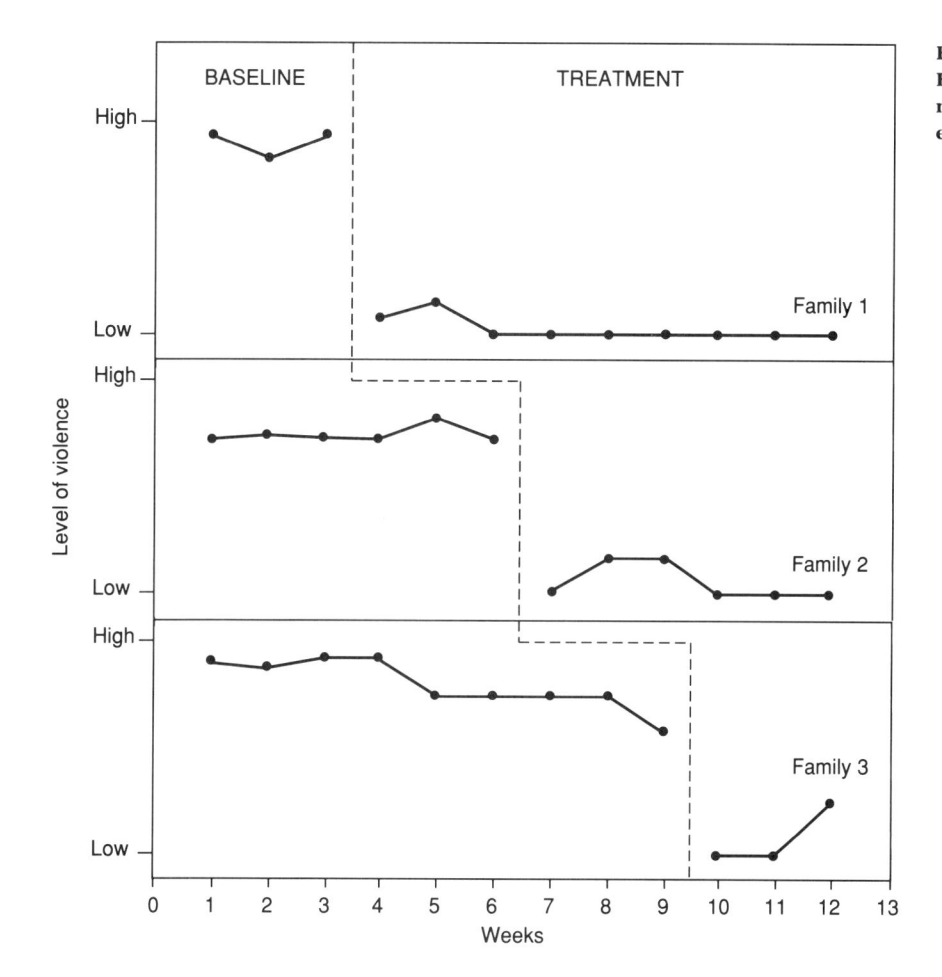

**Figure 6.3
Hypothetical
multiple baseline
experiment**

There are several variations of the multiple baseline design (Barlow & Hersen, 1984). One involves using multiple baselines across subjects; in this case, the behavior of several subjects is measured over time. For each subject, though, the manipulation is introduced at a different point in time. Figure 6.3 shows data from a hypothetical experiment to reduce family violence. The experiment uses three subjects (the subjects are families). Note that the introduction of the manipulation is followed by a change in behavior for each family. Because this change occurs across families and the manipulation is introduced at a different time for each family, we can rule out explanations based on chance, historical events, and so on.

The second type of multiple baseline design involves multiple baselines across behaviors; several behaviors of a single subject are measured over time. At different points in time, the same manipulation is applied to each of the behaviors. For example, a reward system may be instituted to increase the socializing, grooming, and language behaviors of a hospitalized Alzheimer's patient. The reward system is applied to each of these behaviors at different points in time. Demonstrating that each behavior increases when the reward system is applied evidences the effectiveness of the manipulation.

The third variation is multiple baselines across situations; the same behavior is measured in different settings such as at home and at work. Again, a manipulation is introduced at a different time in each setting with the expectation that a change in the behavior in each situation will occur only after the manipulation.

Single-subject design with replications

The procedures for use with a single subject can be replicated with other subjects, greatly enhancing the generalizability of the results. That is, it is desirable that our findings generalize to entire populations and are not limited to a single case. Usually reports of research that employ single-subject procedures do present the results from several subjects. Typically, however, the data from each subject are presented separately. In some clinical research, data are presented separately because the behavior change technique was individually programmed for each individual subject. In other research, however, data from individual subjects rather than group means are often presented because tradition stresses the understanding of responses to the manipulation at the *individual* level. Moreover, grouping the data from a number of subjects by using group means can sometimes give a misleading picture of individual responses to the manipulation of the independent variable. For example, the manipulation may be effective in changing the behavior of some subjects but not others. An emphasis on the individual subject quickly reveals that the manipulation was not effective for some subjects, and steps can then be taken to discover why the manipulation wasn't effective for these individuals.

Most research in the behavioral sciences uses large samples rather than single subjects. Reversal and multiple baseline procedures used in single-subject experiments are really only appropriate for a restricted set of variables. Specifically, these procedures are most useful when the behavior is reversible or when one can expect a relatively dramatic shift in behavior after the manipulation. Single-subject research typically tests predictions derived from the behaviorist tradition and is aimed at producing changes in behavior for specific individuals. Such a therapeutically oriented approach to studying the problems of individuals can be contrasted to studies that investigate questions best answered by looking at behavior averaged over many individuals. Because most researchers wish to discover something about behavior in general, their results must generalize beyond one individual case at a time. Nevertheless, single-subject studies represent an important, if specialized, mode of research.

SUMMARY

In this chapter, we discussed the two major ways subjects can participate in groups in experiments. First, in independent groups (also called between-subjects) designs, each subject participates in only one group. Simple random assignment is a typical means for assigning subjects to groups. Matched random assignment is a more complex method wherein subjects are matched on the basis of characteristics that are strongly related to the dependent variable. Second, in repeated measures (or within-subjects) designs, each subject participates in more than one group. The technique of counterbalancing is used to control for order effects that occur when subjects participate in more than one condition. Repeated measures studies can often be conducted with fewer subjects and have reduced subject error variability compared to independent groups designs. However, researchers must be on the lookout for the susceptibility to demand characteristics and carry-over effects that can occur when subjects participate in more than one condition of the study.

In developmental research, two kinds of designs can be compared. In the cross-sectional design, subjects of different ages are studied at a single point in time. As with any independent groups design, the researcher must worry about the problem of equivalence of the groups studied. Groups with substantially different characteristics are called cohorts, and they can be defined on the basis of various characteristics such as societal landmarks, historical benchmarks, or (most commonly) biological age of the subjects. Researchers wishing to study biological age differences must be aware of possible differences between age groups that have nothing to do with age, per se. These differences are known as cohort differences, and they are a possible source of experimental confounding. In contrast to cross-sectional studies, longitudinal studies test the same subjects at two or more points in time, thus avoiding cohort differences. Longitudinal research has the disadvantages of expense, subject attrition, and delay in obtaining the results, but it has provided some highly valuable insights into how growth and development produce changes in children, adults, and families. Finally, sequential designs involve a combination of cross-sectional and longitudinal approaches.

Time-series experiments are a special class of repeated measures studies, typically involving single subjects. The basic design involves systematically presenting and withdrawing the independent variable and observing changes in the dependent variable. The basic reversal design (also known as the ABA design), involves a control condition, followed by an experimental treatment, followed by another control condition. The ABAB design adds another treatment to ensure that behavioral changes are associated with the independent variable and not other coincidental factors. A multiple baseline design is a variation used when reversal of the behavior of interest is impossible or unethical. Time-series research involving single subjects typically tests predictions derived from the behaviorist tradition and can be contrasted with designs that look at behavior averaged over many individuals.

STUDY QUESTIONS

1. What is the difference between simple random assignment and the matched random sampling procedure?
2. Use the table of random numbers in Appendix C to assign 24 subjects to an independent groups experiment having four conditions.
3. What is the difference between repeated measures and independent groups experiments?
4. Explain why repeated measures studies are usually more sensitive to finding differences produced by the independent variable.
5. What type of questions are best addressed by cross-sectional designs? Longitudinal designs?
6. What is a sequential design? When should it be employed?
7. Suppose you were studying attitudes toward parenting in mothers and fathers who had their children in the 1940s versus the 1980s. How do the cohort differences listed for individuals in Table 6.1 apply to the families that are the focus of your study?
8. Explain how subject attrition in a longitudinal study can produce systematic bias in the results as the study progresses.
9. Why is an ABAB design better than an ABA design?
10. Distinguish three types of multiple baseline studies.

CHAPTER 7

Complex Experimental Designs

CAREER PROFILE

Kathleen C. Guy / Bereavement Counselor

Kathy holds a B.S. in Psychology from Denison University; an M.A. in Educational Psychology from the University of California, Berkeley; and an Ed.D. in Counseling and Guidance from the University of Nevada, Reno. She is the Bereavement Counselor for the St. Peter's Community Hospital Hospice Program, Helena, Montana.

Kathy's responsibilities include (1) provision of individual and group counseling services; (2) oversight of special peer support groups such as survivors of suicide, widows support, pregnancy loss, and SIDs parents; and (3) provision of educational and other support services to organizations, businesses, and professional groups, as well as concerned individuals regarding the grieving process and how to help others deal with losses. "I use a variety of therapeutic techniques to facilitate a normalization of grieving behavior, provide opportunities to express emotions, remember and come to terms with the lost relationship, and facilitate the building of a new life.... Bereavement is a crucible in which family function/dysfunction becomes quite evident. In assisting with the grief process, we have an opportunity to encourage growth and change in nearly all areas of a client's life.

"Research provides information that enables me to differentiate normal and pathological grief, which is especially important because our society does not recognize and facilitate healthy grief responses. Instead, it encourages denial and control that impede the process. New research findings are beginning to help us differentiate the impact of different kinds of losses—for example, child versus parent; accidental versus expected; and violent death versus suicide—that will facilitate appropriate bereavement services."

The basic experimental designs we have described thus far address simple questions about differences between groups such as "Do 3-year-old children and 5-year-old children differ in the number of letters of the alphabet they can identify?" or "Will experience with an alphabet computer game increase letter identification ability in children?" Although basic designs are useful, the information they can provide is limited. More complex designs are usually required to answer the questions advanced in research. For example, Kathy Guy featured in the career profile indicates that research findings help differentiate the effects of different kinds of loss such as child versus parent or accidental versus expected. The effects of both kinds of loss on grieving can be studied simultaneously with a complex experimental design, and these types of designs are considered in this chapter.

FACTORIAL DESIGNS

Most experimental research consists of the evaluation of more than one independent variable in a single experiment. Typically, two or three independent variables are considered simultaneously. Such designs allow for greater approximation of real-world conditions in which independent variables do not exist by themselves. Researchers recognize that behavior is affected by a combination of variables, so they design complex experiments that provide more complete evidence about the factors that affect behavior and development.

Factorial designs are designs with more than one independent variable (or factor). In a factorial design, all levels of each independent variable are combined with all levels of the other independent variable. The simplest factorial design has two independent variables, each with two levels; this kind of design is referred to as a 2 × 2 (read: two by two) *factorial design*.

Consider the following hypothetical experiment designed to evaluate simultaneous questions about possible age (3 years versus 5 years) and instructional treatment (computer game versus no computer game) differences on children's alphabet identification. When the two levels of the two independent variables are combined, a total of four groups—or conditions—is produced:

1. Three-year-olds, no computer game
2. Three-year-olds, computer game
3. Five-year-olds, no computer game
4. Five-year-olds, computer game

This 2 × 2 factorial design thus consists of two independent variables with two levels each.

Interpretation of results from factorial designs

Factorial designs provide different kinds of information. One type regards the effect of each independent variable by itself. The second kind of information provided is the interaction between the independent variables. For a design with two independent variables, there are two main effects and one interaction (or three sources of effects). The interaction in this type of 2 × 2 factorial indicates whether the influence of one independent variable is contingent or dependent on the level of the other independent variable.

To illustrate main effects and interactions, we can look at the results of our hypothetical experiment concerning alphabet identification. Table 7.1 illustrates a common method of presenting the means for the groups in a factorial design. The numbers in each cell represent the mean number of letters in the alphabet correctly identified in the four conditions.

Main effects A *main effect* is the influence each independent variable has by itself. In Table 7.1, the main effect of age (independent variable A) is the relationship between the child's age and the number of letters identified. Similarly, the main effect of the computer game (independent variable B) is

Age Group (independent variable A)	Condition (independent variable B) No computer	Computer	M (marginal means for main effect of independent variable A)
Three	3.00	13.00	8.00
Five	16.00	21.00	18.50
M (marginal means for main effect of independent variable B)	9.50	17.00	

Table 7.1
Mean number of letters identified in the computer game experiment

the effect that playing an alphabet computer game has on subsequent letter identification.

The main effect of each independent variable is the overall relationship between the independent variable and the dependent variable. In other words, it resembles a simple, two-group experiment. For independent variable A, is there a relationship between age and letter identification performance? Let's look at the overall (or marginal) means in Table 7.1. We refer to these means as *marginals* because they are shown in the margins of the table (outside the cell or group means). The marginal mean for the older children is 18.50, whereas the marginal mean for younger children is 8.00. The calculations of these means for the main effect of the age variable are as follow (assuming equal numbers of subjects in each group):

$$\bar{X} \text{ (age 3)} = \frac{3 + 13}{2} = \frac{16}{2} = 8.00$$

$$\bar{X} \text{ (age 5)} = \frac{16 + 21}{2} = \frac{37}{2} = 18.50$$

Overall, it can be seen that older children may be associated with more letter identifications than younger children. Statistical tests can determine if this apparent developmental (age-related) difference is reliable; if so, this effect is then referred to as a statistically significant main effect.

The main effect for computer game (variable B) is the overall relationship between this variable, by itself, and the dependent variable of the number of correct letter identifications. The calculations of the marginal means for the no computer versus computer conditions are as follows:

$$\bar{X} \text{ (no computer)} = \frac{3 + 16}{2} = \frac{19}{2} = 9.50$$

$$\bar{X} \text{ (computer)} = \frac{13 + 21}{2} = \frac{34}{2} = 17.00$$

The marginal means show that the computer game group (mean number of identifications = 17.00) identified more letters than the no computer game group (mean number of identifications = 9.50). Again, a statistical test is required to determine if the difference is significant. An observed statistically significant main effect indicates that a reliable difference between the conditions has been found.

Interaction An *interaction* between independent variables indicates that the effect of one independent variable is different at different levels of the other independent variable. An interaction is evident in our example study. The effect of computer play is greater for 3-year-old children than for 5-year-old children: That is, younger children benefited more from the computer game in terms of alphabet identification than the older children did. Thus, understanding the effectiveness of a computer learning experience depends on the age of the child; in this example, it is more effective with younger children.

Interactions can easily be seen when the means for all conditions are

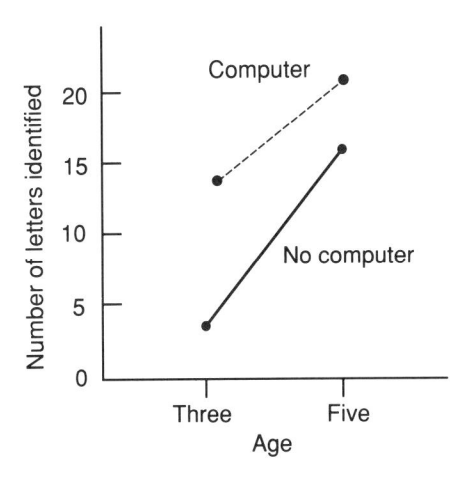

Figure 7.1 Interaction between computer game exposure and age

presented in a graph. Figure 7.1 presents a graph that depicts the results of our alphabet identification study. Note that all four cell means have been depicted and that there are two lines to describe the performance relationship between the groups. In contrast to Table 7.1, no explicit information about the overall effect (represented by the marginal means) of each independent variable is presented in the graph. The fact that the difference between the means of the no computer versus computer groups is larger for 3-year-olds than for 5-year-olds indicates an interaction. In other words, the gap between the two computer groups is larger at one age level than the other.

The concept of interaction is a relatively simple one that you probably use all the time: When you say "it depends," it usually indicates that some sort of interaction is operating. For example, a decision to go to a party may reflect an interaction between two variables: (1) Is an exam coming up (yes or no)? and (2) Is a specific person going to be there (yes or no)? If you have an exam coming up, you may not go to the party under any circumstances (probability of attendance is low). If you do not have an exam coming up, your decision may depend on the presence of the other person; that is, you will go only if he or she will be there.

Outcomes of 2 × 2 factorial design

A 2 × 2 factorial design has two independent variables, each with two levels. When analyzing the results, there are several possibilities:

1. There may or may not be a significant main effect for independent variable *A*.
2. There may or may not be a significant main effect for independent variable *B*.
3. There may or may not be a significant interaction between the independent variables.

When a 2 × 2 factorial design is used, the researcher has usually predicted an interaction between the two independent variables. Much of the time, the researcher is less interested in the main effects per se than in understanding the contingent relationships between the two variables. The *form* of the interaction predicted depends on the hypothesis; different hypotheses are associated with different forms of the interaction. Figure 7.2 presents six possible outcomes in a 2 × 2 factorial design, some containing interactions and some without. For each outcome, the means are given, and they are also depicted in a graph. Note that on each graph the dependent variable is placed on the vertical axis, and independent variable A is placed on the horizontal axis. The two means for B1 are plotted, and a line is drawn to represent this level of B. Similarly, the B2 means are plotted, and a second line is drawn to represent this level.

The means that are given in the figure are idealized examples. Such perfect outcomes rarely occur in actual research. Nevertheless, you should study the graphs to determine for yourself why, in each case, there is or isn't a main effect for A, a main effect for B, and an A × B interaction.

Figures 7.2a–7.2b illustrate outcomes in which no A × B interaction takes place. Figures 7.2c–7.2f represent outcomes in which there is an interaction. When there is no interaction, the lines for B1 and B2 are parallel. These parallel lines indicate that the nature of the relationship between independent variable A and the dependent variable is the same at B1 as it is at B2. In Figures 7.2a–7.2b, the lines are parallel, indicating no interaction. An alternate way to conceptualize the absence of an interaction is in terms of differences: The difference between the group means for A1 and A2 at B1 is *not* different from the difference between the group means for A1 and A2 at B2. In other words, the gap between the two conditions is the same at each level of the other variable. Thus, there is no interaction. If the researcher had predicted an interaction, an outcome with main effects and *no* interaction may indicate that the researcher's hypothesis requires modification and/or a more decisive test of the predicted interaction is required.

When the lines are not parallel, an interaction is present. Note in Figures 7.2c–7.2f that the lines do not actually have to cross on the graph; any deviation from parallelism indicates a possible interaction. Such outcomes indicate that the nature of the relationship is different, depending on the specific level of B. That is, the effects of independent variable A are different at each level of independent variable B. In Figures 7.2c–7.2f, the two lines are not parallel, which indicates interactions between the independent variables. In addition, note that in Figure 7.2f neither independent variable has an effect by itself; however, the interaction shows that independent variable A has strong (but opposite) effects, depending on the level of B. The interaction means that both independent variables must be considered if the relationships involved are to be understood. To make sure that you fully understand these graphs, try testing yourself: Cover the answers, or draw a new set of graphs, and see if you can say whether or not there are main effects or an interaction.

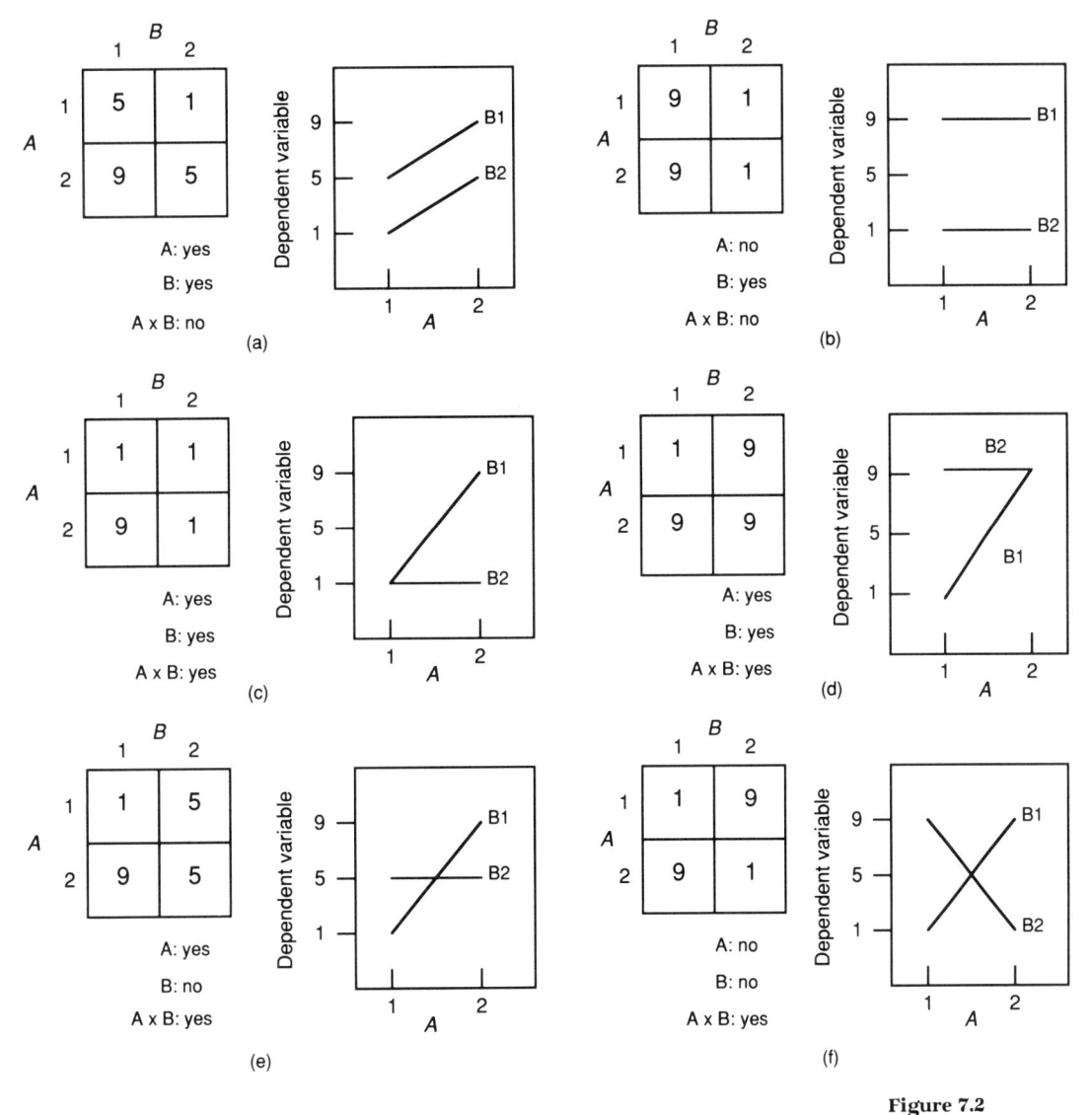

Figure 7.2 Outcomes of factorial designs with two independent variables: (a)–(b) no $A \times B$ interaction, (c)–(f) interaction

An alternate way to assess the presence of an interaction, without drawing a graph, is to find the differences between the group means of $A1$ and $A2$ at each level of B (i.e., $B1$ and $B2$). If the two differences are different, then an interaction is present. For example, Figure 7.2e illustrates an interaction because the two lines are not parallel. The presence of this interaction can also be assessed by taking the differences between the means: The difference between the $A1$ and $A2$ means ($A1 = 1$, $A2 = 9$: $9 - 1 = 8$) at $B1$ is 8, whereas the difference between $A1$ and $A2$ means ($A1 = 5$, $A2 = 5$: $5 - 5 = 0$) at $B2$ is 0. Since the two differences are different (i.e., $8 \neq 0$), an interaction is suggested. Try this method of taking the differences between the means for Figure 7.2a or 7.2b, in which no interaction is suggested by the graph. Are these differences appreciably different?

Kinds of factorial designs

The 2×2 factorial design illustrated in the preceding discussion includes a selected subject variable (age) and a manipulated variable. This kind of design is common in the human development and family literature. Other kinds of subject variables typically considered are sex, socioeconomic status, ethnic group membership, marital status, family size, birth order, personality characteristics, ability grouping, and clinical diagnostic category. As discussed in Chapter 6, this kind of design can be distinguished from experimental designs in which all of the independent variables are manipulated.

In Chapter 3, we also learned that cause-and-effect relationships can be inferred when differences on the dependent variable can be directly attributed to the manipulation of an independent variable (assuming, of course, that all extraneous variables are controlled). For example, in the alphabet identification study, we can infer that differences in letter identification can be directly attributed to the manipulation of children's exposure to computer game activities. As discussed in Chapter 6, subject variables such as age are *not* manipulated; their levels or categories are selected by the researcher. Thus in our alphabet study, the higher level of letter identification observed for older children in comparison to younger children is referred to as an age-related difference. A direct causal attribution cannot be made. That is, we cannot conclude that age per se caused the differences in letter identification. By stating that the difference is age-related, we acknowledge that

1. Cause and effect should not be assumed when the independent variable is *not* manipulated.
2. Other factors that systematically vary with our selected subject variable may be truly responsible.

Regarding the age variable, maturational and experiential factors are probably involved in the age-related differences we observe. What experiential factors do you think may contribute to improvement in letter identification? Can you think of different ways of manipulating experiential factors as independent variables in an experiment?

Another distinction discussed in Chapter 6 was independent groups versus repeated measures designs. Recall that in independent groups designs, different subjects are randomly assigned to the levels of the independent variable (experimental conditions). In complex designs that include more than one independent variable, an independent groups comparison is frequently referred to as a *between-subjects independent variable* or *factor*. This type of comparison indicates that the manipulation of the independent variable occurs *between* different groups of subjects. Thus, in a 2 × 2 factorial in which both independent variables are between subjects, four different groups of subjects participate in the experiment. Figure 7.3a illustrates the assignment of 40 subjects, 10 to each of four different conditions, in an independent groups design.

Recall that in a repeated measures design the same subjects participate in more than one condition. This kind of comparison is frequently referred to as a *within-subjects independent variable* or *factor* in complex designs which include more than one independent variable. This designation indicates that the manipulation of the independent variable occurs *within* the same subjects. For example, for a 2 × 2 factorial with repeated measures on both independent variables, each subject participates or is measured in each condition. Subject assignment for this kind of design in which conditions are evaluated *within* the same group of subjects is illustrated in Figure 7.3b. An advantage of this kind of design may be in terms of the number of subjects required. But, certain disadvantages must be overcome or controlled such as the effects of repeated testing and potential contamination produced by carry-over effects due to subjects' participation in more than one condition.

A combination of between- and within-subjects independent variables can be used in factorial designs. This kind of approach is common when the

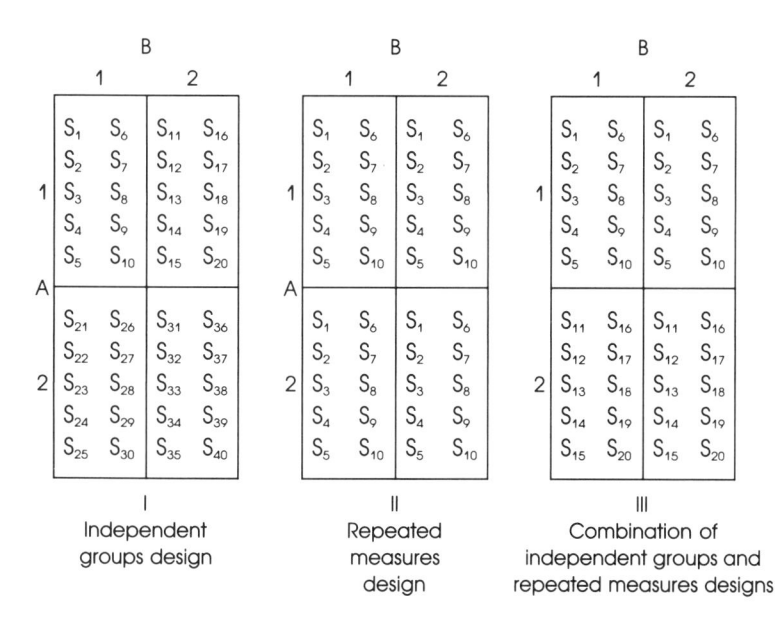

Figure 7.3
Examples of subject assignment for experimental designs: (a) independent groups design, (b) repeated measures design, and (c) combination of independent groups and repeated measures designs

design consists of a selected independent variable as the between-subjects factor and a manipulated independent variable as the within-subjects factor. For example, Figure 7.3c illustrates how two different groups of subjects comprise independent variable A, whereas both levels of independent variable B are represented within both groups of subjects. This kind of design is used in studies that examine the influence of sex role stereotypes. For example, subjects may be asked to listen to a story that describes a person engaged in both sex role appropriate and sex role inappropriate activities. After hearing the story, the subject is asked to recall all the activities engaged in by the story character. The comparison of appropriate versus inappropriate activities is the within-subjects independent variable, because each subject is exposed to both levels of this factor. The selected between-subjects factor may be the subject's sex (male versus female) or age group (e.g., young versus old).

Whether to test variables between subjects versus within subjects and whether to combine the different kinds of independent variables in complex designs are decisions based on many considerations. Most important is the relevance of the experimental design to the hypotheses examined. Secondary considerations may be those of cost and convenience. For example, if we are interested in examining people's proficiency at using their left versus right hand, we examine the independent variable of "hand" as a within-subjects variable. In contrast, questions that concern the manual proficiency of left-handed versus right-handed persons require a between-subjects comparison of the handedness variable. As you may guess, a 2 × 2 factorial design is used to determine if there is an interaction between handedness (left-handers versus right-handers) and manual proficiency (use of left hand versus use of right hand). In this example, the design should be mixed, consisting of both a within- and a between-subjects independent variable. If the dependent variable in this experiment is the time required for subjects to write the letters of the alphabet, what kind of outcome can you predict? Remember, a 2 × 2 design provides three sources of information: main effect of variable A, main effect of variable B, and the interaction. It may help you to graph the different kinds of interactions. (*Hint:* One of the graphs in Figure 7.2 is a likely outcome.)

ADDITIONAL COMPLEXITY

Adding levels to the independent variable

In the simplest experimental design, there are two levels of the independent variable. There are several reasons why a researcher may want to design an experiment with more than two levels. First, when the design includes only two levels, the research may not provide a completely accurate description of the nature of the relationship between the independent variable and the dependent variable. If there are only two levels of the independent variable, it is only possible to show linear relationships. For example, Figure 7.4 shows

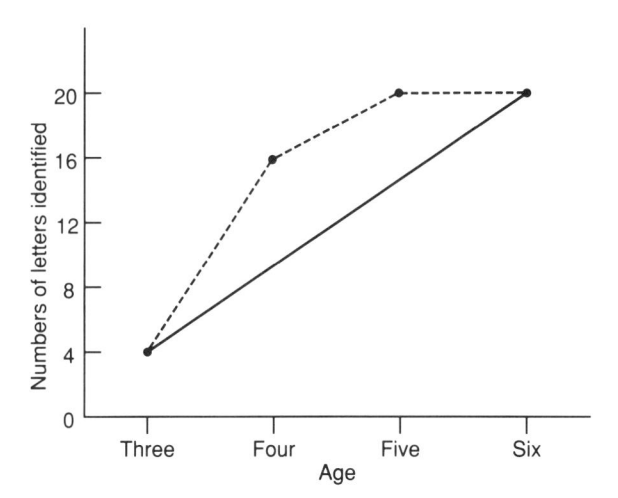

Figure 7.4 Comparison of hypothetical outcomes with two versus four levels of the independent variable

the outcome of a hypothetical experiment on the relationship between age and alphabet identification. The solid line describes the results when there are only two levels (3-year-olds versus 6-year-olds). Because there are only two levels, the relationship can only be described as a straight line. We don't know what the relationship would look like if intermediate age groups had been sampled. The dashed line in the figure shows the results when additional levels of the age variable (ages 4 and 5) are sampled. In this experiment, growth of letter identification ability is most rapid at the younger ages and levels off at the older ages.

An experiment that is designed to map out the exact relationship between variables is called a *functional design*, and it is intended to show how scores on the dependent variable change as a function of changes in the independent variable. For example, a parent may be interested in the functional relationship between amount of reward (none versus 25 cents or 50 cents, 75 cents versus 1 dollar) to number of homework problems completed.

Characterizing functional changes is especially important in developmental and aging research that focuses on understanding the manner in which behavior changes with age. Remember, with only two levels to the variable of age, only linear trends are exposed. Thus, such evidence would be misleading and would obscure growth spurts and declines with age.

One kind of relationship not detected with only two levels of the independent variable is a curvilinear relationship between variables. If a researcher predicts a curvilinear relationship, at least three levels of the independent variable must be used (Figure 7.5). As the figure shows, if only levels 1 and 3 of the independent variable are used, there appears to be no relationship between the independent and dependent variables.

Examples of such curvilinear relationships exist in the literature. For example, changes in the speed at which we process visual information over the human life span are presumed to be curvilinear: Children are slower than young adults, who in turn, are faster than elderly adults (Ross & Ward, 1978). Similarly, changes in "fluid" intelligence also appear curvilinear. Fluid

**Figure 7.5
A curvilinear relationship**

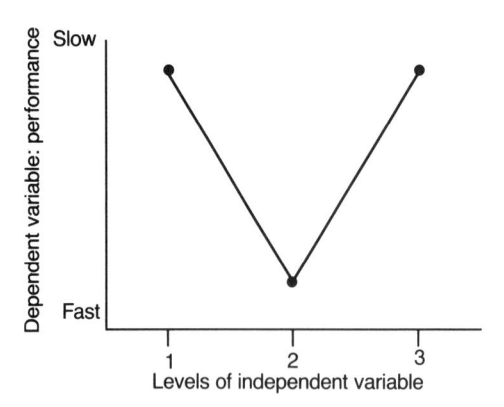

intelligence test performance increases with chronological age into adulthood, although it then may decline as early as middle adulthood (Baltes, Dittmann-Kohli, & Dixon, 1984).

Finally, the research problem itself often dictates more than two levels of the independent variable. For example, a researcher may be interested in determining what type of nutritional instruction is most effective with older adults. The researcher may compare the four or five most popular methods suggested by nationally recognized nutrition experts. As another research possibility, investigators concerned with the effects of maternal employment status on child development may include multiple levels of the variable, for instance, full-time employment versus part-time employment versus none.

Keeping the preceding discussion in mind, let's now consider our example 2 × 2 factorial design that consists of two levels of the age variable (age 3 versus age 5) and two levels of the computer game condition (no game versus game). The age variable can be increased to chart the functional relationship between computer game experience and alphabet identification across the early childhood period (e.g., 3, 4, 5, 6 years). This comparison provides more complete information on how computer game experience affects identification ability during the period in which children normally acquire the alphabet. The general format for describing factorial designs is as follows:

(Number of levels of the first independent variable) ×
(Numbers of levels of the second independent variable) ×
and so on

Thus for this experiment, we have a 2 × 4 factorial with two levels of computer game experience and four levels of subjects age—for a total of eight experimental conditions. The design increases to a 3 × 4 factorial if we also add another level to the computer game condition (e.g., no computer game versus computer game without sound effects versus computer game with sound effects)—for a total of 12 experimental conditions. As the number of levels of the independent variable(s) increase(s), more subjects are required for the experiment, especially for between-subjects manipulations.

To review, the format for describing factorial designs indicates how many independent variables are included and the number of levels (conditions) for each of the independent variables. In this section, we presented factorial designs with two independent variables: Thus, there were two numerical entries in the design statement. The values of each entry (i.e., 2, 3, or 4) refer to the number of levels (conditions) associated with each independent variable.

Increasing the number of independent variables

Since the 2 × 2 factorial design is basic, it can be enhanced in a number of ways. One common approach often suggested by the empirical question under study is the addition of independent variables. For example, to the basic 2 × 2 factorial design we can add an additional independent variable with two levels. Using our computer game example, we may consider the effect of group size: Children play the game alone or with a partner. Thus, our new design is a 2 (computer game: no versus yes) × 2 (age: 3 versus 5) × 2 (group size: alone versus pairs) factorial. This addition also increases the number of subjects required for the experiment.

Remember our discussion in the previous section concerning the format for factorial design statements? The addition of an independent variable to the design adds an additional numerical entry to the statement, but it does not alter the values of the original entries associated with the first two independent variables. Table 7.2 illustrates a 2 × 2 × 2 factorial design that includes a combination of two manipulated variables (computer game and group size) and one subject variable (subject age).

This three-factor design can reveal information about the following:

1. Main effects (overall influence) of each independent variable by itself
2. Two-way interactions between the independent variables (computer game versus age, computer game versus group, and age versus group)
3. Three-way interaction between all of the independent variables (computer game versus age versus group)

Because interactions that involve more than two independent variables are quite complex, a frequently used analytical strategy is to *decompose* complex designs. For example, notice that this 2 × 2 × 2 design can be viewed as two 2 × 2 designs: one for subjects participating alone versus in pairs and one for 3-year-olds versus 5-year-olds. By decomposing the 2 × 2 × 2 (three-

	Condition			
	No computer		Computer	
Age	Alone	Pairs	Alone	Pairs
Three				
Five				

Table 7.2
A 2 × 2 × 2 design

way) factorial design into two 2 × 2 (two-way) factorial designs, we can evaluate whether or not the form of the two-way interaction is different at the different levels of the third independent variable. The manner in which we decompose complex interactions depends on the nature of our hypotheses and outcomes from statistical analyses.

Sometimes when students design experiments they are tempted to include as many independent variables as they can think of. They may do so under the mistaken impression that a more complex design is necessarily more useful and "impressive." Usually, such designs are needlessly complex and are more costly because of the additional subjects required. The investigator is probably not interested in all of the main effects and interactions that may accompany complex designs such as a 2 × 2 × 2 × 2 design. Basic 2 × 2 factorial designs are very powerful when

1. The investigator has clearly articulated the different interactions predicted by current research and theory.
2. The independent variables have been carefully selected to offer the best test of the hypotheses.

Increasing the number of dependent variables

Increasing the number of dependent variables is another way to add to the information provided by either simple or complex designs. In this way, the researcher can measure more than one aspect of the subject's behavior in the experiment. Care must be taken to select measures that are sensitive to the independent variable. In other words, variables should be selected that will "capture" the presumed differences in the level of the independent variable(s). Note, there may be different ways to measure the same performance in an experiment. For example, researchers in studies of infant perception may evaluate preference for target stimuli by measuring both visual fixation times and heartrate changes. Parent–child studies may include a number of measures of language behavior (e.g., requests for identifications, positive comments, directives, questions, and negative comments) and physical activities (e.g., hugging, kissing, caretaking, and modeling). Investigation of sensorimotor skill changes during the adult years typically includes measures of speed, accuracy, and variability. In some kinds of research, experiments are conducted with a primary dependent variable. Secondary dependent variables are included to provide collateral and/or converging information on the effects of the manipulated variables. For example, the number of correct responses is frequently used as the primary dependent variable in studies on memory development. Evaluation of the kinds of memory errors made is a frequent secondary dependent variable that is included to provide additional insights into the nature of the memory process under study. Secondary dependent variables that have proven useful in past research may become the focus of attention in later studies (remember Piaget's success with studying children's errors and the reasons for these errors at different ages). The selection of dependent variables should always be determined by your hypotheses. Suggestions from current theory and the feasibility of collecting the additional information should also be considered. Generally speaking, new dependent variables are not and should not be added capriciously!

HUMAN DEVELOPMENT AND FAMILY RELATIONS QUESTIONS AND COMPLEX EXPERIMENTAL DESIGNS

Problems studied in human development and family relations often require the use of complex factorial designs or multiple dependent variables. In this section, we consider three examples.

Example 1: age-group comparisons

Developmental research is concerned with explaining the changes that occur with age. During childhood, many developmental improvements are observed. For example, major improvements in children's learning abilities are evident. Developmental theory identifies a number of processes and/or structures that are presumed to be responsible. For example, the more proficient learning of older children is generally attributed to their spontaneous use of learning strategies like the imagery mnemonic discussed in Chapter 1. In contrast, young children may not think of using imagery spontaneously when faced with a learning or problem-solving task. These children are labeled "production deficient," since they can usually use the imagery strategy effectively if they receive explicit prompts to produce it.

A 2 × 2 factorial design may be used to verify the hypothesis that developmental differences in learning are due to corresponding age differences in the spontaneous use of effective learning strategies. In this experiment, age is the first independent variable in the design. The age groups selected represent the period for which the developmental increase in learning is most evident. For example, large increases in learning are typically observed in children between the ages of 10 and 18. Thus, the age groups selected for a developmental learning experiment may be ages 10 versus 18. The second independent variable is a treatment or manipulated variable (no treatment versus treatment). The treatment condition is designed to prompt or induce younger subjects to use the process presumed to be used by the older subjects for their superior performance (one that is apparently absent for the younger subjects). Thus, the levels of the second variable are no imagery instructions versus imagery instructions. The no imagery condition serves as a control condition and allows us to demonstrate the developmental improvement in learning that we wish to explain. If we are correct about the process that is responsible for the superior performance of the older subjects and have designed a treatment that effectively induces the younger subjects to use this process (i.e., the imagery mnemonic), the treatment condition should only

103

Figure 7.6 Outcome for the imagery experiment

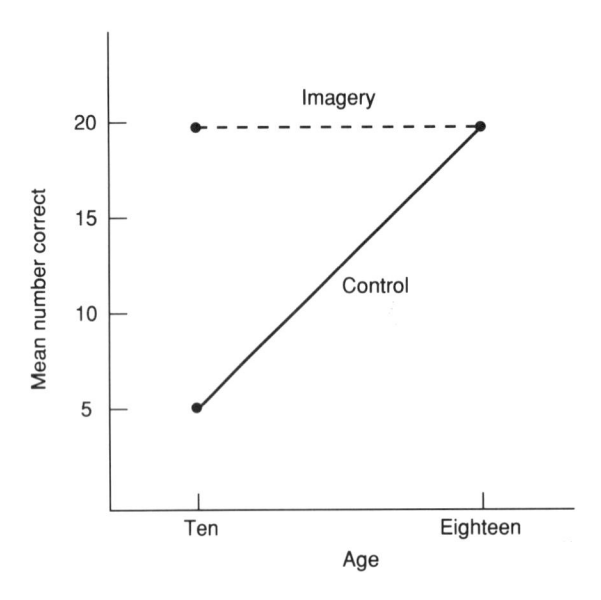

affect the performance of the younger subjects. The older subjects should not be affected since they already have or use what is represented in the treatment condition. The form of the interaction predicted for this kind of study is presented in Figure 7.6. Notice that for the no imagery instruction condition a large improvement in learning is observed between ages 10 and 18. However, for the imagery condition, the age difference is eliminated. Such an outcome suggests that it is the use of imagery that distinguishes the learning performance of the two age groups. That is, requesting that the subjects use the strategy helps the younger children (who presumably don't normally use the strategy) but does not affect the performance of the older subjects (who already use this method). If the age difference is not completely eliminated by the treatment, other sources for the developmental improvement may be evaluated in subsequent research.

A detailed discussion of the use of factorial designs for evaluating age differences in learning is provided in a paper by William Rohwer (1976), titled "An introduction to research on individual and developmental differences in learning." Also, a comprehensive review of current research concerning imagery strategies is presented in a book edited by Mark McDaniel and Mike Pressley (1987), titled *Imagery and related mnemonic processes: Theories, individual differences, and application.*

Example 2: special populations

Age may not always be the subject variable of interest. For example, differences in ability level, social status, or family background may be the focus of research. In such studies, the researcher is usually testing a hypothesis that some treatment has differential effects (i.e., an interaction) for the groups studied. For example, an investigator may wish to assess the story comprehension ability of learning disabled children versus nondisabled children. One independent variable is the clinically diagnosed group of the child (nondisabled versus learning disabled). The investigator selects two methods for presenting the stories: Students read stories versus students listen to the stories. The investigator hypothesizes, based on available evidence, that learning disabled children may differ from nondisabled children primarily in their ability to process and understand printed material. The number of correct story questions answered can serve as the dependent variable for this hypothetical experiment, and the results are presented in Figure 7.7. Notice that the form of the interaction indicates that nondisabled children have better comprehension than learning disabled children for both the read and listen conditions. However, the difference between the two groups of children is greater in the read condition. The investigator may conclude that the ability to process printed material is one factor that distinguishes nondisabled from learning disabled children, but other factors may also be involved. As such, additional research is required to identify the other factors involved. It is especially important in this kind of research to make sure that the population differences cannot be attributed to subject characteristics that co-vary with the selected variable of population membership. In our example, such variables as subject's sex and IQ must be considered. Finally, the results of such studies have practical significance, as they indicate that comprehension can be improved in learning disabled children by presenting stories verbally.

The *Handbook of cognitive, social, and neuropsychological aspects of learning disabilities*, edited by Stephen Ceci (1987), is an excellent reference on the topic of learning disabilities. Theory, research, and methods are discussed in this comprehensive, two-volume set.

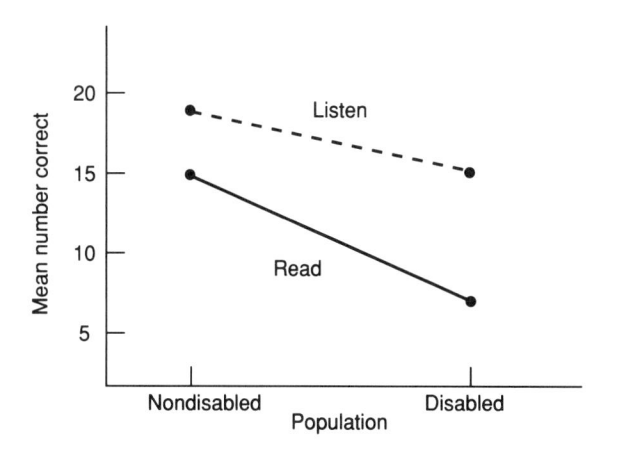

Figure 7.7 Outcome for the special population experiment

Example 3: family variables

In the preceding examples, specific hypotheses concerning interactions among the independent variables were advanced. In some areas, especially in the formative stages of inquiry, the researchers may use complex designs or simple designs with multiple dependent variables to obtain a comprehensive picture of possible phenomena for future investigation. These designs are often applied in the analysis of longitudinal data such as that discussed in Chapter 6. For example, this tactic may be applied when studying the effects of maternal employment status on family dynamics and child development. Researchers would like to establish if maternal employment affects the family and if so in what ways. Thus, a two-group comparison may be suggested: mothers working outside of the home versus full-time mothers. The independent variable of maternal employment status with the two identified levels is a selected subject variable, since under normal circumstances it would not be manipulated. Dependent variables are selected to evaluate the impact of the independent variable on family activities and child development. Examples of dependent variables selected to evaluate the impact of maternal employment on family life include measures of marital satisfaction and fathers' involvement in child-rearing activities. Dependent variables selected to evaluate the impact of maternal employment on child development include measures of school achievement and behavior adjustment.

Figure 7.8 presents hypothetical results for the dependent variables of father involvement in child-rearing and children's school achievement scores. These results are presented as a function of the independent variable of maternal employment. In Figure 7.8a, a high score represents more time spent in child-rearing activities. As can be seen, greater father involvement is observed for households in which mothers work outside the home in contrast to households in which mothers stay at home. In Figure 7.8b, no difference is observed in the school achievement of the children of the two groups of mothers. These outcomes may suggest that although family dynamics may be affected, children may not be at a scholastic advantage or a disadvantage if their mothers work. Undoubtedly, you can probably identify other dependent variables that should be considered in this kind of study. Any findings should also offer suggestions for additional studies to isolate more clearly the impact of maternal employment on the family and child development. An appropriate extension and refinement of our illustrative study would be to increase the number of levels of the independent variable of maternal working status. (Do you recall why this might be a good idea?)

Current research concerning the influence of maternal employment is presented in a book edited by Adele and Allen Gottfried (1988), titled *Maternal employment and children's development: Longitudinal research*. This book provides a fascinating discussion of the effects of maternal employment status on human development and families.

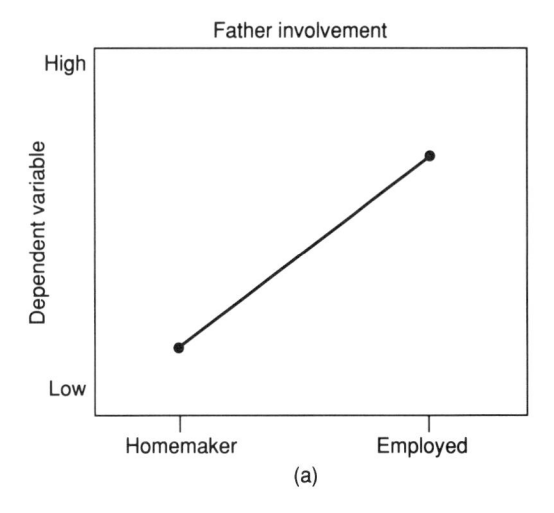

Figure 7.8
Outcomes of the maternal employment experiment (independent variable): (a) father involvement (dependent variable), (b) children's achievement in school (dependent variable)

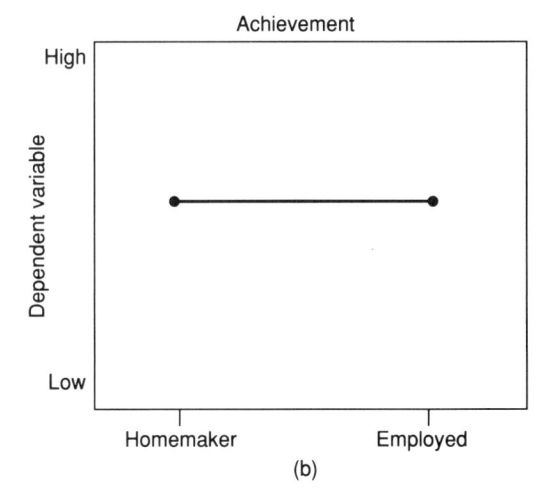

SUMMARY

Complex experimental designs are used to answer many of the questions advanced in research on human development and family relations. Factorial designs include more than one independent variable. The simplest factorial design is a 2 × 2 design, in which there are two independent variables with two levels each. Factorial designs provide information on the effect of each independent variable by itself—the main effects—and the interaction between the independent variables. An interaction between independent variables indicates that the effect of one independent variable is different at different levels of the other independent variable.

Factorial designs can include a combination of a manipulated variable and a selected subject variable such as age, ethnicity, or family status. A combination of between-subjects (independent groups) and within-subjects (repeated measures) independent variables can also be used.

The complexity of factorial designs can be increased by (1) adding levels to independent variables, (2) increasing the number of independent variables in the design, and/or (3) increasing the number of dependent measures. Experimental designs do *not* need to be overly complex: The basic 2 × 2 factorial design is quite useful.

STUDY QUESTIONS

1. What is a factorial design? Why would a researcher use a factorial design?
2. What are main effects? What does a significant interaction tell us about main effects?
3. Why would a researcher add levels to an independent variable?
4. Identify some reasons for increasing the number of dependent variables in an experiment.
5. What is the difference between adding levels to independent variables versus increasing the number of factors in the design?
6. Identify the number of conditions associated with a 2 × 2 design, a 2 × 3 design, and a 2 × 2 × 2 design.
7. How many subjects do you need for each of the designs in Question 6, assuming that each condition requires 10 subjects and all the independent variables are between-subjects variables?

CHAPTER 8

Nonexperimental Methods

CAREER PROFILE

Juan Castanon Garcia / Marriage and Family Counselor

Juan's initial training was in Anthropology; he received his B.A. from the University of California, Santa Cruz and an M.A. from Stanford University. Subsequently, he received an M.S. degree in Clinical Psychology with an emphasis in Community Psychology. He then returned to his studies in Anthropology for a Ph.D. Juan is employed as a Marriage and Family Counselor with Family Court Services, Probation Department, Fresno County, California.

"My primary responsibility is to help parents in the process of divorce or separation come to a mutual understanding and agreement about where their children shall live and arrange a visitation plan for the out-of-home parent. If an agreement is not possible, then it is my job to make a recommendation to the court about what arrangement would be in the best interest of the child regarding custody and visitation. I use models from family therapy to help parents recognize what's in the best interest of their children so that they can make joint decisions about their children. A complete social study of the family is also conducted that evaluates its dynamics, roles, rules, and related emotional issues. This information is used as the basis of objective recommendations to the court regarding custody issues." Because the central California area has become an endpoint to secondary migration in the United States for Southeast Asian refugees, Juan is also involved with helping these groups through "bicultural effectiveness training."

Juan credits his training in anthropology for enabling him to understand individuals and their families from a cultural framework. "This has multiple implications for assumptions regarding family dynamics and decisions regarding clinical approaches when dealing with different families from diverse ethnic groups." He recommends that students "combine theoretical learning with practicum. Once out of school, continue learning from established authorities. The more you gain your own experience, the more the theories make sense, and thus, the more you can contribute to theory."

Chapters 5–7 have focused on research using the experimental method. This chapter explores nonexperimental methods. In contrast to the experimental method, nonexperimental methods do not manipulate any of the variables of interest. Instead, behaviors are observed as they occur naturally. Such observational techniques may be performed by asking people to describe their behavior, by directly observing behavior, or even by examining existing records of behavior such as census data or hospital records. In this chapter, we consider five nonexperimental research techniques:

    Field observation

    Systematic observation

    Case studies

    Surveys

    Archival research

Juan Garcia's profile illustrates the practical applications of careful observation. Juan is often faced with the need to conduct a study of a family by observing family dynamics, roles, rules, and emotional outcomes. His observations form the basis for recommendations that concern legal and clinical issues confronting the family.

WHY CONDUCT NONEXPERIMENTAL STUDIES?

The distinction between nonexperimental and experimental methods was made in Chapter 3. In that chapter, we focused on the correlational approach to studying relationships between variables in contrast to the experimental approach. We noted several reasons why the correlational approach is useful, including the fact that ethical and practical considerations sometimes make use of any other method impossible. The nonexperimental methods that we discuss in this chapter may be employed in correlational studies that are designed to test specific hypotheses about relationships between variables. However, there are two additional reasons why researchers use nonexperimental methods to study behavior:

Description

Exploration

Description

A major goal of science is to provide an accurate *description* of events. Nonexperimental methods, including observational techniques, case studies, and surveys, are used to provide descriptions of behavior. Such descriptions also allow us to more fully understand the behaviors in question. For example, Piaget carefully observed the behaviors of his own children as they matured, and he described in detail the changes in their ways of thinking about and responding to their environment (Piaget, 1952). These observations led to a theory of cognitive development that is still being tested and refined by researchers using both experimental and nonexperimental methods (cf. Brainerd, 1976; Flavell, 1985).

Another example is Paul Rosenblatt's study entitled *The family in business* (Rosenblatt, de Mik, Anderson, & Johnson, 1985). In that study, extensive interviews were conducted with family members who jointly ran their own businesses. The researchers were able to identify and examine many sources of tension in these families—for example, role conflicts that arise when people must interact with one another as both family members (spouse, child) and workers in the business (supervisor, employee). Many other potential areas of conflict were identified as well, along with ways that family members respond to and cope with problems. The Rosenblatt study provided important insights into theories of family interaction, techniques for family therapy, and methods of business management.

Exploration

Researchers sometimes begin with nothing more than an intense curiosity about some phenomenon. The goal in the research project is simply to *explore* the phenomenon. They may observe and interview people with the aim of finding out what people think, what variables are important, and what questions should be asked in future research. For example, if you are interested in the general topic of women who return to college after many years as a homemaker, you may talk to a number of women about their experiences, telephone the directors of women's centers at several colleges, and ask professors to tell you about their impressions of returning women students. You may also explore data available from college admissions officers on the age distribution of women students over the past 10 or 20 years. Eventually, you would develop some specific ideas about these students and conduct further research to test these ideas systematically (see Ballmer & Cozby, 1981).

FIELD OBSERVATION

Observation in natural settings

Field observation is sometimes called *field work* or *naturalistic observation* (see Lofland, 1971, 1976; Douglas, 1976). In a field observation study, the researcher makes observations in a specific natural setting (the field) over an extended period of time using a variety of techniques to collect information. The report includes these observations and the researcher's interpretations of the findings.

Gans's (1962) study of "urban villagers" living in Boston's West End is a good example of a field observation study. To examine the impact of living in what was considered a "slum" environment, Gans used a variety of techniques to watch people and listen to conversations in stores, bars, and other public settings. He attended meetings and public gatherings and made friends with people who provided him with information. Gans concluded that, contrary to the beliefs of many city planners and urban renewal advocates, the West End was viewed by its inhabitants as a secure place. The effect of urban renewal (constructing new dwellings to replace the "slum") was to disrupt lives and break strong family and ethnic bonds that existed in the neighborhood.

Field observation is undertaken when a researcher wants to describe and understand how people in a social setting live, work, and experience the setting. If you want to know about bars as a social setting, you must visit one or more bars over an extended period of time, talk to people, observe interactions, and become accepted as a "regular" (cf. Cavan, 1966). If you are interested in how people "become" part of some social group (e.g., marijuana users, prostitutes, a religious cult), you can arrange to meet members of such groups to interview them about their experiences (cf. Becker, 1963, on marijuana users). If you want to know what it is like to be a patient in a mental hospital, you must get yourself admitted as a patient (cf. Rosenhan, 1973). Of course, you may not want to do any of these things; however, if these questions interest you, the written reports of the researchers who entered these situations are fascinating.

Field observation demands an immersion in the situation. The field researcher observes everything—the setting itself, the patterns of personal relationships, people's reactions to events that occur, and so on. The goal is to provide a complete and accurate picture, not to test hypotheses formed prior to the study. To achieve this goal, the researcher must keep detailed field notes: On a regular basis (at least once each day), the researcher must write down or dictate everything that happened during the day. Further, the field researcher uses a variety of techniques to gather information—observing people and events, using key "informants" to provide information, talking to people (interviewing them), and examining documents produced in the setting (e.g., newspapers, newsletters, or memos).

Interpreting the data

The field researcher's first goal is to describe the setting, the events, and the persons observed. The second, equally important goal is to provide an analysis of what was observed. The researcher must interpret what occurred, essentially generating hypotheses to explain and understand the data. Such an analysis is accomplished by building a coherent structure to describe the observations. The final report, although sensitive to the chronological order of events, is usually organized around an analytical structure developed by the researcher. Specific examples of events that occurred during observation are used to support the researcher's interpretations.

A good field observation report provides support for the analysis using multiple confirmations. For example, there may be several instances in which similar events occurred, similar information was reported by two or more people, and several different events all supported the same conclusion.

The data in field observation studies are primarily *qualitative* in nature: That is, the data are the descriptions of the observations themselves rather than *quantitative* statistical summaries. However, there is no reason why quantitative data cannot be gathered in a field observation study. Thus in a study of family businesses (see the Rosenblatt study described previously), data can be gathered on income, family size, education levels, and other easily quantifiable variables. Such data can be reported and interpreted along with qualitative data gathered from interviews and direct observations.

Issues in field observation

Participation and concealment   Two related issues face the field observation researcher:

> Whether to be a participant or nonparticipant in the social setting
> Whether to conceal one's purposes from the other people in the setting

Is it better to become an active participant in the group or to observe from the outside? Do you conceal your purposes or even your presence? Do you openly let people know what you are doing?

A *nonparticipant observer* is an outsider who does not become an active part of the situation; a *participant observer* is an active participant who observes from the inside. Participant observation allows the researcher to observe the setting from the "inside" and experience events in the same way as natural participants do. Friendships and other experiences of the participant observer may yield valuable data. However, a potential problem in participant observation is that the observer may lose the objectivity that is necessary in scientific observation. Such a situation may be especially problematic when the researcher already belongs to the group being studied (e.g., a researcher who belongs to Parents Without Partners who undertakes a study of that group). Remember that field observation requires accurate description and objective interpretation with no prior hypotheses. If a researcher has some prior reason either to criticize people in the setting *or* to give a glowing report of a group, then the research simply should not be performed. In such cases, there are too many reasons to expect that problems will arise and a lack of objectivity will occur in the results.

Should the researcher be "concealed" or be open about the research purposes? *Concealed observation* may be preferable because the presence of the observer may influence and alter the behavior of those being observed. Imagine how a nonconcealed observer may alter the behavior of high school students in many situations at a school. On the other hand, *nonconcealed observation* may be preferable from an ethical viewpoint—consider the invasion of privacy when researchers hid under beds in dormitory rooms to discover what college students talk about (Henle & Hubbell, 1938)! As well, in nonconcealed observation situations, people often quickly become used to the observer and behave naturally in the observer's presence. One widely viewed example of nonconcealed observation was the public television documentary series, "An American Family," in which one family's activities were filmed over a period of several months. Many viewers of this series were surprised to see how quickly family members forgot about the cameras and spontaneously revealed many private aspects of their family life.

Whether to conceal your purpose or presence is a decision that must be dependent on the specific group and setting being studied. Sometimes a participant observer is nonconcealed to certain members of the group who give the researcher permission to be part of the group as a concealed observer. Often, a concealed observer decides to say nothing directly about his or her purposes but may completely disclose the goals of the research if asked by anyone. Nonparticipant observers are also not concealed when they gain permission to "hang out" in a setting or use interview techniques to gather information (e.g., in Becker's study of marijuana users, some of the subjects who were interviewed first introduced Becker to their network of friends who were also marijuana users). In actuality, then, there are degrees of participation and concealment: A nonparticipant observer may not become a member of the group, for example, but over a period of time he or she may become accepted as a friend or simply part of the ongoing activities of the group. You can see that field observation researchers must carefully determine what they want their role in the setting to be.

External validity *External validity* refers to the generalizability of results. Field observation research typically tells us what occurs in one setting as reported by one observer; it is reasonable to ask whether such results are generalizable. Such results *are* generalizable to similar settings—for example, similar neighborhoods, similar bars, or similar groups. In addition, many researchers worry about generalization and include in their research two or more settings: Sometimes both settings are similar; sometimes two or more dissimilar settings are studied (e.g., a "working class" bar and an "upscale" bar).

Defining the scope of the observation A field observation researcher may want to study *everything* about a setting. However, such research may not be possible simply because a setting and the questions you may ask about it are quite complex. Thus, it is often necessary for researchers to limit the scope of their observations to behaviors that are relevant to the central issues of the study. For example, rather than try to study everything that happens in a bar, a researcher may focus only on ways that males and females meet and interact in a bar setting.

Limits of field observation Field observation cannot be used to study all questions. The approach is most useful when investigating complex social settings; it is less useful for studying simple settings such as a single family or a single classroom.

Field research is also quite difficult to perform (cf. Green & Wallaf, 1981). Unlike a typical laboratory experiment, field research data collection cannot always be scheduled at a convenient time and place. In fact, field research can be extremely time-consuming and often places the researcher in an unfamiliar setting for extended periods of time. Also, in experimental research, the procedures are well-defined, the same for each subject, and data analysis is planned in advance. In field observation research, there is an everchanging pattern of events, some important and some unimportant; the researcher must record them all and maintain flexibility to adjust to them as the research progresses. When the research is completed, the analysis is not simple: The researcher must sort through the data again and again, develop hypotheses to explain the data, and make sure all the data are consistent with the hypotheses. When some of the observations are not consistent, the researcher must perform more analysis. Kidder and Judd (1986) emphasize the importance of *negative case analysis*—a *negative case* is an observation that does not fit the explanatory structure devised by the researcher. When a negative case is found, the researcher revises the hypothesis and again makes sure that all data are consistent with the new hypothesis. The researcher may even collect additional data to examine more closely the circumstances that led to the negative case. The main point here is that field observation research is a difficult and challenging scientific procedure. When carried out well, knowledge gained from this procedure can be invaluable.

SYSTEMATIC OBSERVATION

Systematic observation refers to the careful observation of one or more specific behaviors in a specific setting. This research approach is much less "global" than field observation research: The researcher is interested in only a few specific behaviors, the observations are quantifiable, and frequently the researcher has developed prior hypotheses about the behaviors. For example, Bakeman and Brownlee (1980; also see Bakeman & Gottman, 1986) were interested in the social behavior of young children. Three-year-olds were videotaped in a room in a "free play" situation. Each child was taped for 100 minutes; observers viewed the videotapes and coded each child's behavior every 15 seconds. The following coding system was used by the observers:

Unoccupied: Child is not doing anything in particular or simply watching other children.

Solitary play: Child plays alone with toys but is not interested in or affected by the activities of other children.

Together: Child is with other children but is not occupied with any particular activity.

Parallel play: Child plays beside other children with similar toys but does not play with the others.

Group play: Child plays with other children, including sharing of toys or organizing play activities among a group of children.

Bakeman and Brownlee were especially interested in the sequence or order in which the different behaviors were engaged in by the children. For example, they found that the children rarely went from being unoccupied to engaging in parallel play. However, they frequently went from parallel play to group play, indicating that parallel play is a transition state in which children decide whether to go ahead and interact in a group situation.

Coding systems

Numerous behaviors can be studied using systematic observation. The researcher must decide which behaviors are of interest, choose a setting in which these behaviors can be observed, and most important, develop a *coding system* that observers can use to measure the behaviors. Sometimes the researcher develops the coding system to fit the needs of the specific study. Coding systems should be as simple as possible, allowing observers to categorize behaviors easily. Ease of use is especially important when observers are coding "live" behaviors rather than viewing videotapes that can be reviewed or even coded on a frame-by-frame basis. An example of a simple coding system comes from a study by Barton, Baltes, and Orzech (1980) in which nursing home residents and the nursing home staff were observed. In this study, five categories were used: Resident independent behavior (e.g., doing something by oneself such as grooming), resident dependent behavior (asking for help), staff independence-supporting behavior (praise or encouragement for independence), staff dependency-supportive behavior (giving assistance or encouraging taking assistance), and other, unrelated behaviors of both residents and staff. Their results illustrate one of the problems of care facilities; staff perceive themselves as "care providers" and so most frequently engage in dependency-supportive behaviors. Does such behavior lead to greater dependency by the residents and perhaps a loss of feelings of control? If so, the consequences may be serious (recall the Rodin and Langer experiment [1977] discussed in Chapter 3 in which feelings of control led to greater happiness and general well-being among nursing home residents).

Sometimes researchers can use coding systems that have been developed by others. For example, the Family Interaction Coding System (FICS; see Patterson & Moore, 1979) consists of 29 categories of interaction; these are grouped as aversive (hostility), prosocial (helping), and activities. Most of the research using the FICS has centered on how children's aversive behaviors are learned and maintained in a family. Another coding system is the Interaction Process Analysis developed by Bales (1970) to code interactions in small groups. In this system, 12 categories are organized into four general types of interactions: positive social-emotional (e.g., expresses agreement), negative social-emotional (shows antagonism), task-related answering (gives opinion), and task-related questioning (asks for information). The interaction Process Analysis system has been used to study such topics as leadership in groups and group satisfaction. A major advantage of using an already developed coding system is that there is an existing body of research in which the system has proven useful, and there are usually training materials available.

Methodological issues

We should briefly mention three issues in systematic observation. The first concerns *equipment*. Systematic observation can be conducted with paper on a clipboard and a pencil to make observations; a stopwatch is sometimes useful to record the duration of events or the interval between events; a handheld mechanical counter can be used to record the rate of events such as the number of people entering a setting. Alternatively, you can use a computer recording device that is not much larger than a calculator. Keys on the device are pressed to code the behaviors observed as well as to keep track of duration. These recorders add to the expense of the research, and initial training of observers may take longer. However, for research that requires observing several types of behavior, recording behavior duration is facilitated by using computer devices. Also, data analysis may be easier when using a computer device because the data can automatically be transferred from the device to the computer in which the analyses are performed.

The second issue is *reactivity*—the possibility that the presence of the observer will affect people's behaviors. As we noted in Chapter 4, reactivity can be reduced by concealed observation. Alternatively, reactivity can be reduced by allowing enough time for people to become used to the presence of the observer and any recording equipment.

Reliability is the third issue. Recall from Chapter 4 that *interrater*, or interobserver, reliability is an index of how closely two observers agree when coding the same observations. Very high levels of agreement are reported in virtually all published research using systematic observation. For some large-scale research programs in which many observers are employed over a period of years, observers are first trained using videotapes, and their observations during training are checked for agreement with previous observers (Bakeman & Gottman, 1986).

CASE STUDIES

A *case study* provides a description of an individual. This individual is usually a person, but it may also be a setting such as a business, school, or neighborhood. Sometimes a field observation study is called a case study, and in fact there is overlap between the field observation and case study approaches. We discuss case studies here as a separate section because they do not necessarily involve field observation. Instead, the case study may be a description of a child by a school psychologist or a historical account of an event such as a model school that failed. Case studies may use such techniques as library research and telephone interviews with persons familiar with the case. In fact, there may be no "direct" observation of the case at all (cf. Yin, 1984).

Depending on the purpose of the investigation, the case study may present the individual's history, symptoms, characteristic behaviors, reactions to situations, or responses to treatment. Typically, a case study is presented when an individual possesses a rare, unusual, or noteworthy condition. One famous case study was "Sybil," a woman with a rare multiple personality disorder (Schreiber, 1973). During the course of therapy, it was discovered that Sybil had experienced severe beatings and other traumatic experiences during childhood. One explanation of Sybil's disorder, then, is that she unconsciously created other personalities who would suffer the pain instead of her. A case study in language development was provided by "Genie," a child who was kept isolated in her room tied to a chair and never spoken to until she was discovered at age 14 (Curtiss, 1977). Genie, of course, lacked any language skills. Her case provided psychologists and linguists the opportunity to attempt to teach her language skills and discover which skills could be learned. Apparently, Genie was able to acquire some rudimentary language skills such as forming childlike sentences but did not develop full language abilities.

Case studies are valuable in informing us of conditions that are rare or unusual and thus not easily studied in any other manner. Insights gained through the case study may also lead to the development of hypotheses that can be tested using other methods.

SURVEY RESEARCH

Surveys use self-report measurement techniques to question people about themselves—their attitudes, behaviors, personality, and demographics (age, income, race, marital status, etc.). They may employ careful sampling techniques to obtain an accurate description of an entire population (e.g., the Gallup Poll conducts surveys to find out what people are thinking about issues such as abortion or to obtain data on preferences among political candidates). Surveys can be much less systematic, however. A researcher may survey a sample of high school students to investigate who they talk to about personal problems; in this case, the researcher would probably obtain the sample in an unsystematic fashion (e.g., going to a local high school and distributing questionnaires to students in classes in which teachers gave permission to conduct the research). The researcher's concern in this case is not to describe accurately high school students in the United States; rather, the researcher's goal is to focus on finding out who they talk to, whether there are gender differences, or whether the students talk to different people about different types of problems. Sampling is discussed in more detail later in this section and in Chapter 9.

Of the various methods used by researchers, you are probably most familiar with surveys. They are all around us! As a student, you may be asked by your school to be part of a survey. An area agency on aging may survey elderly citizens to determine which services are most needed by that population. A sample of teachers may be asked to evaluate training programs sponsored by the school district. You have probably seen marketing survey researchers at shopping malls or been called by a survey organization. Often surveys such as these are aimed at providing information needed for important policy or marketing decisions. This section describes some of the important issues to be considered when conducting survey research.

Questionnaires versus interviews

Survey research may use either questionnaires or interviews to ask people questions about themselves. With questionnaires, the questions are presented in written format, and the subjects write their answers. Interviews involve a one-on-one verbal interaction between an interviewer and respondent, either face-to-face or over a telephone. The questionnaire approach is generally cheaper than interviews. Questionnaires can be administered in groups, or they can be mailed to people. Also, questionnaires allow anonymity of the subjects. However, questionnaires require that the subjects can read and understand the questions. Also, many people find it dull to sit alone reading questions and writing answers; thus, the written format may pose some problems of motivation. With interviews, there is a greater chance that the interviewer and the subject can establish a rapport, that the subject will find it interesting to talk to the interviewer, and that all questions are understood. Telephone interviews are less expensive than face-to-face interviews, because of the higher time and labor costs of face-to-face interviews.

Constructing questions

When constructing questions for a survey, the first thing the researcher must do is explicitly determine the research questions: What is it that he or she wishes to know? The survey questions must be tied to the research questions. Too often, surveys get out of control when researchers begin to ask any question that comes to mind about a topic without considering exactly what useful information is to be gained by asking it.

It is also important to think about how people will respond to the questions. As we noted in Chapter 4, self-report questions may be closed or open-ended. Open-ended questions, which ask people to respond freely in any manner they choose, are especially useful in exploratory research or as questions at the end of a survey. With closed-ended questions, the response alternatives are provided. These answers must make sense to people in the context of the question asked. Also, there must be a sufficient number of alternatives to allow people to express themselves—for example, five- or seven-point scales ranging from "agree to disagree" or "good to bad" may be preferable to simple "yes or no" or "agree or disagree" alternatives.

Once the questions have been written, it is especially important to edit them and test them out on others. You should look for "double-barreled questions" that ask two things at once; a question such as "Senior citizens should be given more money for recreation centers and food assistance programs" is difficult to answer because it taps two potentially different attitudes. Researchers must also avoid questions that "lead" people to answer in a certain way or that may be easily misinterpreted. For example, the questions "Do you favor eliminating the wasteful excesses in the public school budget?" and "Do you favor reducing the public school budget?" are likely to elicit different answers. It is a good idea to give the questions to some people and have them "talk aloud" while answering them—for example, asking them to tell you how they interpret each question and how they are deciding to respond to the response alternatives. This procedure can provide valuable insights to be used when editing the questions (see Chapter 9 on the importance of pilot studies).

Survey designs

Surveys most frequently study people at one point in time. However, there are numerous occasions when researchers wish to make comparisons over time. One way to study changes over time is to conduct a *panel study* in which the same people are surveyed at two or more points in time. In a "two-wave" panel study, people are surveyed at two points in time; in a "three-wave" panel study, there are three surveys; and so on. Panel studies usually seek to examine changes over time: That is, how do people change as they grow older? How does interest in political campaign information change as the election draws nearer? Also, panel studies allow researchers to study questions such as whether similarity of attitudes among dating couples is a predictor of whether the couples are still together at some time in the future (cf. Hill, Rubin, & Peplau, 1976).

Panel studies can be quite difficult and expensive; it isn't easy to track the same people over long periods of time. Another way to make comparisons over time is to conduct a similar survey with a different sample at a later point in time. For example, Sebald (1986) compared surveys of teenagers in 1963, 1976, and 1982. The questions focused on who teenagers seek advice from on a variety of issues. The primary result was that seeking advice from peers rather than parents had increased from 1963 to 1976, but this peer orientation decreased from 1976 to 1982.

Sampling

Sampling is an extremely important consideration when planning surveys. Sampling methods are described in detail in Chapter 9, but for now, you should understand that sampling refers to selecting people for a study from some larger *population* of people. Thus, if you survey residents of nursing homes about their general life satisfaction, you have sampled from the population of nursing home residents. An important consideration when sampling people is the generalizability of the results to the larger population.

When the research is intended to tell us precisely what a population is like (e.g., state or national opinion polls), careful sampling procedures must be used. Such precision requires defining the population and sampling people from it in some random fashion so that no biases are introduced. Thus, to learn about what elderly people think about the social services available to them, a careful sample of the elderly population is needed. Obtaining the sample by going only to nursing homes could bias the results, because these individuals are not representative of all elderly people in the population.

Other survey research is less concerned with sampling issues. If your main interest is comparing the life satisfaction of nursing home residents as compared to elderly individuals who live at home or with relatives, you will want a representative sample of these groups. However, in this case, you will not be worried about whether the life satisfaction ratings are typical of all elderly people in your city, state, or the nation. Thus, surveys aimed primarily at discovering relationships between variables may use less sophisticated sampling techniques. For such a survey, you should sample residents of several nursing homes and other elderly people in several different settings to ensure that your samples are fairly representative. For this survey, you need not concern yourself with random sampling from a defined population of individuals.

When evaluating survey data, it is important to examine how the responses were obtained and what population was investigated. When the research is intended to provide accurate information about a population, you must ask how that population was sampled. Major polling organizations typically take great care to obtain representative samples of adults in our society. However, many other surveys, such as surveys on marital satisfaction or sexual practices published in magazines, have limited generalizability because the results are based on people who read the magazine and are sufficiently motivated to complete and mail in the questionnaire. When Dear Abby asks readers to write in to tell her whether they have ever cheated on their spouse, the results may be interesting, but they cannot give an accurate estimate of the true extent of extramarital activity in our society.

Interviewer bias and response sets

Two major sources of bias can arise when questionnaires and interviews are used:

Interviewer bias

Response sets

Interviewer bias refers to all of the biases that can arise from the fact that the interviewer is a unique human being interacting with another human. Thus, one potential problem is that the interviewer can subtly bias the subject's answers by inadvertently showing approval or disapproval of certain answers. Or if there are several interviewers, each interviewer can possess different characteristics (e.g., level of physical attractiveness, age, or race) that may influence the way subjects respond. Another problem is that interviewers may have expectations that would lead them to "see what they are looking for" in the answers of a subject. Such expectations can bias their interpretations of responses, or they may result in probing further for an answer from certain subjects but not others (e.g., when questioning whites but not blacks or when testing boys but not girls). Careful screening and training of interviewers help limit biases, but they remain a possibility in interview research.

A *response set* is a tendency to respond to all questions from a specific perspective rather than to provide answers that are directly related to the questions. Thus, response sets can affect the usefulness of data obtained from self-reports.

The most common response set is called *social desirability*, or "faking good." The social desirability response set leads the individual to answer in the most socially acceptable manner—the way that "most people" are perceived to respond, or the way that reflects most favorably on the subject. Social desirability can be a problem in many research areas, but it is probably most acute when the question concerns a sensitive topic such as violent or aggressive behavior, substance abuse, or sexual practices. However, it should *not* be assumed that people consistently misrepresent themselves. Jourard (1969) has argued that people are most likely to lie when they don't trust the researcher. If the researcher openly and honestly communicates the purposes and uses of the research, promises that there will be feedback about the results, and assures anonymity, then there is every reason to believe that subjects will provide honest responses.

Another response set is the tendency of some subjects to consistently agree or disagree with questions ("yea-saying" or "nay-saying"). The solution is relatively straightforward. Several questions are asked and are posed in both "positive" and "negative" directions. For example, a study of family communication patterns may ask people how much they agree with the following questions: "The members of my family spend a lot of time together" and "My family members don't usually eat dinner together." Although it is possible that someone could legitimately agree with both items, consistently agreeing or disagreeing with a set of related questions posed in both directions is an indicator that the subject is using a response set.

However, this method of posing both positive and negative questions does not work well with children. Benson and Hocevar (1985) have studied the difficulty children have with negative items on such questionnaires. As pointed out by Marsh (1986), the double-negative logic required for such items may be cognitively more difficult for children than positive items are. That is, "My family members don't usually eat dinner together" requires the answer "false" to indicate that the family usually eats together. Young children (and poorer readers) may not employ this logic appropriately and may give the opposite answer from what they intend. Marsh (1986) demonstrated how such misunderstanding of the question could incorrectly suggest that younger children have lower self-esteem than older children if the self-esteem measure contains confusing, negatively worded questions.

Other potential response sets exhibited by children include a tendency to say "yes" to every question, to alternate answers, or to choose the last possibility mentioned in a multiple-choice format. Variations on such response sets include a tendency to pick round numbers or favorite numbers or consistently to choose the item presented on the right (or left). If the measure is carefully designed, such response sets will result in essentially chance-level scores, and the researcher can thus detect the child's guessing behavior. If the measure is poorly designed (e.g., the correct answers systematically alternate), the scores of subjects who exhibit certain response sets (e.g., answer alternation) will be highly misleading.

The problem of retrospective memory

One final issue in self-report measures should be mentioned. Frequently, researchers must ask subjects to recall something about past behaviors. How accurate are such retrospective memories? In some cases, terrible; in other cases, surprisingly good.

An example of terrible memory can be found in an investigation of how well people could reconstruct one of the most familiar of common objects: a penny (Nickerson & Adams, 1979). Hardly anyone could recognize an actual penny from an array of possibilities that varied in the direction Lincoln faced, location of the date, the presence of various slogans, and so on. The authors speculated that details of visual stimuli are not retained in memory unless there is some functional reason for them to be. Thus, people have great difficulty remembering such details as exactly how many buttons their favorite shirt has.

People also have great difficulty remembering *anything* from before they were 3-years-old. This *childhood amnesia* was investigated by Sheingold and Tenney (1982), who asked people about a salient event, the birth of a younger sister or brother. People who were 0 to 3-years-old when their younger sibling was born had practically no recall for the event; however, people who were 4-years-old had good memory for such details as what they were doing when their mother left for the hospital, whether they visited their mother in the hospital, and what presents the baby received. The accuracy of these memories was checked by asking the mothers to respond to the same questions.

The birth of a sibling is an especially noteworthy event in life. Other studies suggest a gradual fading away of much information for several years, coupled with a surprising resistance to forgetting of certain salient events and facts (Bahrick, Bahrick, & Wittlinger, 1975; Squire & Slater, 1975). What influences which facts will be retained and which will be forgotten is one of the more interesting mysteries in memory research today.

We know that memory is selective, and our memories are "updated" as we learn new information or acquire new attitudes. For example, Robbins (1963) asked parents about their infant care practices three years later. Their memory was generally quite inaccurate, and in some cases extremely distorted. She asked them questions about the age of weaning, beginning of toilet training, end of the 2 A.M. feeding, and so forth. Accuracy was assessed using a diary that the parents had kept for the researchers during their child's infancy. Most disturbing from the point of view of research methods was the tendency to remember the course of development as easier and smoother than it really was. The parents also remembered their child-rearing practices as more closely conforming to expert opinion about what parents *should do* than what they actually did. This variation represents the general tendency to modify self-reports to enhance social desirability. In this case, parents' memories of their earlier behavior with their children became more socially desirable without any real awareness that their memories had changed. It is also known that people often cannot remember what they used to believe, if their attitudes have subsequently changed (Goethals & Reckman, 1973). All of these findings have made researchers cautious about collecting data based solely on retrospective memories.

ARCHIVAL RESEARCH

Archival research is the use of already existing information to answer research questions; the researcher doesn't actually collect the original data. Instead, he or she analyzes existing data such as statistics that are part of public records (e.g., number of divorce petitions filed), reports of anthropologists, the content of letters to the editor, or information contained in computer data bases. Kidder and Judd (1986) distinguish between three types of archival research data:

Statistical records
Survey archives
Written records

Statistical records

Statistical records are collected by many public and private organizations. The U.S. Census Bureau maintains the most extensive set of statistical records that is available for analysis by researchers. There are also numerous, less obvious sources for statistical records, such as public health agencies for public health statistics and testing organizations (e.g., Educational Testing Service) for records of test scores.

Researchers Lillian Belmont and Francis Morolla used such statistical records when they examined the intelligence test scores of all 19-year-old men in the Netherlands. They discovered an interesting pattern in the data. Intelligence was systematically related to both birth order and family size: It was higher in families with fewer children and also higher among early-born rather than later-born children. Later, Zajonc (1975) developed a mathematical model to explain the data, a model that is based on the amount of intellectual stimulation received by children of differing family size and birth order: As the number of children in a family increases, the intellectual climate decreases. Zajonc was also able to replicate the original findings by studying a database that consisted of test scores obtained in the United States.

Various public records can also be used as sources of archival data. For example, Gwartney-Gibbs (1986) used marriage license applications in one Oregon county in 1970 and 1980 to study changing patterns of premarital cohabitation. She found that only 13 percent of the couples used the same address on the application in 1970, whereas 53 percent gave the same address in 1980. She was also able to relate cohabitation to other variables such as age and race. The findings were interpreted as support for the notion that premarital cohabitation has become a new step in patterns of courtship leading to marriage.

Survey archives

Survey archives consist of data from surveys that are stored on computer tapes and are available to researchers who wish to perform analyses of the data. Major polling organizations make many of their surveys available. Many universities are part of the Interuniversity Consortium for Political and Social Research (ICPSR) that makes survey archive data available. One useful data set is the General Social Survey, which is a series of surveys funded by the National Science Foundation and is intended as a resource for social scientists. Each survey includes over 200 questions covering a range of topics such as attitudes, life satisfaction, health, religion, education, age, gender, and race. These survey archives are extremely useful because most researchers do not have the financial resources to conduct large surveys that carefully obtain national samples; the archives allow researchers to access such samples to test their ideas. For example, Weissert (1986) was able to predict the institutionalization of elderly persons using demographic data (age, race, gender) from the National Health Interview Survey and the National Nursing Home Survey.

Although most survey archives consist of data obtained from adults, there is one major survey of children. The National Survey of Children is a 1981 sample of elementary through high school students that has been used to study a variety of questions including the effects of divorce on behavior problems of children (see Peterson & Zill, 1986).

Written records

Written records consist of a variety of documents such as diaries and letters that have been preserved by historical societies, ethnographies of other cultures written by anthropologists, public documents such as speeches by politicians, and mass communications including books, magazine articles, movies, and newspapers.

Researchers de Charms and Moeller (1962) examined achievement motivation in American history by rating the amount of achievement imagery—concern with success—expressed in the themes of children's readers published between 1800 and 1950. The researchers predicted that the achievement values expressed in the readers would be related to technological development. Indeed, they found that increases in achievement imagery were followed by increases in the number of patents issued several years later by the U.S. Patent Office. Declines in achievement imagery were associated with declines in patents. Analysis of archival data (children's readers and patent information) allowed the researchers to investigate how achievement motivation and technological development are related in a nation's history.

Archival data may also be used in cross-cultural research. Such research examines aspects of social structure that differ from society to society. A variable such as the presence versus the absence of monogamous marital relationships cannot be studied in a single society. For example, in North America monogamy is the norm, and bigamy is illegal. By looking at a number of cultures, some monogamous and some not, we can increase our understanding of the reasons that one system or the other comes to be preferred. This method was pursued in a study by Rosenblatt and Cozby (1972) on the role of freedom of choice in mate selection. In some societies, considerable restrictions exist as to whom one can marry, whereas other societies give great freedom of choice to young people in selecting a spouse. In the study, anthropologists' descriptions (called *ethnographies*) of a number of societies were used to rate the societies as being either low or high in terms of freedom of choice of spouse. The ethnographies also provided information on a number of other variables. The results indicated that when there is freedom of choice of spouse, romantic love and sexual attraction are important as a basis for mate selection, and there is also greater antagonism in the interactions among young males and females. The Rosenblatt and Cozby study used the Human Relations Area Files, a resource available in many university libraries, to obtain information from the ethnographies. The Human Relations Area Files consist of anthropologists' descriptions of many cultures that have been organized according to categories such as courtship and marriage customs, child-rearing practices, and so on. Thus, it is relatively easy to find specific information from many societies by using the Human Relations Area Files.

Content analysis of documents

Content analysis is the systematic analysis of existing documents (see Holsti, 1969; Viney, 1983). Like systematic observation, content analysis requires researchers to devise coding systems that raters can use to quantify the information in the documents. Sometimes the coding is quite simple and straightforward—for example, it is easy to code whether the addresses of the bride and groom on marriage license applications are the same or different. More often, the researcher must define categories to code the information. In the Rosenblatt and Cozby cross-cultural study, for example, raters had to read the ethnographic information and determine whether each culture was low or high on freedom of choice of spouse. Raters were trained to use the coding system, and reliability coefficients were computed to ensure that there was high agreement among the raters. Similar procedures may be used in studies that examine archival documents such as speeches, magazine articles, television shows, or letters.

SUMMARY

Field observation is the observation of activities in a natural setting over an extended period of time. Information is gathered in a variety of ways, and it is interpreted by the researcher. The researcher must consider the advantages and disadvantages of being either a participant or nonparticipant observer and whether or not to conceal the observation.

Systematic observation is the observation of one or more specific behaviors in a specific setting. A coding system must be used to allow observers to record behaviors.

A case study is a description of a single "case," which may be an individual or a specific event. Case studies are especially useful for studying rare, unusual events.

In survey research, self-report measures are used to question people. Questionnaire techniques are generally cheaper than interviews, but people are often less motivated to fill out questionnaires than they are to answer an interviewer's questions. Questions must be carefully chosen, and they may be either open or closed-ended. "Double-barreled" and "leading" questions should be avoided. Sampling procedures are especially important in survey research. Survey researchers must try to eliminate interviewer bias and response sets such as social desirability and consistent agreement or disagreement with questions.

Archival research is the use of existing information such as statistical records, survey archives, and written documents. Content analysis procedures are used to code the information in written documents.

We have now presented the fundamental concepts of design of both nonexperimental and experimental research investigations. In the remaining chapters, we discuss some practical issues in the conduct of research including obtaining subjects, conducting pilot studies, and the statistical analyses of results.

STUDY QUESTIONS

1. What is field observation? How does a researcher collect data when conducting field observation research?
2. What is negative-case analysis?
3. Why are the data in field observation research primarily qualitative?
4. Distinguish between participant and nonparticipant observation. Distinguish between concealed and nonconcealed observation.
5. What is systematic observation? Why are the data from systematic observation primarily quantitative?
6. What is a coding system? What are some important considerations when developing a coding system?
7. What is a case study? When are case studies used?
8. What is a survey? When would you use a panel survey design?
9. What are the advantages and disadvantages of using questionnaires versus interviews in a survey?
10. Define interviewer bias.
11. Describe some types of response sets.
12. What are the issues and problems associated with retrospective information?
13. What is archival research? What are the major sources of archival data?
14. What is content analysis?

CHAPTER 9

Preparations for Conducting Research

CAREER PROFILE

Maryhelen Campa / Montessori Teacher

Maryhelen received an A.A. in Liberal Studies from San Bernardino Valley College. She holds Montessori preschool accreditation through the American Montessori Society and a Montessori pre-primary teaching certificate from the Montessori Western Teacher Training Program. Maryhelen is the Head Teacher and School Director at the Montessori Greenhouse School, Los Alamitos, California.

"As a Head Teacher, I work with an educationally qualified assistant in a classroom of 24 children ranging in age from 2½ to 6 years. My activities include the preparation of an environment responsive to each child's developmental needs, which includes maintenance of a clean and safe classroom that provides educationally appropriate materials and an opportunity for the child to explore within clearly defined limits. As Director, I spend a great deal of time consulting and problem solving with children and parents. I am constantly involved with teacher–child, teacher–parent, and parent–child issues. I began working at Montessori with no formal training. I realized immediately that I needed an understanding of not only the Montessori Method but also child psychology and human development as well. I must say, one of the most important things I studied was communications. I learned how to speak effectively and to listen carefully.

"To anyone planning a career with young children, I feel they must have a wealth of patience and love. You must be willing to share your creativity and be willing to be flexible in responding to the constantly changing needs of each child. The adult must appreciate each child's unique abilities and have respect for that child as an individual. Look within yourself; for you cannot be honest with a child until you are honest with yourself."

Suppose Maryhelen Campa, the Montessori teacher in the profile, wanted to study how teachers' communication styles affected children. After she has decided on a topic to study, what next? There is still a great deal of planning to do before the project gets under way. Before an abstract idea can become a research project and be tested, numerous decisions must be made. The evolution of an idea from conception to publication is a long one, but it is an exciting process for the researcher who initiates the idea. This chapter provides a detailed, behind-the-scenes look at the process of conducting research. We examine some of the general principles researchers use when they are planning the details of their studies, so that you will understand some of the important practical considerations that influence the design and execution of research.

RESEARCH PROPOSALS

Planning what is to be done

A *research proposal* details why the study is being done, poses the questions the research is designed to answer, and discusses the variables to be studied. It describes the specific procedures that are to be used to test the idea. A research proposal is similar to the introduction and method sections of a journal article.

Such proposals are required as part of applications for research grants; they are also used as the basis for qualifying to undertake master's or doctoral thesis research. They are a useful part of the planning process for any type of research project. Simply putting thoughts into words helps to organize and systematize ideas. The proposal can be shown to colleagues who provide useful feedback about the adequacy of procedures and design. Others can sometimes see problems that the researcher didn't anticipate. Research proposals often lead to ways of improving the research.

Estimating costs

Another important function served by a research proposal is *cost estimation*. Research sometimes requires expensive equipment, although technological advances have reduced the costs of much common research equipment (e.g., the personal computer and the portable videocassette recorder). For example, Gregg (1978) investigated the difficulties preschoolers had driving a remote-controlled turtle through a maze. The turtle was connected by a cable to an expensive and bulky computer. The turtle required a special computer program to execute its movements. Today, remote-control toys are so inexpensive that they are popular Christmas gifts, and this kind of research can now be conducted by anyone who can afford to buy such a toy.

In addition to equipment, supplies must be purchased such as blank audio or videotapes, computer diskettes, paper and pencils, and so forth. Frequently, stimulus materials must be prepared or questionnaires duplicated. There also may be costs associated with paying and training research assistants, such as observers or survey takers. If subjects are going to be paid for their participation, the experimenter must determine what would be a fair reimbursement (research in social psychology suggests that people's behavior can be affected if they receive either too little or too much compensation). If children are involved, researchers sometimes reward them with a trinket of some sort or with candy (although giving children anything to eat without obtaining prior parental permission is unwise).

Another important cost to consider is time. Research projects range tremendously in the amount of time they take. Inexperienced researchers sometimes conceive projects that exceed their time and financial resources; therefore, experienced researchers try to plan carefully to avoid these problems. On the one hand, there are relatively fast and easy projects such as the study of occupational sex typing conducted by Garrett, Ein, and Tremaine (1977) with large classrooms of first, third, and fifth graders. The researchers compiled a set of 40 occupations that were either predominantly male, female, or gender-neutral (based on census data). Children were given answer sheets that depicted a five-point rating scale with both words and pictures ("only women," one cartoon female head; "mostly women, a few men," two females and one male head; "women and men," one female and one male head; "mostly men, a few women," two males and one female head; "only men," one male head). The experimenter simply read each occupation ("Who do you think can be [*each of the 40 occupations*]?"). Subjects marked their answers in their booklets. All that remained was for the researchers to tally the checkmarks in the booklets and analyze the data.

On the other hand, consider the observational study conducted by Sigel (1982). He videotaped 120 children performing two tasks (story telling and paper folding) with each of their parents. The coding system focused on parental and child behaviors such as degree of engagement in the interaction, evaluative comments, emotional support, spoken utterances, and so forth. So many variables were measured that the researchers had to develop a special manual specifying their definitions. Six coders were necessary to score the 800 videotaped sessions generated by the study. When you consider that each hour of videotape probably took several hours to be coded, you can appreciate the huge scope of this study.

FINE-TUNING MANIPULATIONS, MEASURES, AND CONTROLS

Even though the researcher has identified the hypothesis and the variables to study, many additional decisions are required to help the researcher achieve a fruitful outcome.

Strength of the manipulation

The simplest experimental design has two levels of independent variable. In planning to conduct an experiment, the researcher must choose these levels. One principle worth considering is to make the manipulation as strong as possible. A strong manipulation maximizes the differences between the two groups and increases the chances that the independent variable will have an effect.

To illustrate, consider a study by Byrne, Ervin, and Lamberth (1970) on the relationship between attitude similarity and attraction in dating couples. Male and female students who held either similar or dissimilar attitudes were matched, and each couple had a brief date on campus. When the researchers measured how much the members of each couple liked one another they found that couples who were similar were more attracted to each other than couples who were dissimilar. A researcher who wanted to conduct this type of study would have to decide on the amount of similarity. Figure 9.1 shows the hypothesized relationship between attitude similarity and attraction at 10 different levels of similarity (from least to greatest similarity). To achieve the strongest manipulation, the subjects in one group would be matched at level 1 similarity, and the subjects in the other group would be matched on the basis of level 10 similarity. Such a manipulation would result in the greatest difference in the means of the levels of liking one another; it would result in a nine-point difference in mean liking of one another. A weaker manipulation—using levels 3 and 7, for instance—would result in a smaller mean difference.

A strong manipulation is especially important in the early stages of research, when the researcher is most interested in demonstrating that a relationship does, in fact, exist. If the early experiments are successful in

Figure 9.1
The hypothesized relationship between attitude similarity and attraction at 10 different levels of similarity. Independent variable: amount of attitude similarity. Dependent variable: amount of liking one another.

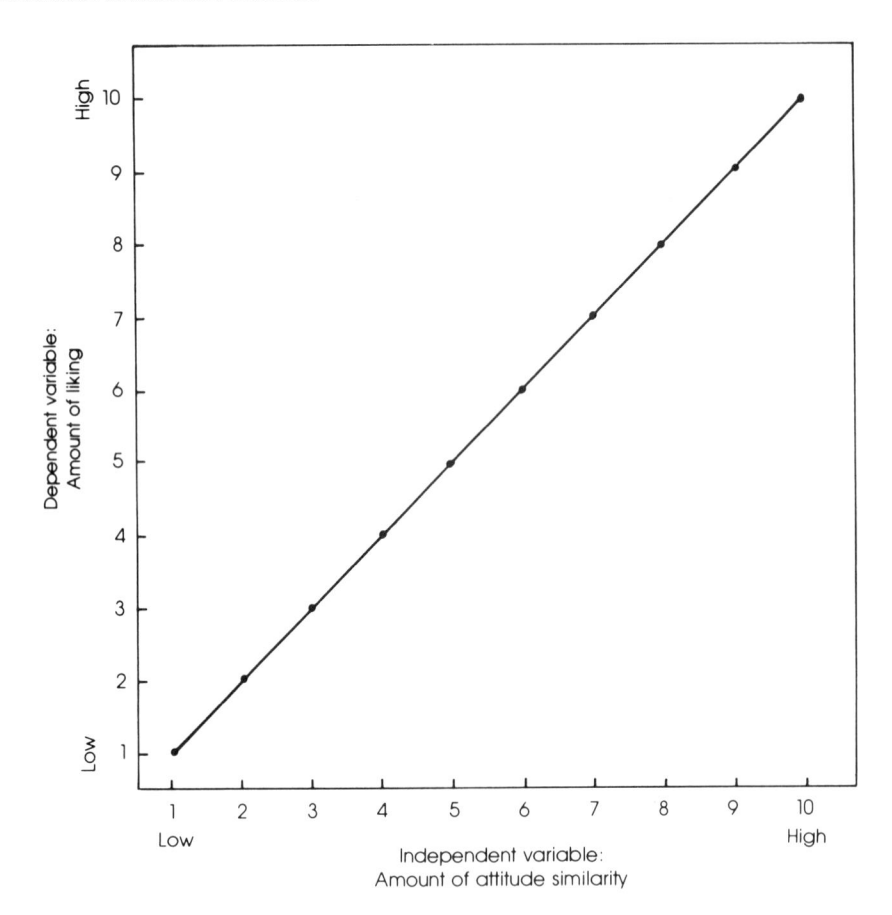

finding a relationship between the variables, later research can systematically manipulate the other level of the independent variable to provide a more detailed picture of the relationship.

The principle of using the strongest manipulation possible should be tempered by at least two considerations. First, the strongest possible manipulation may involve a situation that rarely, if ever, occurs in the real world. For example, suppose a researcher is interested in the effects of crowding on classroom learning and behavior. An extremely strong crowding manipulation may involve placing so many children in a room that no one can move, which may result in a significant effect on a variety of behaviors. However, we wouldn't know if the results were similar to those occurring in regular classrooms that are less crowded.

A second consideration is ethics. When considering the strength of the manipulation, it is important to remain within the bounds of ethics. A strong manipulation of punishment, for example, may not be possible because of the physical and psychological harm that may result.

Types of manipulations

Straightforward manipulations   Researchers may be able to manipulate a variable with relative simplicity by presenting written or verbal material to the subjects—which is sometimes referred to as *instructional manipulation*. For example, Weissberg and Paris (1986) gave children from 3 to 7 years of age six items to remember. In one condition they used a direct lesson format ("Now I am going to tell you some words. Listen carefully, because I will ask you to tell them all to me later."). In another condition they used a game-like "shopping" situation—the children were asked to buy a list of six remembered items from a play grocery store. There was also a "party" situation in which the child was asked to remember the names of six stuffed animals to introduce them to another animal. Weissberg and Paris found that, in contrast to a famous earlier study conducted by Soviet psychologist Istomina (1975), the children remembered more in the lesson than in the game contexts. Weissberg and Paris interpreted their data as showing unexpected evidence of deliberate memory processes in very young children. This example illustrates the use of a straightforward manipulation in that it was clear to the subjects what their task was—even though in some conditions the memory task was couched in a game-like situation.

Staged manipulations   Other manipulations are less straightforward. Social psychologists often stage events that enable them to study various aspects of social behavior—which is sometimes called *event manipulation*. Frequently these experiments involve a confederate—a person who poses as a subject but is actually part of the manipulation. Staged manipulations demand a great deal of ingenuity and even some acting ability. They are used to involve subjects in an ongoing social situation, which the subject perceives not as an experiment but as a real experience. Researchers assume that the result will be natural behavior that truly reflects the feelings and intentions of subjects. However, such procedures allow for a great deal of subtle interpersonal communication that is hard to put into words. As well, staged manipulations may make it difficult for other researchers to replicate the experiment, and a complex manipulation is difficult to interpret. If many things happen to the subject, what *one* thing is responsible for the results? In general, it is easier to interpret results when the manipulation is relatively straightforward. However, the nature of the variable you are studying sometimes demands complicated procedures.

For example, Ceci and Bronfenbrenner (1985) investigated children's prospective memory ("Don't forget to take the cupcakes out of the oven!"). The subjects (10-year-olds and 14-year-olds) baked cupcakes for 30 minutes, during which time they played the popular and engaging videogame, Pac Man. The experimenter recorded the number of times the children checked the clock located on the wall behind them. Two contexts were investigated: Subjects either baked cupcakes at home or were brought to a university laboratory. The results showed that children as young as 10 years of age were able to employ a sophisticated strategy for monitoring the passage of time before the cupcakes were ready, but they were far more likely to do so at home than in the lab. The purpose of manipulating the setting in this fashion was to determine whether the behavior of time monitoring is influenced by familiar versus unfamiliar surroundings—as it was. If the research had only been conducted in the lab, the results would have underestimated the children's ability "to remember not to forget."

In the previous memory example, the "staging" involved two different settings for the cupcakes task. Social science researchers sometimes employ even more elaborate staging that involves complex events and confederates, but more elaborate staging is unusual in research on child development. The following present a few examples of such staged manipulations. Milsoky, Wilkinson, Chiang, Lindow, and Salmon (1986) used child actors to prepare videotapes of two elementary school students working together on math problems. Subjects judged the adequacy of the children's explanations of the math problems to one another. In another case, mothers were trained to feign "depressed" facial expressions and bodily movements, and their infants' reactions were measured (Cohn & Tronick, 1983). Another study measured mothers' reactions to infants' cries. In actuality, the mothers listened to the same tape recording of a crying infant; the staging involved labeling the infant as either "fussy and irritable" or "easy to care for" (Donovan & Leavitt, 1985). However, note that most research on child development focuses on straightforward rather than staged situations.

Sensitivity of the dependent measure

An investigator who is conducting an experiment must find a specific way to measure the dependent variable. The means of measurement vary widely in accordance with the experiment, but some general considerations apply to measuring and observing behavior.

Reliability Recall from Chapter 4 that the measurement of the dependent variable should be *reliable*. An unreliable measure contains a great deal of measurement error, which will be reflected in greater variability in scores. That is, scores on an unreliable measure will have greater variability about the group mean than scores on a reliable measure. When there is a large amount of error variance, it is difficult to obtain a significant difference between the means.

Sensitivity The dependent measure should also be *sensitive* enough to show a difference between groups. For example, a measure of marital satisfaction that asks, "Do you have a satisfying marriage?" (answer yes or no) is less sensitive than one that asks, "How satisfying is your marriage?" (answer on a specific scale). The first measure allows only for a yes or no response; many subjects may be polite and say "yes" regardless of how they actually feel. The second measure allows for gradations of satisfaction—a continuous scale that can range from "extremely satisfied" through "neutral" to "extremely unsatisfied." Such a scale makes it easier to detect differences in terms of amount of satisfaction. The main point is that the dependent measure should be able to detect the effect of the independent variable. Rating scales can be adapted for use with children under some conditions. For example, children who do not yet read can use scales with pictures of happy, neutral, and frowning cartoon faces (Adams & Worden, 1986). With very young children, it is necessary to train them how to use the scale with several examples. Age-appropriate examples should be tested to see if children respond correctly (i.e., on a scale indicating likelihood, a 5-year-old should point to the "never" end of the scale for the question "do you eat mud at a birthday party?"—or else he or she is not using the scale correctly). Again, the point is that scales that measure a range of responses enable a more sensitive measurement than simple "yes/no" responses.

Ceiling and floor effects   Dependent measures can be insensitive to differences on tasks that are either too easy or too difficult for the subjects (Levin, 1985). A *ceiling effect* occurs when a task is so easy that subjects tend to achieve perfect or near perfect performance. Suppose you wish to test cognitive status in healthy, nonhospitalized retirement community residents by asking them to count from 1 to 50 and measuring their errors. Their performance would probably not differ significantly from a comparison group of younger adults. However, any time performance is "on the ceiling," the researcher cannot be sure that a more sensitive measure would not have detected differences that are obscured by an upper limit on performance. A more difficult task (e.g., having subjects count backwards from 582 by 3's) might have revealed cognitive differences between the young and elderly adults. On the other hand, a task that is too difficult can result in a *floor effect*. Asking subjects to perform mental multiplication with three-digit numbers would probably not reveal any meaningful differences between the young and elderly adults, because so few of them could do the task!

Multiple measures   Scientists feel they have the best understanding of a phenomenon when they have multiple measures of the same dependent variable. There are usually several ways of actually measuring a variable, and confidence in the results is increased if the same results are found with a variety of operational definitions. For example, in Harlow's classic studies of the effects of isolation on infant monkeys, the researchers measured numerous indices of normal and abnormal behavior, such as locomotion, rocking, stereotypy, self-clasping, huddling, social contact, tactile–oral exploration, and social play (see Novak & Harlow, 1975). It is sometimes possible to take multiple measurements in a single experiment, but it is usually necessary to conduct a series of experiments, each with different measures.

Additional control groups

The basic design of an experiment uses two groups. In the simplest case, an experimental group receives the manipulation and a control group does not. Use of a control group makes it possible to eliminate a variety of alternative explanations based on history, maturation, statistical regression, and so on.

Sometimes more than one control group may be necessary. The general purpose of a control group is to provide a basis for eliminating alternative explanations for the results. Different research problems may demand specific additional control groups. The need for such additional groups becomes a factor in planning the experiment.

Placebo controls In drug research, one specific control group is called a *placebo* group. Consider an experiment that is investigating whether a drug improves the behavior of a group of hyperactive children. One group receives the drug; the other group does not. Now suppose the drug group shows an improvement. We don't know whether the improvement has been caused by the properties of the drug or whether it was caused by a placebo effect. A child's behavior can be affected by many things, including expectations. If the child is told "this pill will calm you down," he or she may calm down in the expectation that the drug is going to help control his or her activity level. In other words, simply administering a pill may be enough to cause an observed improvement in behavior. To control for this possibility, a placebo group can be added. Subjects in the placebo group receive an inert pill but do not receive the drug given to subjects in the experimental group. Sometimes both groups of subjects are found to improve, but if the improvement results from the active properties of the drug, the subjects in the experimental group should show *greater* improvement than those in the placebo group.

When subjects are unaware of whether they are receiving the experimental drug or the placebo, the procedure is called a *blind procedure*. However, if the experimenters know which group is which, their observations may bias their expectations. That is, if the observers expect the drug to calm the hyperactive children, they may rate a given behavior as more calm than if it were seen in one of the placebo subjects. For this reason, it is common that even the experimenters do not know which group is receiving the experimental drug and which the placebo; subjects and medications are coded, and their actual conditions are revealed only after the data have been collected and analyzed. This procedure is called a *double-blind procedure*.

The importance of minimizing both the subjects' and the experimenters' awareness of the expected results cannot be underestimated. A famous demonstration of how experimenter expectancy can bias the results was conducted by Rosenthal and Fode (1963). They gave two groups of graduate student experimenters rats that supposedly had been selectively bred to be "maze bright" or "maze dull." Even though the rats were actually from the *same* strain, the bright rats ran the mazes faster than the dull ones. There have been many speculations about why this outcome occurred. Because the experimenters with the "bright" rats expected them to perform better, perhaps they trained them more thoroughly. Another possibility is more indirect—because the rats were thought to be "bright," the students reported that they liked them better and accordingly handled them more, promoting better growth, development, and performance. A third possibility is that minute errors of measurement could have been produced by the experimenters' expectations—those with "bright" rats could have clicked their stop watches a split second faster than those with "dull" rats. The cumulative effect of this unconscious measurement bias could have added up to a significant difference between the two groups. Thus, the placebo control group and procedures for both the subjects and experimenters to be "blind" to the expected outcome are important remedies for the problems of expectancy effects.

Attention controls Even if people are not aware of the purpose of the research, they are prone to change their behavior simply because they know they are being observed. As discussed in Chapter 4, a technical term for such behavior is *reactivity*. Reactivity sometimes produces predictable behavior. If someone measures your waist, you tend to suck it in a little; if someone measures your height, you tend to stand straight and tall. In other cases, reactivity effects are unpredictable and counterintuitive. The most famous demonstration of how simply being studied can affect behavior took place in the Hawthorne, MA, manufacturing plant of the Western Electric Company (Mayo, 1946). The researchers made a variety of changes in the workers' environment (e.g., both raising and lowering the level of illumination) to see under what conditions production levels would improve. The surprising finding was that production increased in *every* condition; after awhile, the researcher realized that it was the workers' awareness that they were in a study that produced the results—not the experimental manipulations. This phenomenon has ever since been known as the *Hawthorne effect*. A possible remedy is to add a group to the design that receives either no treatment or a treatment that is not, in and of itself, expected to produce an effect, that is, to add an *attention control*. If the treatment group shows a greater effect than the attention control group, then we can conclude that the result was not due to the Hawthorne effect.

It is more difficult to predict what will happen to children's behavior when they know they are being observed. Some children become uncharacteristically shy; others become shameless hams. For this reason, any time we single out a group of children to participate in an experimental treatment, there also should be a group that merely receives an equal amount of attention (without receiving the treatment). For example, Cazden (1965, cited in Cazden, 1972) was interested in the effect of a specific linguistic experience, called *expansion*, on linguistically deprived preschool children's language development. The treatment group was taken from their preschool classrooms to a special room for 40 min per day of deliberate expansion of all of their utterances by specially trained teachers. The attention control group was also given a one-on-one experience with the special room and teachers, but it was not given the intensive experience with expansions. After the 12-week experimental period, Cazden found that *both* the expansion group and the control group showed growth in linguistic ability—and to the same degree. The most parsimonious explanation for these results is that the improvement was due to the special attention received by the children rather than to the expansion manipulation itself. Without the attention control group, the researcher might have concluded incorrectly that the expansion treatment was responsible for the children's linguistic improvement.

Maturation control group A final control group that must be considered in developmental research is the *maturation control group.* In the Cazden (1965, cited in Cazden, 1972) research just discussed, another possible explanation for the results is that the children had simply matured over the 12-week duration of the study. It could be that their linguistic performance was improved at the end of the study as the result of the natural maturational process of language development—and not as a result of either the expansion manipulation or the increased attention of participating in the study. A maturation control group is simply a group of subjects who are the same age as the experimental subjects at the beginning of a study. These subjects are given the same pretest and posttest as the experimental subjects, but they otherwise do not participate in the study. A maturation control group would show whether the training was effective or whether the children had simply matured over the 3-month period.

OBTAINING SUBJECTS AND SAMPLING

Sources of research participants

A major practical problem facing the researcher is where to find subjects. Locating groups of children or families to participate in research can challenge the researcher's ingenuity, patience, ability of persuasion, and in some cases can be the single most time-consuming aspect of the project. No wonder so many researchers restrict their studies to college sophomores! For those who are interested in studying people from the wider population, the following are some suggestions for finding subjects.

Infants can be found by contacting hospitals, obstetricians, or pediatricians. Other sources are newspaper birth announcements, classes for prospective parents and babies (e.g., YMCA and Lamaze). Toddlers can be found at day care centers and churches. Elementary school children are almost as easy to find as college sophomores, because they are conveniently rounded up for several hours a day in schools, and they usually stay in the same classrooms most of the day. Moreover, elementary schools are often cooperative in providing useful demographic information on their student population. Older school children (junior and senior high school students) are more difficult to schedule for research studies, because they typically move from class to class throughout the school day, and they often take part in a variety of extracurricular activities. Older adolescents become progressively harder to locate, as some of them drop out of the school system and enter the work force or otherwise disappear. Adults are especially difficult to recruit (outside of college). But, they can be recruited from church groups, clubs, political associations, conventions, class reunions, singles bars, newspaper solicitations, and so on (if you are thinking about the possible sampling problems associated with these suggestions, these are addressed in the next section). Finally, elderly adults are a little easier to locate, and because most of them are retired, they usually have more time to volunteer for research. You can find them in retirement centers, senior citizens clubs, and increasingly, in college.

Once you have identified a potential source of subjects, the next task is to obtain permission to include them in your study. Obtaining access can range from trivially easy to simply impossible. At one end of the spectrum is field observation, which at most requires only a minimum of explanation (e.g., if you are going to observe families in a shopping mall, at a swap meet, or in a public park, it may be a good idea to get permission from the management). This statement is not to imply that field observation is necessarily easy—it can be technically difficult, tedious, or even dangerous (e.g., as in gathering information on street gang warfare). Research in university settings involves submitting a prospectus to a university committee that reviews the procedures, especially for protection of the rights of the subjects. Submitting a prospectus involves a moderate amount of work, but most universities are familiar with research and are geared up to deal with such requests. Research in outside institutions can be more difficult, because frequently they have no established procedure for dealing with requests to conduct research. If you want to test a few children in a classroom, you may have to write a prospectus and present it to the teacher, the principal, or even the school board at a public hearing before permission can be granted—which can delay your research for weeks or even months. The most difficult process, however, probably takes place in medical settings, in which there tend to be layers and layers of review, extending at times into the state and even federal government. Of course, the purpose of this bureaucratic review is to protect the subjects, who have important rights in the research situation. The rights of human research subjects, including their right to free informed consent to participate, are so important that we have devoted an entire chapter to this critical issue (see Chapter 12).

There are a few suggestions that can smooth the review process. A well-prepared prospectus is a key ingredient; it should describe the essentials of the project, and it should be as brief as possible. Make yourself readily available to answer further questions about your project. If possible, meet the people in authority in person (e.g., the school principal). Be prepared with good answers to questions such as "What is the point of your study? What use is to be made of the results?" Successful researchers learn to convey these ideas in terms that can be understood by and will sound interesting to nonscientists. Whenever possible, the procedures should be tailored for the convenience of the subjects, their teachers, and/or their families. In other words, to the extent that you can make it easy, fun, and interesting, most people are willing if not eager to participate in research studies.

Samples and populations

Suppose we have identified a good source of subjects and have obtained ready access to them. Whether the subjects are children, college students, retired people, archival data, mammals, fish, or insects, they must somehow be selected. The method used to select subjects has implications for the generality of the research results. Most research projects involve *sampling* subjects from a population. The population is composed of all of the individuals of interest to the researcher. For instance, the population of interest to a major pollster may be all people in the United States who are eligible to vote. This statement implies that the pollster's population of interest does *not* include people under the age of 18, people serving prison terms, visitors from other countries, and other people ineligible to vote. With enough time and money, a pollster can, conceivably, contact everyone in the population who is eligible to vote. Fortunately, the pollster can avoid this massive undertaking by selecting a sample from the population of interest. With proper sampling, the pollster can use information obtained from the sample to estimate the opinion of the population as a whole, with only a small margin of error. Not only has the pollster saved money and time, but with proper sampling techniques, the results will be so accurate that virtually no new information would be gained if the whole population were contacted.

There are two basic types of sampling techniques:

Probability sampling

Nonprobability sampling

In *probability sampling*, each member of the population has a specifiable probability of being chosen. In *nonprobability sampling*, we don't know the probability of any specific member of the population being chosen.

Nonprobability sampling

Haphazard sampling Nonprobability sampling is quite arbitrary and sloppy. One form of nonprobability sampling is called *haphazard sampling*, which is a "take them where you find them" method of obtaining subjects. For example, a representative of a television station may poll people who happen to walk past a specific street corner at a specific time of day and are willing to say a few words to the camera. The population of interest may be "people who live in this city," but the results of this poll cannot really be generalized to this population. It is not possible to specify the probability of a city resident being chosen as a participant in this poll. The probability is high for some people (those who live or work near the street corner) and low for others. This haphazard sampling technique excludes everyone who, for any reason, isn't present at the specific location at the specific time. Thus, any generalization of the results to the entire city is probably inaccurate.

Quota sampling Another form of nonprobability sampling is called *quota sampling*. A researcher who uses this technique chooses a sample that reflects the numerical composition of various subgroups in the population. For instance, suppose a high school district has the following composition: 60% White, 20% Black, 10% Chicano, 5% Asian, and 5% Native American. A quota sampling technique that uses nationality and ethnic subgroups produces a sample that numerically reflects these percentages. Thus, a sample of 100 adolescents from this school district would have 60 Whites, 20 Blacks,

10 Chicanos, 5 Asians, and 5 Native Americans. Similarly, subgroups may be based on age, sex, socioeconomic class, handedness, height, weight, and so on. Quota sampling is a bit more elegant than haphazard sampling; however, problems are associated with such sampling because no restrictions are placed on how individuals in the various subgroups are chosen. Although the sample reflects the numerical composition of the population of interest, subjects within each subgroup are selected in a haphazard manner.

The advantage of nonprobability sampling techniques is that the investigator can obtain subjects without spending a great deal of money or time on selecting a specific sample group. For example, many researchers commonly select "adult" subjects from students in introductory college classes. Often these students are required to participate in experiments; they can usually choose the experiments in which they wish to participate. However, with this kind of sampling technique, it is difficult even to define the population of interest. Usually, researchers want to generalize to "people in general" or at least to "adults who live in the United States." Obviously, generalizing to these populations is risky when the haphazard sample is composed of students at a specific college who have decided to take a specific class and have volunteered for a specific experiment. Similarly, elderly adults chosen from a specific nursing home are not truly representative of all senior citizens in the society.

If generalization is such a problem, why do researchers use these techniques? First, they are practical and cheap. It is impossible to find a truly representative sample of the general population that is willing to come into the lab to volunteer for an experiment, and even telephone or mail surveys are quite expensive compared to the costs of collecting data from college students. Second, researchers are often primarily interested in finding relationships between variables. The purpose of the research is to test a hypothesis that certain variables are related to one another. If a relationship is found, one can then ask whether the same relationship between variables would be observed in some other population of subjects. In some research, such as studies of perceptual processes, there isn't a compelling reason to expect that the relationship would not be found among other groups. When there is a reason to hypothesize that other groups would behave differently (e.g., younger or older children, the elderly, or various ethnic or cultural groups), researchers usually conduct further research to test their hypotheses in these new groups. For instance, when it is suspected that findings may depend on conditions present in our specific culture, researchers try to replicate the findings in other cultures. An example of such cross-cultural research are the studies of Barbara Rogoff, who tested people in rural Guatemala on "traditional" Piagetian concepts and tasks and found that the usual North American and European results are by no means universal (Rogoff, 1981).

In spite of our growing awareness of the possible influence of different cultures and contexts on behavior, scientific studies designed to test ideas about relationships between variables tend to be more concerned with measuring those relationships accurately than with wide generalization of the results. It is important to be aware, then, that these relationships may not hold in all contexts or for all groups of subjects. However, when the research goal is to describe some specific aspect of a specific population, probability sampling techniques must be used. For example, research that is aimed at determining how many people will vote for a specific political candidate or assessing the needs of the elderly in a specific city must use a truly representative sample. Let's examine three general types of probability sampling:

Simple random sampling
Stratified random sampling
Area sampling

Probability sampling

Simple random sampling With *simple random sampling*, every member of the population has an equal probability of being selected for the sample. If the population has 1,000 members, each has 1 chance out of 1,000 of being selected. Suppose you want to sample college students who attend your school. A list of all students is needed; from that list, students may be chosen at random to form the sample. This procedure doesn't introduce any biases about who is chosen; a haphazard procedure in which you sampled from students walking by a certain location at 9 A.M. may involve all sorts of biases. For example, such a haphazard procedure eliminates students who don't frequent the location, and it may also eliminate afternoon and evening students.

Stratified random sampling A somewhat more complicated procedure is called *stratified random sampling*, which is analogous to quota sampling in that the population is divided into subgroups (or *strata*). Random sampling techniques are then used to select sample members from each stratum. Stratified random sampling has the advantage of a built-in assurance that the sample will accurately reflect the numerical composition of the various subgroups. This kind of accuracy is especially important when certain subgroups comprise a very small percentage of the population. For instance, if blacks comprise 5 percent of a city of 100,000 population, a simple random sample of 100 people may not include any blacks, whereas a stratified random sample would include five blacks chosen randomly from blacks in the population. A number of dimensions can be used to divide the population. The dimension (or dimensions) used should be relevant to the problem under study. For instance, a survey about attitudes toward occupational gender stereotyping should stratify on the basis of age, gender, and amount of education, because these factors are related to people's attitudes about sex roles. Stratification on the basis of height or hair color is unlikely.

Area sampling It may have occurred to you that obtaining a list of all members of a large population (e.g., the residents of an entire city) may be difficult. In such situations, a technique called *area sampling* can be used. Rather than random sampling from a list of individuals, the researcher can sample from a list of geographical areas. For instance, a city can be described by a list of city blocks, and the researcher can then take a random sample of the city blocks and survey all the people who live on the blocks that are chosen.

All attempts to form a representative sample of the population can be fouled up in the data collection phase. Biases are still possible if some people in the sample are not contacted. For example, if the researcher were to by-pass dilapidated houses, low-income individuals might be systematically excluded from the sample. As another example, what would happen to the sample if an interviewer conducting a phone survey neglected to call people whose names he or she couldn't pronounce? A random sample can quickly become nonrandom unless care is taken to collect data from the entire sample.

SETTING THE STAGE

There is one more general area that must be planned before the researcher is ready to begin conducting a study. He or she must give serious consideration to the question of how to present the research situation to the subjects.

Instructions

In setting the stage, you usually have to explain to subjects why the research is being conducted. Sometimes the rationale given is completely truthful, although rarely will you want to tell subjects the actual hypothesis. For example, subjects can be told that you are conducting research on dual-career couples when, in fact, you are studying the effects of stress on dual-career couples. Although it is important that each and every subject receive the same orientation, such presentation can be accomplished in various ways. Subjects can be given a written description of the task, or the experimenter can read the same written text to all subjects. However, procedures are sometimes modified to suit the needs of the subjects (such as slowing the pace or increasing the size of the print for elderly adults).

Instructions to children

Young children cannot read well enough to absorb a page of written instructions. They do not process information well by listening passively to an experimenter reading a script. Some children do not respond well to an adult acting in a distant, clinically objective manner. More success may result if the researcher exudes warmth, friendliness, and transmits an impression that the activity is designed to be fun. The researcher must be sensitive to the child's level of comprehension and explain the research so that each child ends up with a good understanding of what is expected. It may take some experience for the researcher to learn to interpret the child's reaction to the instructions. The experimenter must look the child in the eye and assess frequently whether the child understands what is expected. It is not sufficient merely to ask "Do you understand?" because young children are poor at indicating their lack of understanding (Flavell, Speer, Green, & August, 1981; Markman, 1977). Having the child repeat back or paraphrase what is expected is a better way to assess comprehension. It is sometimes necessary to explain a given concept in several alternative ways before a child grasps your intention. Precise terms may have to give way to language more appropriate to the child's level. For example, it is common to describe the experiment as a game you are going to play together.

The point is that uniformity of understanding is the true goal of instructions to research subjects, not just uniformity of instructions. In addition to the instructions themselves, other conditions may have to be adjusted to suit the child's personality and developmental level. Some very young children can be tested by themselves; others may need a parent to be present for reassurance. In all of these instances, the researcher seeks to balance the need to set the stage most appropriately for each subject against the need for uniformity of conditions. If the researcher is not confident that a specific factor (e.g., presence of parents) won't contaminate the results, consideration should be given to testing that factor explicitly (e.g., by studying the effects of parents present versus parents absent on young children's performance).

Deception

Sometimes the researcher conceals the actual purpose of the experiment from the subjects. For example, *deception* is common in social psychological research, because researchers often feel that subjects behave most naturally when they are unaware of the variable that is being manipulated. If subjects know what you are studying, they may try to confirm the hypothesis, or they may try to "look good" by behaving in a socially acceptable manner.

Thus, deception may frequently be necessary if the study is to be conducted successfully. However, you must recognize that deception is ethically questionable and should be used only when necessary. Further, when subjects have been deceived, it is important that the researcher debrief the subjects after the research is completed. Of course, subjects may in fact know or suspect that some deception will occur in the experimental procedures. However, they generally do not know exactly which aspects of the experiment are part of the crucial experimental manipulation.

Debriefing

If human subjects have participated in research, the final part of the study is a *debriefing session*. During debriefing, the researcher explains the purpose of the study and tells the subjects what kinds of results are expected. The practical implications of the research may also be discussed. In some cases, it may be possible to contact subjects later on to inform them of the actual results of the study. The purpose of a debriefing is educational, especially for subjects recruited from college classes. Both deception and debriefing in research are important ethical issues that are discussed in depth in Chapter 12.

If subjects have been deceived in any way, debriefing is necessary for ethical reasons. The researcher needs to explain why the deception was necessary and must assure the subjects that the research problem required the deception. If the research procedure altered the subjects' physical or psychological state in any way—for example, by lowering self-esteem or increasing anxiety—the subjects must be returned to their original condition. Debriefing, then, is an important part of the experiment. The subjects should be able to leave the experiment without any ill feelings toward the field of behavioral research or themselves. They may even leave with some new information about their own behavior.

In the case of children, however, debriefing usually cannot involve the level of information we would give to adult subjects. The goal should be to give the children a debriefing commensurate with their ability to understand. Infants are never debriefed, although their parents should be. Preschoolers may only understand that you "wanted to learn more about children." Elementary school children may understand general hypotheses ("We are studying who is more generous, girls or boys."), but detailed descriptions of the technicalities may exceed their understanding or even confuse them.

PILOT STUDIES AND MANIPULATION CHECKS

When the researcher has finally decided on all the specific aspects of the procedure, it is possible to conduct a *pilot study*, which is a miniproject in which you test your procedures with a small number of subjects. Thus, the researcher can learn whether the planned procedures really work before efforts are expended on the full-blown study. The pilot study should reveal whether most subjects understand the instructions, whether the research situation seems plausible, and how long it takes to run the experimental session or conduct the interview. Further, a pilot study allows the researcher and confederates (if there are any) to practice, to become comfortable with their roles, and to standardize their procedures.

In an experiment, the pilot study also provides an opportunity for a *manipulation check* of the independent variable. Obviously, it is important that the independent variable manipulation has the intended effect on subjects, which is what a manipulation check verifies. Suppose you wish to study whether anxious infants show more attention to cuddly, soft toys than nonanxious infants. You manipulate anxiety by having the infants' mothers leave them alone in the playroom. A manipulation check can tell you whether subjects in the high-anxiety group really are more anxious than subjects in the low-anxiety condition. A number of manipulation checks can be made. One may involve having the mothers observe their infants through a one-way mirror and report whether their infants seem anxious. A behavioral measure can be taken by a trained observer (who can record facial expression, vocalization, activity level, etc.); or a physiological measure (e.g., heartrate) can be recorded. Manipulation checks can be included in the actual experiment, although you may want to avoid a check in the actual experiment if you are trying to disguise the purpose of the project.

Conducting a manipulation check in a pilot study is a good idea, because if the check shows that your manipulation was not effective, you can save the expense of the actual experiment. You can also turn your attention to changing the manipulation to make it more effective. For instance, if the manipulation check shows that neither the low- nor the high-anxiety group of infants is very anxious, you can change your procedures to increase the anxiety in the high-anxiety condition, perhaps by introducing an unfamiliar adult into the room with the infant.

WORKING WITH CHILDREN AND OTHER SPECIAL POPULATIONS

Finally, a few words of practical advice about the special challenges of conducting research with people. We have already mentioned the difficulties in locating and gaining access to subjects in real-world settings. This last section is designed to alert you to the special difficulties that are sometimes encountered in actually testing the subjects.

Infants, of course, are notoriously difficult to study because of the transitory nature of their behavioral states. Toddlers have especially short attention spans and limited understanding of the role of a research participant (they would much rather play a game with you than answer your silly questions). Elementary school children can adapt their understanding of the teacher–student role to perform adequately in the research setting, but unexpected problems tend to occur nevertheless. Epidemics of childhood illnesses, field trips, or school events can make large segments of the school population unavailable without warning. Individual subjects can become sick, have to use the bathroom, or pull out a loose tooth during the experimental session. Schools usually lack space, and the "research facility" is often the janitor's closet, the back of the stage, a corner of the lunchroom, the detention room, or the nurse's office (which is the least recommended location, since a highly distracting emergency inevitably interrupts the testing). Children are highly influenced by time of day (proximity to naps, meals, or recess) and exciting upcoming events (holidays or the end of the school year).

Other populations also present their own special difficulties. Married couples must juggle work and child-care schedules, and they may not be available at the convenience of the researcher. Elderly people may have transportation difficulties. In contrast to busy young adults, older adults may wish to chat and socialize with the experimenter after the testing period. These groups can also be influenced by time of day, proximity to meals, or rest periods. Finally, upcoming holidays and special events can influence adult behavior as well. A research project on memory in older adults (Worden & Sherman-Brown, 1983) was seriously disrupted for several weeks because of activities in anticipation of a campaign visit to the retirement community by Ronald Reagan.

In spite of these difficulties, conducting research outside the university setting can be a fun, interesting, and an educational experience for the researcher. In this chapter we have reviewed the practical matters that must be considered to conduct an actual research study. In the next chapter, we discuss the outcome of this endeavor and how to understand research results.

SUMMARY

Research proposals help investigators plan their studies by estimating the time, materials, and costs involved. If the researcher is planning an experiment, the strength of the manipulation(s) should be considered, as well as whether the manipulation will involve a straightforward instructional manipulation or a staged event manipulation. A number of decisions must be made about the dependent measure(s), including the reliability and sensitivity of the measure(s). The researcher must also take care to avoid ceiling or floor effects. In some cases, multiple measures are especially useful to give a full picture of the phenomenon under study.

In experimental research, various control groups should be considered. In the traditional control group, the subjects simply do not receive the manipulation given the experimental group. A special kind of control group is called a placebo group, in which subjects are given an inert treatment (e.g., a sugar pill in medical research) to control for the effects of expectations. When subjects are unaware of whether they are receiving the active treatment or the placebo, the procedure is called a blind procedure. When neither the subjects nor the researchers know which group is receiving the treatment, the procedure is called a double-blind procedure. In nonmedical settings, researchers sometimes employ an attention control group to counter the effects of reactivity (the tendency of people to change their behavior simply because they know they are being observed). A third kind of control group used in developmental research is the maturation control group. If the study involves an experimental treatment administered over time, the maturation group is one that is measured at the beginning and end of the study to control for the effects of growth and development.

Obtaining subjects is one of the most challenging practical aspects of research in the behavioral sciences. Once a target population has been accessed, the researcher then has the task of sampling. Nonprobability sampling is quite informal. One type of nonprobability sampling is haphazard sampling, in which no specific effort is made to select subjects according to specific characteristics. Quota sampling involves selecting a sample that reflects the numerical composition of various subgroups in the population. Probability sampling is more involved, and it requires more systematic information about the population's characteristics. With simple random sampling, for example, every member of the population has an equal probability of being selected for the sample. A somewhat more complicated procedure is called stratified random sampling, which involves dividing the population into subgroups (or strata) and selecting proportions of subjects in the sample that correspond to proportions in the strata. Area sampling uses geographical areas as the basis for sampling, and is commonly used in survey research.

Once subjects are identified and selected, the researcher must decide how to set the stage with instructions. Instructions should be adjusted to the needs of the subjects so that all participants have a uniform understanding of their role in the study. Some studies involve deception, and the researcher needs to provide for appropriate debriefing in such cases. Experienced researchers know the value of pilot studies, which are trial projects in which the instructions, procedures, apparatus, and so forth are tested with small numbers of subjects. Pilot studies enable manipulation checks to ensure that the independent variables have the intended effect on the subjects. Finally, researchers in the area of human development and family studies need to be aware of the special problems sometimes encountered in testing subjects, such as attention, fatigue, interest, testing environment, and scheduling. As you can see, there is much more to conducting research than simply selecting a hypothesis and designing a study!

STUDY QUESTIONS

1. What kinds of costs can be anticipated in a proposed study of play interactions of twins versus non-twins?
2. Describe how an event manipulation differs from an instructional manipulation.
3. What is a ceiling effect? A floor effect? Why are they such serious problems?
4. What does it mean for the dependent measure to be reliable? Sensitive?
5. Name three kinds of additional control groups that are commonly used in child development research.
6. Think of a study in the area of human development or family relations you would be interested in conducting. How would you go about obtaining subjects for your study?
7. Distinguish between probability and nonprobability sampling techniques. What are the implications of each?
8. Distinguish between haphazard and quota sampling. How do stratified random, simple random, and area sampling differ?
9. When is debriefing necessary?
10. What is a manipulation check? What is the purpose of a pilot study?

CHAPTER 10

Understanding Research Results

CAREER PROFILE

R. Max Learner / Department of Health Coordinator

Max received a B.A. in Psychology from the University of North Carolina, Chapel Hill. His M.S. and Ph.D. degrees were awarded by the University of North Carolina, Greensboro, in Child Development and Family Relations with minors in counseling and nutrition.

Max is the Coordinator of Planning and Research for the Office of Program Management, South Carolina Department of Health and Environmental Control. Prior to that, he served as the Director of Research and Evaluation for Maternal Health and as Research Director for the South Carolina Community Long-Term Care Project. "My work involves conducting social science research on issues in public health on such topics as the efficacy of home-based services to impaired elderly and the factors that affect women's entry into prenatal care. Knowledge of statistics is important for dealing with the volume of information we evaluate in the management of public health programs. We use vital records, census data, and program data from services such as family planning, home health, and child health. An understanding of where the numbers come from and what the numbers mean is basic in the decision-making process.

"I have worked with human services at both ends of the developmental spectrum—infancy and old age—which gives a broad perspective on the delivery of health care services and the need for such services. It is a major challenge to the public health system to use the available resources wisely and to serve as many people as possible. There is a great need in government for individuals who understand research and statistics. Individuals who have an ability to evaluate the quality of data and to pull together information from many sources are needed to support policy and program development. Work in the public health field offers challenges and opportunities to use research knowledge to improve the health and well-being of our citizens."

Understanding outcomes from research requires both descriptive and inferential analyses. Human development and family relations researchers like Max Learner must have sufficient expertise to evaluate, interpret, and report their findings accurately. Consumers of research must be able to interpret and understand reported results so that they can make informed judgments about the usefulness of the information. In this chapter, we discuss the kinds of basic descriptive and inferential statistics useful to both researchers and consumers. The chapter begins with a discussion of basic descriptive statistics of research data and is followed by a discussion of the inferential statistics used in the analysis of research findings. Although the emphasis of this chapter is on the statistical analysis of experimental designs, the logic of statistical inference applies to all quantitative research.

Let's start with some fictitious data from a hypothetical experiment concerning maternal emotional signaling and infant exploratory behavior. Twenty 12-month-old infants were selected as subjects from an infant care program. The infants were randomly assigned to one of two groups: mother happy versus mother neutral. Infants were tested with their mothers. Each infant–mother dyad was placed in a large room with attractive toys. The mothers of the happy group were trained to exhibit emotional expressions of happiness during the test period, whereas mothers in the neutral group were trained to exhibit a neutral emotional tone. During the test period, the number of child-initiated explorations of toys were recorded as the dependent variable. The scores for each child are presented in Table 10.1. These data are used throughout the chapter in our discussion of the analysis of research results.

DESCRIPTIVE ANALYSES

One of the first activities a researcher undertakes after a study is completed is forming a descriptive analysis of the data. For example, the data can be arrayed in a form like that in Table 10.1.

Frequency distributions

It is useful in this initial phase of analyzing results to construct a *frequency distribution* from the data, which indicates the number of subjects who receive each possible score on the dependent variable. You may already be familiar with these distributions, since they are frequently used to summarize the performance of students on exams by indicating how many students received each score on the exam.

Frequency polygons Frequency distributions can be depicted in line graphs as illustrated in Figure 10.1. The data presented are from the hypothetical experiment concerning maternal emotional signaling, and the figure is a graphical depiction of the scores arrayed in Table 10.1. Two *frequency polygons* are depicted, one for each group, and they show how many infants received each score on the dependent variable of number of child-initiated explorations. The solid line represents the mother–neutral group, whereas the dotted line is for the mother–happy group.

Histograms *Histograms*, or bar graphs, are an alternate method of presenting the same frequency distribution. In a histogram, a bar is presented for each score on the dependent measure; the length of the bar corresponds to the number of persons who received that score. Figure 10.2 provides an example of a histogram for the distribution of scores in Table 10.1.

Table 10.1 Exploration scores in a hypothetical experiment on maternal signaling

	Mother neutral	Mother happy
	1	3
	2	4
	2	5
	3	5
	3	5
	3	5
	4	6
	4	6
	4	6
	5	7
ΣX	31.00	52.00
$\bar{X}$	3.10	5.20
s^2	1.44	1.30
s	1.20	1.14
N	10	10

Figure 10.1 Frequency polygons for distribution of scores in Table 10.1

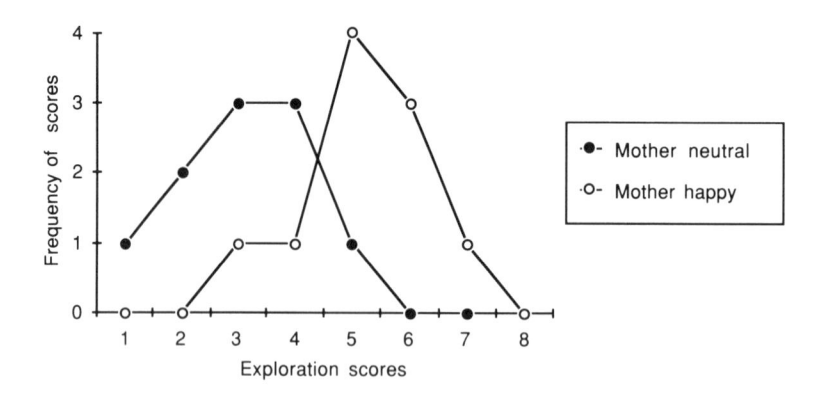

Figure 10.2 Histogram showing the distribution of scores in Table 10.1

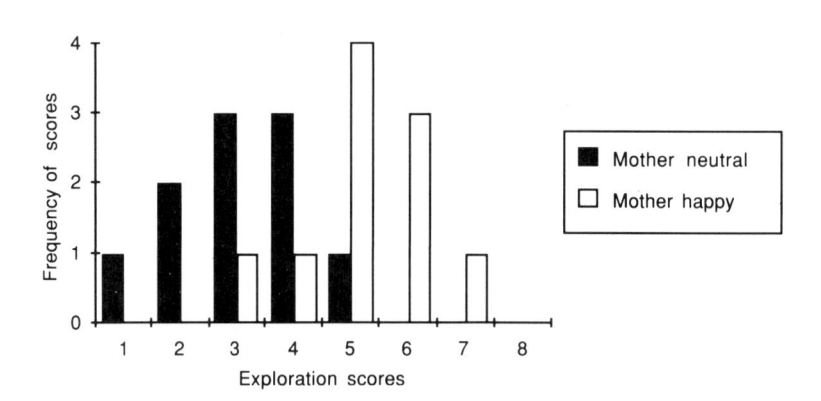

Initial descriptive analyses also include computation of measures of central tendency and variability.

Central tendency

A *central tendency statistic* tells us what the sample as a whole, or on the average, is like. The most common central tendency statistic is the *mean*, which is symbolized as $\bar{X}$. The mean of a set of scores is obtained by taking the sum of all scores and dividing by the number of scores. In Table 10.1, for the dependent variable of number of explorations, the mean score in the mother–happy group is 5.20, and the mean score in the mother–neutral group is 3.10.

In addition to the mean, other measures of central tendency are the *mode*—the most common score—and the *median*—the middle score. Figure 10.3a illustrates a symmetrical distribution in which all three central tendency values are at the same point on the curve. In contrast, when distributions are asymmetrical in shape, the three central tendency statistics fall at different points on the curve (Figures 10.3b and 10.3c). Which central

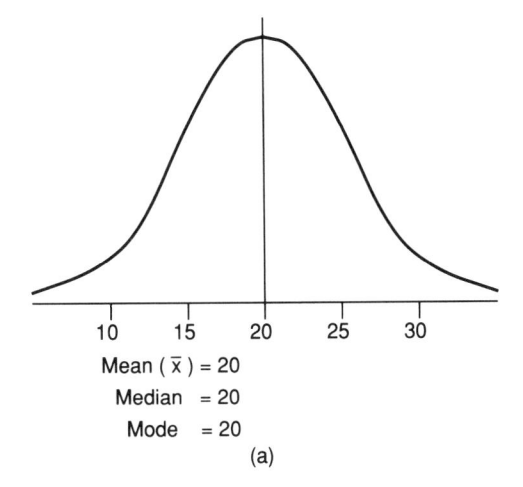

Figure 10.3 Mean, median, and mode for different shaped distributions: (a) is symmetrical; (b) and (c) are asymmetrical

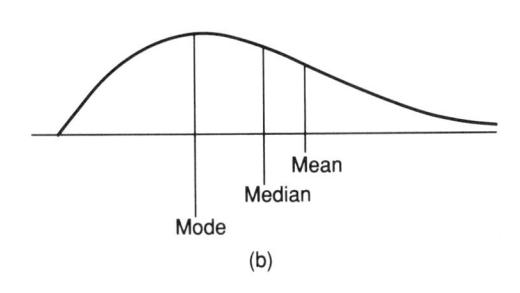

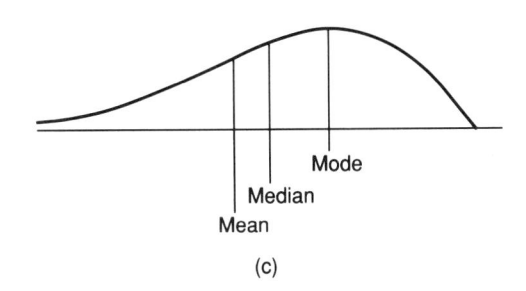

tendency measure is reported will depend on the researcher's objectives. It is never inappropriate to report more than one measure, especially when accuracy is required.

Variability

We can also determine how much variability exists in a set of scores. Measures of *variability* are numbers that characterize the amount of spread in a distribution of scores. One such measure is the *variance*, which is symbolized

155

as s^2. The variance indicates the extent to which the scores deviate from the group mean. The greater the spread about the group mean, the higher the variance. The variance and a related statistic, the *standard deviation*—abbreviated as s—have been calculated for the infant data and are presented in Table 10.1. The standard deviation is simply the square root of the variance. The variance in the mother–happy group is 1.30, and the variance in the mother–neutral group is 1.44.

Graphing means

Graphs can also be used to illustrate the relationships between the experimental groups. Both line and bar graphs are frequently used to express relationships between levels of an independent variable on the dependent variable. Recall that line graphs were used in Chapter 7 to illustrate the concept of interactions in 2 × 2 factorial designs. Figure 10.4 illustrates the graphing of the mean scores for the mother–happy and mother–neutral conditions. Figure 10.4a is a line graph; Figure 10.4b a bar graph. For the line graph, a point is placed on the graph that indicates the means in each group, and a line is drawn to connect the points. For the bar graph, the top of the bar represents the means in each group. Both of these graphs show, as does a comparison of the means in Table 10.1, that happy emotional signaling is associated with more exploration than neutral emotional signaling.

The computation of descriptive statistics such as the mean and standard deviation and the graphing of means provide the researcher with an idea of the relationship between the experimental groups on the dependent variable. The results from the hypothetical experiment presented in Table 10.1 and Figure 10.4 are based on sample data: Researchers rarely if ever study entire populations. In other words, their results are based on sample data that are

**Figure 10.4
Graphing means:
(a) line graph, (b) bar graph**

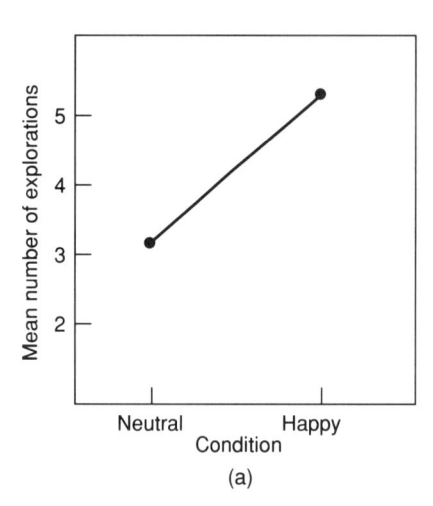

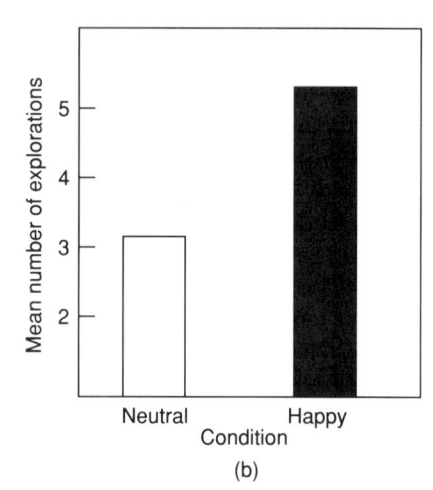

presumed to be representative of the population from which the sample was drawn. Recall that methods for selecting a sample from a population were discussed in Chapter 9. If we want to make statements about the populations from which the samples were drawn, it is necessary to use inferential statistics.

INFERENTIAL STATISTICS

The use of descriptive statistics suggested that the mean scores for the maternal signaling groups were different. Thus, the independent variable seems to have had an effect on infant exploration. *Inferential statistics* enable us to infer, on the basis of the data from the sample, that these differences are reliable and that they hold true for the more general population that the sample represents.

In our discussion of experimental design in Chapter 5, we focused on the importance of making sure that the experimental groups were equivalent in every way except the independent variable that was manipulated by the researcher. Equivalency of groups is achieved experimentally by controlling all other variables or by randomization. The assumption is that if the groups are equivalent, any differences in the dependent variable must be due to the effect of the independent variable.

Although this assumption is usually valid, it is also true that the differences between any two groups is almost never zero. In other words, there is always some difference in the sample means, even when all the precautions of good experimental design are followed. This fact is true because we are dealing with samples rather than populations in which random or chance error may affect the results.

Thus, the difference between the sample means reflects *true* differences between populations *plus any random error*. Inferential statistics allow researchers to make inferences about the true differences in the populations on the basis of the sample data. That is, inferential statistics indicate the probability that the difference between the means reflects random error rather than a real difference.

Hypothesis testing

Experiments are usually designed to uncover and explore differences between groups. In most studies, researchers hypothesize that there will be differences between the groups. The purpose of inferential statistics is to test the *null hypothesis*, which states that the population means do not differ (they are equal), indicating that any observed difference is due to random error. The *research hypothesis* (also referred to as the *alternate hypothesis*) always predicts differences between the groups. In other words, the null hypothesis states that the independent variable has no effect, whereas the research hypothesis states that the independent variable *does* have an effect. In the maternal signaling experiment, the null and research hypotheses are as follows:

H_0 *(null hypothesis):* The population means of the happy and neutral groups are equal.

H_1 *(research hypothesis):* The population means of the happy and neutral groups are not equal.

The logic of the null hypothesis is the following: If we can reject the null hypothesis as incorrect, then we accept the research hypothesis as correct. Acceptance of the research hypothesis means that the independent variable has an effect on the dependent variable.

The null hypothesis is used because it is a very exact statement—the population means are exactly equal. The null hypothesis permits us to know precisely the probability of the outcome of the study that occurs if the null hypothesis is correct. Such precision isn't possible with the research hypothesis, thus we must infer that the research hypothesis is correct only by rejecting the null hypothesis. The null hypothesis is rejected when there is a very low probability that the obtained differences would be due to random error. This fact is what is meant when we say a difference is reliable or is statistically significant. A significant difference is one that has a very low probability of occurring if the population means are actually equal. More simply, significance indicates that there is a low probability that the difference between the obtained sample means is due to random error. Significance, then, is a matter of probability.

Probability

Probability is the likelihood of the occurrence of some event or outcome. We all use probabilities frequently in everyday life. If you say that there is a high probability that you will get an "A" in this course, you mean that it is likely that that will happen. Your probability statement is based on specific information, such as your grades on examinations. The weather forecaster says there is a 10 percent chance of rain today, which means the likelihood of rain is quite low. A high school coach gauges the probability that the school's team will win a specific game based on the past records of the team's success.

Probability in statistical inference is used in much the same way. We want to specify the probability that an event (a difference between means in the sample) will occur if there is no difference in the population. The question is: "What is the probability of obtaining this result if only random error is operating?" If this probability is quite low, we reject the possibility that only random or chance error is responsible for the obtained difference in means.

The use of probability in statistical inference can be understood intuitively from a simple example. Suppose that a friend claims that she has taught her 1-year-old daughter to read by using flash cards. You decide to test your friend's claim by testing her baby with the flash cards. A different word is presented on each card, and the baby is told to point to the corresponding object presented on a response card. In your test, you use 10 different words, presented in a random order. The response card contains pictures of the 10 objects named on the flash cards. Your task is to determine if the baby's responses reflect random error (guess) or whether the answers indicate that something more than random error is occurring. The null hypothesis in your study is that only random error is operating. The research hypothesis is that the number of correct answers shows more than just random or chance guess. (Note, however, that accepting the research hypothesis can mean that the baby can read, but it also can mean that the baby learned to associate the correct objects with the different colors used as backgrounds on the flash cards.)

You can determine the number of correct answers to expect if the null hypothesis is correct. Just by guessing, the subject should get one out of 10 correct (10 percent). If in the actual experiment, more (or fewer) than one correct answer is obtained, can you conclude that the data reflect something more than simply random guessing? Suppose the baby gets two correct answers. Then you probably conclude that only guessing is involved, because you recognize that there is a high probability that the subject may get two correct answers even though only one correct is expected under the null hypothesis. If the baby is guessing, you expect that exactly one out of 10 answers will be correct, if you conduct this experiment with the same baby over and over again. However, small deviations away from the expected one correct answer are highly likely if you repeat the procedure 10 times.

Suppose, though, that your subject gets seven correct answers. Then you probably conclude that the results indicate something other than simply random error. Your conclusion is based on the very low probability of the subject's getting seven correct answers by simply guessing. This outcome of the experiment may be deemed a rare event, and you may say that the result is significant.

How rare does an event have to be before we say that it is significant? The most commonly used probability is 0.05. The outcome of an experiment is considered rare when there is a .05 probability or less of obtaining the results—that is, when there are only five chances out of 100 that the results may be obtained on the basis of random error. If it is unlikely that random error is responsible for the results, the null hypothesis is rejected.

It can intuitively be seen why obtaining seven correct answers out of 10 is a rare event. Fortunately, we don't have to rely on intuition to determine the probability of results occurring by random error. Table 10.2 shows the probability of actually obtaining each of the possible outcomes in the baby reading example. An outcome of two correct answers has the highest probability of occurrence. Also, as intuition indicates, an outcome of one correct answer is highly probable, but an outcome of seven correct answers has a low probability of occurrence and can be considered a rare event.

**Table 10.2
Exact probability of each possible outcome in the baby reading experiment**

Number of correct answers	Probability
10	.0000
9	.0000
8	.0000
7	.0000
6	.0001
5	.0015
4	.0112
3	.0574
2	.1937
1	.3874
0	.3487

The preceding values were drawn from Burington & May (1970).

Example: The *t* Test and *F* Statistic

Different statistical tests allow us to use probability in deciding whether to reject the null hypothesis. A summary of some of the statistical tests developed for the more common research designs is provided at the end of this chapter. In this section, we examine the *t* test, a method to determine whether two groups are significantly different from one another. We also examine the *F* statistic, which is an extension of the *t* test that is used with more complex designs. For both of these statistical tests, interval or ratio-scaled data are required.

The *t* test A value of *t* is calculated from the obtained data and is then evaluated in terms of the probability of obtaining the *t* value if the null hypothesis is true. If the obtained *t* has a low probability of occurrence, then the null hypothesis is rejected. As a general rule, researchers use a significance level of .05 in deciding to reject the null hypothesis. The results are said to be significant when the probability of obtaining the results is .05 or less if the null hypothesis is correct.

The *t* value is a ratio of two measures of the sample data: the difference between the group means and the variability within groups. The ratio may be described as follows:

$$t = \frac{\text{group difference}}{\text{within-group variability}}$$

The greater the *t* value that is obtained (i.e., the larger the group difference relative to within-group variability), the greater the likelihood that the results will be significant. The underlying logic of the *t* test is that the difference in the group means reflects the effect of the independent variable on the dependent variable. In contrast, the within-group variability cannot be accounted for directly and is referred to as "error." It is "error" in the sense that we don't know why individuals within each group differ in their responses to the independent variable.

A concrete example of a calculation of a *t* test may further your understanding of these concepts. The formula for the t test with equal numbers of subjects in each group is as follows:

$$t = \frac{\bar{X}_1 - \bar{X}_2}{\sqrt{\dfrac{s_1^2}{N_1} + \dfrac{s_2^2}{N_2}}}$$

The numerator of the formula is simply the difference between the means of the two groups. In the denominator, we first divide the variance(s) of each group by the number of subjects in the group and add these together. We then find the square root of the result, which yields a measure of the overall amount of variability within the groups.

When this formula is applied to the data in Table 10.1, we find the following:

$$t = \frac{5.2 - 3.1}{\sqrt{\dfrac{1.30}{10} + \dfrac{1.44}{10}}}$$

$$= \frac{2.1}{\sqrt{0.130 + 0.144}}$$

$$= \frac{2.1}{0.523}$$

$$= 4.02$$

Thus, the t value calculated from the data is 4.02. In a scientific paper, this statistic would be reported in the following form:

$$t(18) = 4.02, \quad p < .05$$

Does this value indicate a significant effect? The probability of finding a t value of 4.02, if in fact the population means are equal, is less than .05. In other words, there is less than a .05 probability that we may obtain a t value of 4.02 if the null hypothesis is correct. Obtaining a t value this large is a rare event, thus we may conclude that the means obtained in the two groups reflect a real population difference and that the results are significant.

How do you know how large t must be for the test to be significant? In practice, the researcher uses a table that lists critical values of t: The obtained value must be equal to or larger than the critical value for the test to be significant. In the expression for the t value listed previously, the value in the parentheses (in the example, the value is 18) refers to "degrees of freedom," and this value is used to help locate critical values in the t table. Appendix B provides a more complete discussion of this procedure, and Appendix C (Table C.5) lists critical values of t.

The F statistic   The analysis of variance, or F test, is an extension of the t test. The analysis of variance is a more general statistical procedure than the t test. When a study has only one independent variable with two groups, F and t are virtually identical—the value of F equals t^2 in this situation.

However, an analysis of variance is also used when there are more than two levels of an independent variable and when factorial designs include several independent variables. Thus, the F test is appropriate for the simplest experimental designs as well as for the more complex designs discussed in Chapter 7.

The F statistic is a ratio of two types of variance (hence the term *analysis of variance*). The two variances are called

Systematic variance

Error variance

Systematic variance is the deviation of the group means from the *grand mean*, which is the mean score of all subjects in all groups. Systematic variance is small when the difference between group means is small and increases as the group mean differences increase. *Error variance* is the deviation of the individual scores in each group from their respective group means. In results reported in research articles, you may see the terms *variability of scores between groups* and *variability of scores within groups*, which correspond to systematic and error variance, respectively. The larger the F ratio, the more likely it is that the effect is significant.

As you may recall from our discussion of complex designs in Chapter 7, when 2×2 factorial designs are used, three effects must be explained: main effect of independent variable A, main effect of independent variable B, and the $A \times B$ interaction. In analyses using the F statistic, a 2×2 design may be associated with three F values, one for each of the effects. Significant F values indicate that the null hypotheses can be rejected for the different effects (i.e., the two main effects and the interaction).

To illustrate, we can extend our maternal signaling study to include an age group comparison, making it a cross-sectional study with 12-month-old infants compared to 14-month-old infants. Thus, the design is a 2 (age: 12 months versus 14 months) by 2 (condition: mother happy versus mother neutral) factorial design. The upper portion of Table 10.3 presents the descriptive statistics for the four groups; the lower portion presents the F ratios associated with each of the effects in a 2×2 design. Looking first at the marginal means, it appears that older infants explored more than younger infants and that happy maternal signaling was associated with more exploration than neutral signaling. The cell means indicate an interaction, because the difference in exploration between the two signaling conditions is larger for the 14-month-old infants than for the 12-month-old infants. (You may wish to draw a graph to illustrate the interaction.) The F statistics presented in the lower portion of the table allow us to verify our impressions of the results based on descriptive statistics. Similar to the t test, the F test must exceed a critical value to be significant. For this example, with a probability of .05, the critical F value is 4.08. Each of the F values in the table exceed this value, which indicates reliable or significant main effects and an interaction. Thus, we can reject the corresponding null hypotheses for the three

**Table 10.3
Maternal signaling study with an age group comparison**

Age	Mean Number of Explorations Condition		Mean
	Mother neutral	Mother happy	
12 months	3.10	4.10	3.60
14 months	5.20	8.00	6.60
Mean	4.15	6.05	

Source	Analysis of Variance Summary Table df	MS	F ratio
Condition	1	90.000	65.59
Age	1	36.100	26.31
Condition × Age	1	8.100	5.90
Error	36	1.372	

effects. In a scientific paper, the F statistic for the Condition × Age interaction would be reported in the following form:

$$F(1,36) = 5.90, \quad p < .05$$

Note too that the lower panel of Table 10.3 includes columns of information labeled df (degrees of freedom) and MS (mean squares). In contrast to the column for the F statistics, four entries are listed under the df and MS columns: The mean square for each effect (main effect of age, main effect of condition, and the interaction) are the estimates of systematic variance from the experiment, and the last mean square listed (labeled Error) is the estimate of the error variance from the study. Recall that the F statistic is a ratio of two variances: systematic variance/error variance. Thus, you can compute the F statistic by dividing the estimate of systematic variance by error variance—try it.

The degrees of freedom listed in the table are used to help you locate in an F table the critical value for a significant F ratio. Because sample size influences the detection of significant differences, larger F ratios are required to reject the null hypothesis when we have small samples. Further information on the F test is given in Appendix B, and Appendix C (Table C.6) lists critical values of F.

ISSUES IN DECISION MAKING

Inferential statistics allow us to make decisions about the null hypothesis. The decision to reject the null hypothesis is based on probabilities rather than on certainties. Our decision is made without direct knowledge about the true state of affairs in the population. Thus, the decision may be correct or incorrect.

A decision matrix is presented in Figure 10.5. Notice that there are two possible decisions: (1) reject the null hypothesis, or (2) accept the null hypothesis. There are also two possibilities that may be true in the population: (1) the null hypothesis is true, or (2) the research hypothesis is true. You can see from this decision matrix that there are two kinds of correct decisions and two kinds of errors.

Correct decisions

One correct decision occurs when we reject the null hypothesis, and the research hypothesis is true in the population. Our decision is to say that the population means are not equal, and in fact this is true in the population. The other correct decision is to accept the null hypothesis, and the null hypothesis is true in the population. In this case, the population means are in fact equal.

Type I errors

A *Type I error* is made when we reject the null hypothesis, but the null hypothesis is actually true. Our decision is that the population means are not equal when they actually are equal. Type I errors occur when, by chance, we obtain a large F value. For example, even though an F value of 16.21 is highly improbable if in fact the population means are equal (less than five chances out of 100), it can happen. When we do obtain such a large F value by chance, we incorrectly decide that the independent variable has an effect.

Figure 10.5
Decision matrix: Type I and Type II errors

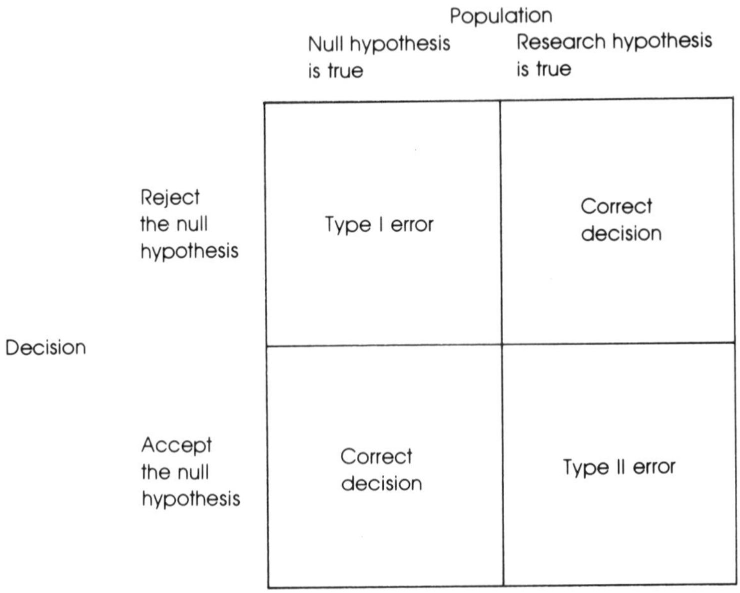

	Null hypothesis is true	Research hypothesis is true
Reject the null hypothesis	Type I error	Correct decision
Accept the null hypothesis	Correct decision	Type II error

The probability of making a Type I error is determined by the choice of significance level. When the significance level for deciding whether to reject the null hypothesis is .05, the probability of a Type I error is .05. The probability of making a Type I error can be changed by the researcher by changing the significance level. If we use a significance level of .01, there is less chance of making a Type I error. With a .01 significance level, the null hypothesis is rejected only when the chance of obtaining the results is one out of 100 (or less) if the null hypothesis is correct.

Type II errors

A *Type II error* occurs when the null hypothesis is accepted, although in the population the research hypothesis is true. The population means are not equal, but the results of the experiment do not lead to a decision to reject the null hypothesis.

The probability of making a Type II error is not directly specifiable, although the significance level is an important factor. If we set a very low significance level to decrease the chances of a Type I error, we increase the chances of a Type II error. In other words, if we make it difficult to reject the null hypothesis, the probability of incorrectly accepting the null hypothesis increases.

Some common examples of Type I and Type II errors

The decision matrix used in statistical analyses is really only one example of the kinds of decisions people frequently make. For example, consider the evaluation of a home pregnancy test. Many families select such a test to provide a preliminary indication of pregnancy prior to consulting a physician. A decision matrix for this example is represented in Figure 10.6. To draw a parallel to the statistical decision, let's assume the null hypothesis is that the woman is *not* pregnant. Thus, rejection of the null hypothesis is to decide that the woman is pregnant, and acceptance of the null hypothesis is to decide that the woman is not pregnant. The decision matrix also shows that the null hypothesis can be true or false. There are two kinds of correct decisions and two kinds of errors that can occur in making the decisions. In this example, a Type I error indicates that the woman is pregnant when she is not (which may raise expectations and perhaps lead to disappointment). A Type II error is to decide that the woman is not pregnant when she really is (which may have an unwanted side effect if the woman smokes and continues to do so after the undetected pregnancy). In contrast to statistical decision making in which the investigator is most concerned with Type I errors, either the Type I or Type II error in this example may be viewed as the more serious.

The decision that a rehabilitation counselor makes to place a recovering adult in a therapy program provides another example of our decision matrix

**Figure 10.6
Decision matrix
for pregnancy**

	True state	
	Null is true (not pregnant)	Null is false (pregnant)
Reject null (conclude pregnant)	Type I error	Correct decision
Accept null (conclude not pregnant)	Correct decision	Type II error

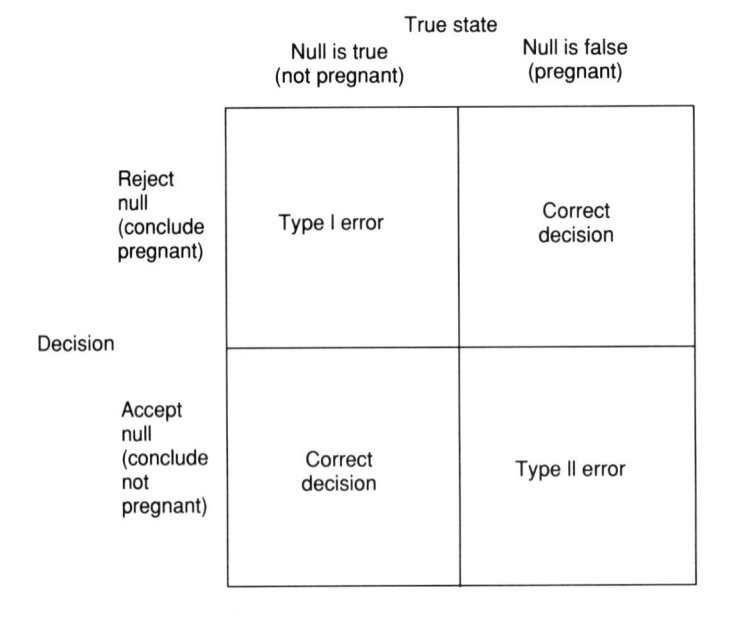

Decision

(Figure 10.7). Here the null hypothesis is that rehabilitation therapy is not necessary. The decision is to reject the null hypothesis and place the person in the program or accept the null hypothesis and not make the placement. In reality, the counselor is faced with two possibilities: Either the therapy is unnecessary (the patient does not need special treatment: the null hypothesis is true), or the therapy is necessary (the patient will not fully recover unless therapy occurs: the null hypothesis is false). Again, which kind of error is most serious (Type I or Type II) may depend on different considerations. For example, if space is limited in the special rehabilitation program, a Type I error may be more serious, since the counselor does not want to take up valuable space with patients that do not require placement. In contrast, if successful recovery is to be guaranteed, a Type II error must be avoided at all costs.

Choosing a significance level

Researchers have traditionally used either a .05 or a .01 level of significance in the decision to reject the null hypothesis. If there is less than a .05 or a .01 probability that the results occurred because of random error, the results are said to be significant. The level of significance is frequently referred to as the *Type I error rate* or *alpha* (α) in research reports.

There is nothing special about the .05 and .01 levels of significance; they merely specify the probability of making a Type I error if the null hypothesis is rejected. The level of significance can be relaxed if you are willing to risk an increase in Type I errors. However, when experiments are designed to find differences, researchers usually feel that the consequences of making a Type

Figure 10.7 Decision matrix for placement in a therapy program

	True state: Null is true (placement not necessary)	True state: Null is false (placement necessary)
Decision: Reject null (place)	Type I error	Correct decision
Decision: Accept null (do not place)	Correct decision	Type II error

I error are more serious than those of making a Type II error. Thus, they want to have a high degree of confidence that the differences they have found are not due to chance. For this reason, researchers are not willing to risk more than five chances out of 100 (.05) or one chance out of 100 (.01) of being wrong. If the null hypothesis is rejected, the researcher may publish the results in a journal, and the results may be reported by others in textbooks or in newspaper or magazine articles. Researchers don't want to mislead others by reporting outcomes that don't exist in the population! This problem can be especially serious in applied research, because consumers may adopt procedures or recommendations based on reported statistical significance. Thus, when a .05 or .01 level of significance is adopted, researchers can share their scientific findings knowing that their chances of an erroneous report are only minimal.

Sometimes an investigator may want to relax the Type I error in some situations. For example, in the early phases of research, the objective may be to decide if it is worthwhile to pursue a line of experimentation. In this instance, it would be a mistake to overlook potentially important data by using too conservative a Type I error rate. Thus, in such exploratory research, a Type I error rate of .10 may be adopted.

Accepting the null hypothesis

Researchers are not generally interested in accepting the null hypothesis. Recall that research is designed to show that a relationship between variables exists rather than to demonstrate that variables are unrelated. More important, nonsignificant results are difficult to interpret. For example, it isn't possible to specify the probability that you may be wrong in the decision to accept the null hypothesis.

Also, a "nonsignificant" outcome may mask meaningful relationships between the variables in the population. For example, the study may *not* have been designed to provide the best test of the hypothesis. A better designed study may be associated with significant results. Such a study may include a stronger manipulation of the independent variable, or a more reliable and sensitive dependent measure may be used.

Nonsignificant results may also have been produced because the researcher selected a Type I error level that was too conservative (e.g., .001). For example, there isn't much of a chance for rejecting the null hypothesis if the researcher is only willing to risk a Type I error one time out of 1,000.

A small sample size in a study can also be responsible for failing to detect a significant relationship between conditions and to prompt the researcher to accept the null hypothesis mistakenly. Generally speaking, the larger the sample size, the more likely it is to uncover "significant" differences, because the larger sample provides a more reliable estimate of the population sampled.

Thus, you should not automatically accept the null hypothesis simply because the results are nonsignificant. The experiment should be conducted again with refined procedures. Perhaps a larger sample of subjects should be tested in a follow-up experiment. If evidence from repeated experiments shows no relationship between the variables of interest, *then* the researcher can accept the hypothesis that no relationship exists.

SELECTING STATISTICAL TESTS

Many statistical tests have been developed for various research designs. The appropriateness of a specific test depends on the design used and the type of measurement scale employed (the dependent variable). This section provides guidelines for selecting appropriate tests for some of the more common experimental designs used in human development and family relations. A statistics text should be consulted for a complete description of statistical tests and guidelines for their selection. Appendix B provides computational illustrations for many of the tests mentioned.

One independent variable—two groups only

Nominal scale data   When subjects are measured using a nominal scale, the appropriate test is a chi-square test. Chi-square tests are used with all nominal data.

Ordinal scale data   If an independent groups design is used, the Mann–Whitney *U* test is appropriate. If a repeated measures or matched design is used, Wilcoxon's *T* or the sign test is used.

Interval or ratio scale data   For independent groups designs, the *t* test described in this chapter or a one-way analysis of variance is used. With repeated measures or a matched groups design, a correlated t test or a repeated measures analysis of variance is used.

One independent variable—three or more groups

Nominal scale data A chi-square test is required.

Ordinal scale data The Kruskal–Wallace H test is appropriate when an independent groups design is used. For repeated measures designs, the Friedman T test is appropriate.

Interval or ratio scale data A one-way analysis of variance is used.

Two or more independent variables

Nominal scale data Again, a chi-square test is appropriate.

Ordinal scale data No appropriate statistical test is available.

Interval or ratio scale data A two-way analysis of variance is used for factorial designs with two independent variables. Analysis of variance can be extended to designs with any number of independent variables. It is appropriate for independent groups (between subjects), repeated measures (within subjects), or mixed (a combination of between and within subjects) factorial designs.

Conclusion

The use of experimental designs permits relatively unambiguous inferences concerning cause and effect, although such designs require a high degree of control over extraneous variables and a strong manipulation of the independent variable. These requirements may present interpretation problems. In contrast, the use of nonexperimental methods allows the researcher to obtain information under natural circumstances. Chapter 11 considers some of the correlational approaches used in the statistical analysis of nonexperimental research data.

SUMMARY

Understanding research outcomes is important for researchers and consumers of research findings. Both descriptive and inferential analyses are used. Descriptive analysis helps you gain an impression of the data. Methods include construction of a frequency distribution; tabulation of measures of central tendency such as the mean, median, and mode; computing measures of variability like the variance and standard deviation; and graphing means.

Because the data collected in studies are based on a sample from the population, inferential analyses are required for the researcher to make inferences about the population. In other words, inferential analysis permits the researcher to infer, on the basis of the sample data, that observed differences are reliable and hold true for the more general population.

Hypothesis testing procedures are based on probability. Two kinds of hypotheses can be identified: A research hypothesis states that the population means are different; a null hypothesis states that the population means are equal. Statistical analysis allows us to test the null hypothesis and to reject it (if appropriate) with a specified probability for making a mistake. Two frequently used statistical tests in experimental designs are the t and F tests. Both of these statistics require ratio or interval data. The t test is appropriate for two-group comparisons, whereas the F test is used when more than two levels of the independent variable are manipulated and with designs with two or more independent variables.

Issues to consider in decision making are the occurrence of Type I and Type II errors. A Type I error is made when we reject the null hypothesis when the null hypothesis is true. A Type II error occurs when the null hypothesis is accepted, although the research hypothesis is true. In experimental research, a Type I error is viewed as more serious than a Type II error, because the researcher wants to have a high degree of confidence that the differences observed are not due to chance. Selecting a .05 or .01 significance level indicates the number of times out of 100 that the researcher will make an incorrect decision and reject the null hypothesis when the null hypothesis is actually true. If significant differences are not found for an independent variable, the researcher may wish to accept the null hypothesis. However, accepting of the null hypothesis should only be done after repeated failures to observe a systematic difference with well-designed and carefully conducted experiments.

STUDY QUESTIONS

1. How are measures of central tendency different from measures of variability?
2. Can you remember how to generate a frequency distribution or graph means?
3. What is the difference between descriptive versus inferential analysis?
4. How is probability used in statistical inference?
5. Distinguish between the research hypothesis versus the null hypothesis. Which hypothesis is tested by experiments?
6. Distinguish between Type I and Type II errors. What determines the probability of each type of error? Which kind of error is viewed as most serious?
7. What factors are involved in selecting a significance level?

CHAPTER 11

Correlation Coefficients

CAREER PROFILE

Jocelyn S. Carter / Convalescent Hospital Administrator

Jocelyn holds a B.S. in Biology and a master's in Health Systems Leadership from the University of San Francisco. She is the Administrator at the San Francisco Community Convalescent Hospital in San Francisco, California.

"I deal with adult children of aging parents and family members of infirm patients. I provide counseling and try to allay their fears, guilt, and doubts about placing their family members in a convalescent hospital. Easing the transition of my patients into an institutionalized setting is another one of my responsibilities. It takes repeated, consistent effort to make them happy. My motto is that we are not perfect, but we will give it our best try—which makes patients and their families realize that there is a *contact person at the top* who cares and is accountable. It is important for patients and relatives to feel that they have a say in making their association with the facility a positive one.

"Research findings play an important role in our activities and suggest ways for us to improve patient care and comfort. This information also helps us anticipate the kinds of patients we can accommodate. For example, Alzheimer's disease is one area in which we can care for people in only certain stages of the disease. Research information is provided to our staff through professional magazines, scientific and medical journals, and in-service training."

Jocelyn offers the following thoughts on aging: "Older people are just as alive as we are and have a lot to offer despite their infirmities. Cherish them for having paved the road for us. None of us are getting younger, and none of us should die alone."

In this chapter, we will discuss the use of correlation coefficients, which are statistics that indicate how strongly variables are related to one another. Jocelyn Carter might say that "positive attitudes of family members and patients' adjustment to a convalescent hospital are highly correlated." Statements such as this refer to the strength of the relationship between the two variables. A correlation coefficient allows us to know how strong the relationship is. Before proceeding, let's make a distinction between "correlation coefficients" and the "correlational method."

CORRELATION COEFFICIENTS AND THE CORRELATIONAL METHOD

As it has been used by researchers over the years, the term *correlation* becomes a bit confusing. In Chapter 3, we reviewed the distinction between the experimental and correlational methods of studying relationships between variables. In this chapter, we discuss the correlation coefficient as an index of the strength of relationship between variables. You may expect that researchers use correlation coefficients only when using the correlational method, since the term *correlation* is common to both. However, this expectation is *not* correct. The term *correlational method* refers to a nonexperimental investigation of the relationship between variables. The term *correlation coefficient* refers to an index of the strength of relationship between variables *irrespective of* whether the experimental or correlational method was used.

This confusion arises because, historically, the results of studies using the correlational method have been described with correlation coefficients, whereas experimental studies have reported mean differences between groups. However, it has become increasingly clear to researchers that correlation coefficients are always used as an index of strength of relationships in both correlational and experimental research.

Several types of correlation coefficients can be calculated. The specific correlation coefficient used depends on the nature of the variables and the type of experimental design. In this chapter, we focus on the *Pearson product-moment correlation coefficient*, which is symbolized by *r*. However, its general principles apply to all correlation coefficients.

INDEXING THE STRENGTH OF A RELATIONSHIP

A correlation coefficient begins with a pair of scores from each subject. In a study of the relationship between watching television violence and aggressiveness among 8-year-old males, you have two scores for each child: a measure of the amount of television violence that the child views each week and a measure of aggressiveness. Table 11.1 shows fictitious data for 20 subjects in such a study. Scores on both variables can range from 0 to 10. The question to be answered is whether and how strongly the two variables are related to one another—which a correlation coefficient will enable us to address.

A correlation coefficient can be calculated using the data in the table. The actual mathematical formula for the Pearson product-moment correlation (*r*) is described in Appendix B, and Appendix C (Table C.8) lists critical values of *r*. The calculated values of *r* can range from +1.00 to −1.00. The plus and minus signs indicate whether there is a positive or negative linear

Table 11.1 Hypothetical data correlating television violence and aggression

Subject #	Television violence	Aggression
1	2	5
2	1	4
3	5	8
4	5	6
5	6	9
6	7	4
7	10	4
8	3	3
9	4	7
10	9	8
11	7	9
12	6	8
13	5	6
14	8	6
15	2	3
16	9	5
17	3	4
18	4	7
19	6	6
20	6	5

relationship between the variables. The absolute size of *r* is an index of the strength of the relationship: The nearer *r* is to 1.00 (plus *or* minus), the stronger the relationship. Indeed, a 1.00 correlation is sometimes called a perfect relationship, because the two variables go together in a perfect fashion. (The correlation coefficient for the data in Table 11.1 is +.32, and we discuss the procedure shortly.)

Data from studies that examine similarities of intelligence test scores illustrate the connection between magnitude of a correlation coefficient and the strength of a relationship. The relationship between scores of identical twins is quite strong ($r = +.86$), demonstrating a strong similarity in test scores in these pairs of individuals. The correlation for fraternal twins reared together is less strong ($r = +.60$). The correlation among non-twin siblings raised together is +.47; the correlation among non-twin siblings reared apart is only +.24. The correlation of intelligence scores among unrelated individuals not reared together is 0.00, indicating that no relationship is present (cf., Bouchard & McGue, 1981).

GRAPHING CORRELATIONS WITH SCATTERPLOTS

Correlation coefficients can be visualized in scatterplots in which each subject's pair of scores is plotted as a single point in a diagram. Figure 11.1 shows scatterplots for a +1.00 correlation and a −1.00 correlation (such relationships are in fact extremely rare). You can easily see why these relationships may be termed perfect relationships. For all subjects, the scores on the two variables fall on a straight line; each subject's score on one variable goes perfectly with the score on the other variable. If we know a subject's score on one of the variables, we can predict exactly what his or her score will be on the other variable.

The scatterplots in Figure 11.2 show patterns of correlation that are

Figure 11.1 Scatterplots of a perfect relationship: (a) $r = 1.00$ (positive relationship) and (b) $r = -1.00$ (negative relationship)

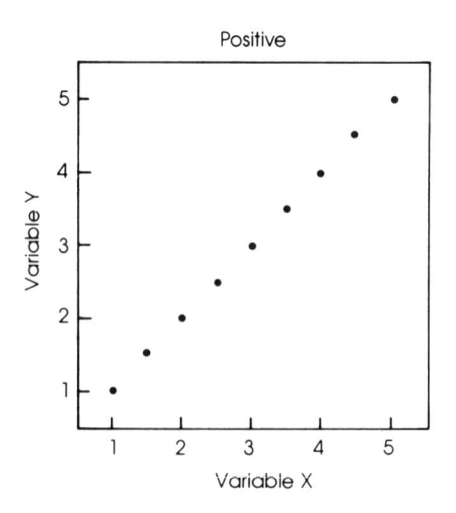

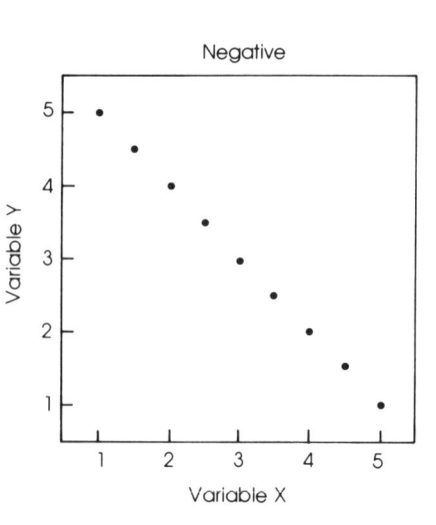

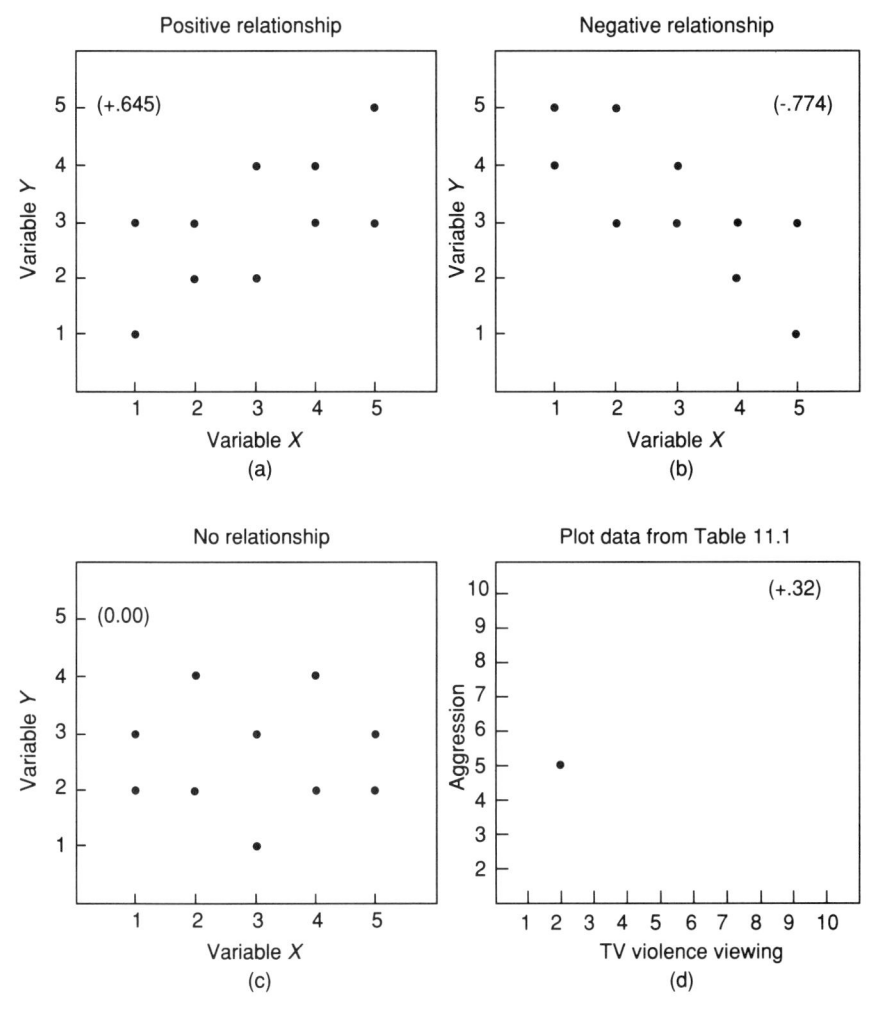

Figure 11.2 More realistic scatterplots: (a) r = +.645 (positive relationship), (b) r = −.774 (negative relationship), (c) r = 0.00 (no relationship), and (d) plot data from Table 11.1 (Subject 1 has been plotted for you; you must plot the others)

somewhat more realistic. Figure 11.2a is a plot of data with a correlation of +.65. Figure 11.2b shows a negative relationship with $r = -.77$. The data points in these two scatterplots show a general pattern of either a positive or a negative relationship, but there is scatter—variability—in the scores. For instance, you can make a general prediction in the first diagram that the higher the score on one variable, the higher the score on the other variable. However, if you know a subject's score on the first variable, you can't *perfectly* predict what that person's score will be on the second variable. To confirm: take a look at value 1 on variable X (the horizontal axis) in Figure 11.2a. For this value, two subjects have a score of 1. One of these subjects has a score of 1 on variable Y (the vertical axis), and the other has a score of 3. This variability represents scatter from the straight line illustrated in Figure 11.1.

Figure 11.2c shows a correlation of 0.00, in which there is no pattern in the plot of the scores. Thus, scores on variable X are not related to scores on variable Y.

Figure 11.2d has been left blank, so that you can plot the scores from the data in Table 11.1. The horizontal axis (X axis) has been labeled "television violence viewing" and the vertical axis (Y axis) has been labeled "aggressiveness." To complete the scatterplot, you must plot the scores for each of the 20 subjects. For each subject, find the score on the television violence variable, then find that subject's aggressiveness score. The common point of the two variables describes the subject's score on both variables. Subject 1's score has been plotted for you. There will be 20 data points in the finished scatterplot.

The correlation coefficient calculated from these data shows that there is in fact a positive relationship: $r = +.32$. Thus, increases in violent television viewing are accompanied by increases in aggressiveness. Note that the .32 correlation, although far from 0.00, is not very strong. We conclude that knowing about television violence watching tells us something about aggressiveness, but it does not tell the whole story. As with many variables, aggressiveness is the result of many factors such as parental aggressiveness, genetic predisposition, or general activity level.

INTERPRETING CORRELATIONS

Restriction of range

It is important that the researcher sample from the full range of possible values of both variables. If the range of possible values is restricted, the magnitude of the correlation coefficient is reduced. For example, if you are studying the relationship between age and verbal ability, studying only 6-year-olds and 7-year-olds reduces the likelihood that you will find a relationship. You are more likely to find a relationship if you include children with a wider range of ages, such as 5 through 12. Similarly, trying to study the correlates of intelligence is almost impossible if your subjects are all similar in intelligence (e.g., the senior class of a prestigious private college).

Curvilinear relationships

The Pearson product-moment correlation coefficient (r) is designed only to detect linear relationships. If the relationship is curvilinear, the correlation coefficient will not indicate a relationship (Figure 11.3). The correlation coefficient calculated from the data in the figure shows $r = 0.00$, although it is clear that the two variables are in fact related.

When the relationship is curvilinear, statistics other than the Pearson r are necessary to determine the strength of the relationship. Because a rela-

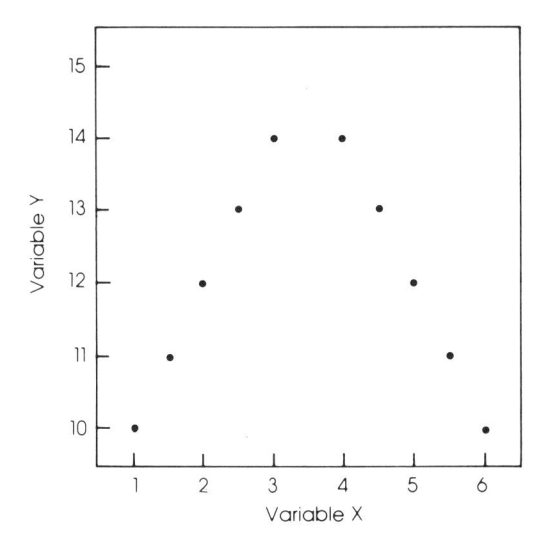

Figure 11.3 Scatterplot of a curvilinear relationship

tionship may be curvilinear, it is important to construct a scatterplot in addition to looking at the magnitude of the correlation coefficient. The scatterplot is valuable because it gives a visual indication of the shape of the relationship.

Significance of a correlation coefficient

The correlation coefficient is a descriptive statistic, as it describes the strength of the relationship between the variables in the sample of subjects studied. Researchers are also interested in learning whether the obtained correlation is statistically significant. That is, would the correlation still be obtained if the study were conducted over and over again with different samples? Issues of statistical significance are discussed in more detail in Appendix B.

Spurious correlation and the third-variable problem

When a correlation coefficient is reported with data obtained using the correlational method, you must remember that the correlation may be spurious; that is, the two variables may not be related at all. Rather, some third variable may be responsible for the apparent relationship between the variables. For example, it is possible that a third variable such as parental aggressiveness or amount of television viewing in general can be responsible for *both* watching television violence *and* aggressiveness. Fortunately, a statistical technique called partial correlation allows researchers to determine whether third variables may have been responsible for the results.

PARTIAL CORRELATION

Researchers face the third-variable problem in correlational research when it is possible that some uncontrolled third variable is responsible for the relationship between the two variables of interest. The partial correlation technique provides a way of statistically controlling third variables. A *partial correlation* is a correlation between the two variables of interest, with the influence of the third variable removed, or *partialled out*, of the original correlation.

Suppose that the results of a survey show that the correlation between residential crowding and school grades among elementary school children is -.50 (the greater the crowding, the lower the grades in school). One potential third variable that may be operating is social class, which may be responsible for both crowding and school grades. The use of partial correlations involves measuring subjects on the third variable in addition to the two primary variables. Thus, the researcher must measure the subjects on all the variables: crowding, school grades, and social class.

When a partial correlation between crowding and school grades, with social class partialled out, is calculated, we can determine whether the original correlation is substantially reduced. Is the original correlation of -.50 greatly reduced when the influence of social class is removed? Figure 11.4 shows two different partial correlations. In both, there is a -.50 correlation between crowding and grades. However, in Figure 11.4a the first partial correlation drops to -.09 when social class is statistically controlled. In Figure 11.4b the partial correlation remains high even when the influence of social class is removed. The outcome of the partial correlation depends on the magnitude of the correlations between the third variable and the two variables of primary interest.

CORRELATION COEFFICIENTS AND PREDICTION OF BEHAVIOR

It is often useful to predict a person's future behavior or performance on the basis of some currently available indicator. This rationale is used in developing tests to determine whether to admit a student to a college, whether a child should be in enriched or honors classes in school, or even whether a couple should reconsider a decision to get married.

Regression equations are used to predict a person's score on one variable

Figure 11.4
Partial correlations between crowding and grades: (a) −.09 and (b) −.49

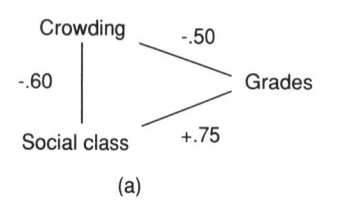

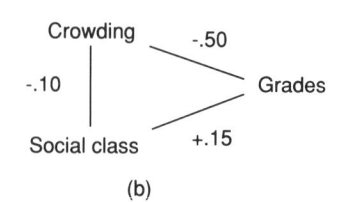

when that person's score on another variable is already known. They are essentially "prediction equations" that are based on known information about the relationship between the two variables. The general form of a regression equation is the following:

$$Y = a + bX$$

where Y is the score we wish to predict, X is the known score, a is a constant, and b is a weight that is multiplied by the value of X. Thus, an equation that predicts college grade point average (GPA) on the basis of a test score (X) may be

$$GPA = 1.0 + .025X$$

If a person scores 80 on the test, the predicted GPA is 3.0; a score of 40 on the test yields a predicted GPA of 2.0. In this case, 40 may become the minimum score necessary for admission.

When researchers or practitioners are interested in predicting some future behavior on the basis of a person's score on some other variable, it is first necessary to demonstrate that there is a reasonably high correlation between the two variables. The regression equation is then calculated from the data, and it provides the method for making the predictions.

MULTIPLE CORRELATION

Earlier we noted that a small correlation between viewing television violence and aggressive behavior ($r = .32$) does not mean that the relationship is unimportant. Rather, there are a number of variables that influence aggression, and television viewing may be only one of them. Recall that many experimental studies manipulate two or more independent variables to study their influence on the dependent variable. Similarly, many correlational studies measure several variables simultaneously. Thus, a researcher may study the correlations between aggressive behavior and the variables of television violence viewing, family income, gender, and parental attitudes toward aggression.

Each of these variables may be expected to be related to aggressive behavior. A technique called *multiple correlation* allows the researcher to evaluate the correlation between aggression and the combined set of variables being studied. The multiple correlation coefficient is symbolized as R, and it can range from 0.00 to $+1.00$. In our hypothetical study of aggression, the researcher may report a multiple correlation (R) of .76, even though each simple correlation (r) may not be greater than .35. Such results demonstrate that the combination of variables is more effective in helping us understand the correlates of aggression than is any single variable. The statistical basis of multiple correlation is beyond the scope of this book. It is, however, a useful research approach that you will undoubtedly encounter when you read research reports in professional journals.

SUMMARY

A correlation coefficient is a statistic that describes the strength of a relationship between two variables. One of the most commonly used correlation coefficient statistics is the Pearson product-moment correlation coefficient, symbolized as r. A correlation coefficient can range from 0.00 to ± 1.00. A positive correlation indicates a positive relationship between the variables; a negative correlation indicates a negative relationship. Scatterplots are useful to inspect visually the relationship between variables.

Partial correlation is a technique for statistically controlling for a third variable. This method allows you to estimate the strength of relationship between two variables with the influence of a spurious third variable removed.

A practical use of correlation coefficients is a prediction equation that allows prediction of a person's score on one variable, such as college GPA, when only a score on another variable, such as high school GPA, is known.

Multiple correlation is a technique to study the relationship between a variable and a combined set of other variables. A multiple correlation coefficient is generally higher than any single correlation between the variables.

STUDY QUESTIONS

1. What is a correlation coefficient? What do the size and sign of the correlation coefficient tell us about the relationship between variables?
2. What is a scatterplot? What happens if the scatterplot shows a curvilinear relationship?
3. What is meant by restriction of range? Why does this restriction reduce the size of the correlation coefficient?
4. What is a regression equation? How may an employer or a school psychologist use a regression equation?
5. How does multiple correlation increase the accuracy of prediction?
6. What is the purpose of a partial correlation?

CHAPTER 12

Ethical Concerns

CAREER PROFILE

Melanie J. Ingle-Nelson / Psychosocial Coordinator

Melanie holds a B.S. in Child Development and an M.S. in Clinical Psychology from California State University, Fullerton. She is the Coordinator for the School Reintegration Program at the Jonathan Jaques Children's Cancer Center of Miller Children's Hospital, Memorial Medical Center, Long Beach, California.

"Practically every job that I've had has been working with children. My current position involves educating children about illness. If I am to explain why chemotherapy has caused a child to lose his or her hair, then I need to do so in a developmentally appropriate manner. After the child understands his or her medical problem, I then go into the classroom to explain to classmates 'why Johnny looks different' or 'why Brenda is absent so often.' I especially enjoy my job because it involves so many systems. As medical knowledge advances, I am able to share that information with laypersons through in-services and school conferences. My job is also unique because I am able to see the same child in different environments. One day I may help a child get through a painful medical procedure, and the next day I am able to see him or her participating in school 'just like a normal kid.'

"If you are interested in a specific human development or family relations field, get out there and get some experience. And then, once you have decided it is for you, jump in and start swimming, rather than sitting back and compiling all the reasons why you shouldn't. This kind of practical experience is invaluable for understanding all the theory and research."

Because Melanie Ingle-Nelson, the Psychosocial Coordinator in our profile, works in a medical setting, she is undoubtedly aware of the ethical concerns raised by medical research; her own behavioral research on educating children about illness must also be considered in the context of ethical questions. Throughout the book, ethical concerns and their impact on research in human development and family relations have been mentioned. In this chapter, we explore in detail the nature of ethical problems that arise in research, especially with subjects from different populations. Because research with children presents specific problems in this area, it is important to consider these special problems carefully. Through a brief historical vignette, we begin by introducing the concept of *psychological risk*.

THE PRINCIPLE OF PSYCHOLOGICAL RISK

Milgram's research

Although it has always been assumed that biomedical research has inherent physical risks, it was not always recognized that studies of human behavior can potentially have harmful psychological effects on the participants. This lack of recognition changed with a controversial series of experiments by Stanley Milgram (1963, 1964, 1965). Milgram studied obedience to authority in a staged situation disguised as a "scientific study of memory and learning" conducted at Yale University. Volunteer subjects who reported to the laboratory were met by a scientist dressed in a lab coat and another "subject" (who was really a confederate). The scientist explained that he wished to examine the effects of punishment on learning. One subject would be a "teacher" who would administer the punishment, and the other subject would be the "learner." A rigged drawing always resulted in the volunteer subject being the teacher and the confederate being the learner.

The scientist attached electrodes to the learner and placed the volunteer subject in front of an impressive-looking shock machine. The machine had a series of levers that would supposedly deliver shocks to the learner, who was in a booth nearby. The first lever was labeled 15 V, the second, 30 V, then 45 V, and so on up to 450 V. The levers were also labeled "Slight Shock," "Moderate Shock," and so on up to "Danger: Severe Shock," followed by red Xs above 400 V.

The confederate was instructed to learn a series of word pairs. Every time the learner made a mistake, the teacher was to deliver a shock as punishment, and for each subsequent mistake the learner was to receive a higher level of shock. The learner never actually received any shock, but the real subject didn't know that. In the experiment, the learner made frequent mistakes. When the teacher got to the 300-V level, the confederate began making sounds of distress and did not provide any further answers. Usually the teachers became upset at this point and expressed reluctance to continue. The scientist told the teacher he must continue, using a series of prods ranging from "Please continue," to "The experiment requires that you continue," to "You have no other choice, you *must* go on!"

If you had been a subject in this experiment what do you think you would have done? Before the experiment was conducted, Milgram asked people to predict how many subjects would administer all the shocks, and most predicted that at least 97 percent of the subjects would refuse to continue shocking the learner. The actual result was that 26 of 40 subjects (or over 60 percent) continued to deliver shocks all the way to the maximum 450 V! Factors that might have induced this blind obedience by most of the subjects included the presence of an authority figure (the scientist), his authoritative apparel (the lab coat), the experiment's affiliation with a prestigious institution (Yale University), the scientific laboratory setting, the lack of time for reflection, the novelty of the situation, and so forth. Milgram's study has important relevance for understanding the violence inflicted by human beings on one another in such tragic historical events as the Nazi Holocaust, the Killing Fields of Cambodia, or the Jonestown mass suicide.

But, the Milgram research had another important effect. It dramatized the question of whether experimental procedures themselves might be unethical. Even though no actual physical pain was experienced by either the confederate or the volunteer subjects, the situation produced extraordinary tension in the participants. Subjects were observed to "sweat, tremble, stutter, bite their lips, groan, and dig their fingernails into their flesh" (Milgram 1963, p. 375). Often they fell into nervous laughing fits or even paroxysms of hysterical laughter. Because of the obvious stress caused by the experiment, Milgram was careful to debrief his subjects, to explain that they hadn't actually hurt anyone. But what about the long-range effects of knowing that you had administered shocks to another human being, even if it turned out the shocks weren't real?

Milgram's study is not the only example of research that potentially caused stress, anxiety, self-doubts, and/or lowered self-esteem for the participants. It is, however, the one that most readily comes to mind, whenever the question of psychological risk in behavioral research is raised.

Stressful research with children

In research with children, there probably has not been an equally extreme counterpart to Milgram's studies. Nevertheless, there have been experimental situations devised that cause children a certain amount of stress. For example, Mary Ainsworth's classic research involved briefly leaving a baby alone in an unfamiliar room (Ainsworth, Blehar, Waters, & Wall, 1978). The situation was designed to be mildly distressing to assess the infant's attachment to his or her mother. Although this paradigm deliberately causes some minor upset, note that being left alone briefly is not an unusual situation for most infants. A more deliberately contrived situation was devised by Mischel and his colleagues (Mischel & Ebbesen, 1970; Mischel, Ebbesen, & Zeiss, 1972) to study children's ability to delay gratification. Preschool children were left alone in a room at a desk with a bell for 15 min, while the experimenter surreptitiously observed them. The children were given a choice: They could have a desirable treat (such as a marshmallow) if they could wait for the whole 15 min, or they could have a less desirable snack (a pretzel) if they couldn't wait and rang the bell to bring back the experimenter. Mischel and his colleagues were interested in various factors that influenced how long the children could delay gratification, such as whether they had a toy to play with while they waited or whether they were encouraged to think happy or sad thoughts. Mischel, Ebbesen, and Zeiss (1972) reported various activities the children engaged in to reduce the "distress of waiting," such as making up songs, hiding their heads in their arms, pounding the floor with their feet, fiddling with the bell, praying to the ceiling, and falling asleep. Thus, sometimes children have been placed in research situations that make them uncomfortable.

Other research paradigms have induced children to exhibit undesirable behaviors. Perry and colleagues (Perry & Perry, 1974; Perry & Bussey, 1977) studied aggression in boys using an "aggression machine" that contained 10 push-button switches to administer tones of varying intensities to another boy wearing earphones while learning arithmetic problems. In actuality, the noise was not administered to the learner, because he was a confederate just as in the Milgram situation. The aggressors were given feedback on the pain the learners were supposedly feeling, ranging on a scale from (1) "did not hurt my ears at all" to (5) "hurt my ears so much that my whole head aches." During the arithmetic task the confederate made 50 percent errors, and the subjects decided how loud a tone to administer. The findings showed that denial of pain caused the subjects to escalate their aggression until they became "extraordinarily hostile" (Perry & Perry, 1974, p. 60). This finding was an important one for understanding the circumstances under which bullying boys become more aggressive toward their victims. The research also raises ethical questions, however, in that the subjects were prompted to engage in (and therefore practice) a socially unacceptable behavior. A similar concern can be raised about the classic studies of children's imitation of aggressive models (Bandura, Ross, & Ross, 1961; 1963). Briefly, Bandura and his associates arranged to have young children watch an adult sit on a Bobo doll and punch it in the nose, hit it on the head with a mallet, throw it in the air, and kick it about the room. The children subsequently exhibited nearly twice as much aggression as did subjects who had not witnessed the aggressive adult, and they faithfully imitated the adult models, inflicting the same idiosyncratic punishments on a Bobo doll in their playroom. In this case, not only were the children induced to behave more aggressively than usual, the behavior was induced (and presumably condoned) by adult role models. Bandura's studies were pioneering demonstrations of the extent to which children's behavior can be learned by imitation, but what about the effects on the children who participated in these studies?

THE PRINCIPLE OF INFORMED CONSENT

Behavioral research justifies exposing subjects to potentially risky situations by relying on the principle of *informed consent*, which requires that experimental subjects be told beforehand about potential stresses. Armed with this knowledge, subjects can then make an informed decision about whether to expose themselves voluntarily to such risks for the sake of science. In the abstract, this principle guarantees that the research is ethically grounded. In practice, however, there are problems with both components, "information" and "consent."

Information

Do people really understand what is being asked of them when they serve as experimental subjects? For example, it is doubtful that children fully understand the concept of research or experimentation until at least early adolescence. For younger children, the closest situation in their experience is likely to be school, which means that children may mistake the experiment as a kind of a test or evaluative situation. Therefore, instructions to children need to clarify whether the research is evaluative ("I want you to try to throw this bean bag as far as you can.") or not ("I'm interested in finding out more about your feelings about different kinds of music."). Very young children, especially those without school experience, may not understand the situation at all. They may not be willing to execute their role in a research situation, that is, to exhibit a specific behavior that an adult wishes to observe and study. Indeed, the mere presence of the strange adult may affect their behavior in artificial ways.

Because children have an incomplete understanding of the research situation, parents are asked to give informed consent on behalf of their children. The information given to parents may be more complete and technical than that given to children. For example, a researcher may elicit a 3-year-old's participation by inviting him or her to play a "game," but only if the parent is informed about the real purpose of the activity.

There are other populations for which informed consent is a special problem. People of all ages with mental handicaps that preclude their full understanding need to be represented by someone who can evaluate what it means to participate in the research. Such advocates can be parents of developmentally delayed adults in institutions, institutional officials, or in the case of institutionalized elderly with mental limitations, perhaps their spouse or their children. The point is that it is not up to the researcher to decide whether it is appropriate for a subject to participate in research; the subject or a qualified advocate has the right to make that decision.

Deception

Subjects in the Milgram experiment agreed to participate in a study of memory and learning. They actually took part in a study on obedience. There were several levels of deception in this study. First, who would expect that a memory and learning experiment would involve delivering high-intensity, painful shocks to another person? If subjects had been fully informed, how many would have volunteered?

1. Those who did volunteer under these circumstances would probably constitute a biased sample. If the experiment were conducted with such a sample, one could say that the obedient behavior occurred simply because the subjects were sadists in the first place.

2. The shocks weren't actually administered (if so, this experiment would have been a truly inhumane study). When subjects were debriefed about this aspect, they were relieved of a great deal of their distress (we discuss debriefing presently). If Milgram's subjects had known about the nonexistence of the shocks beforehand, the meaning of the experiment would have been entirely different.

3. Knowledge that the research was designed to study obedience would no doubt have altered the subjects' behavior. Few of us like to think of ourselves as blindly obedient, and we would probably go out of our way to prove that we are independent.

Thus, in the Milgram situation, even limited informed consent might have distorted the results obtained.

In other words, outright deception is sometimes necessary for the success of the study. Although some degree of deception may be involved in any study using concealed or participant observers, milder forms of deception (which may be termed "incomplete information") occur more frequently, as in the incidental recall paradigm in which subjects are given a surprise memory test. When is deception acceptable? Never, if there is another way to elicit and study the behavior. If deception is a critical element of the research, however, it depends on the extent of the deception and the importance of the information that is to be yielded by the research. The researcher cannot make this judgment alone; research involving outright deception must be reviewed by an *institutional review board (IRB)*, consisting of other scientists and educated laypersons. IRB's did not exist at the time of Milgram's studies. It is interesting to speculate whether an IRB would consider his findings sufficiently valuable to justify the extreme level of deception necessary to obtain them. This question has inspired much debate on the subject of research ethics—with strong support on both sides of the argument.

Consent

Suppose subjects *are* fully informed about all aspects of the research situation. If they agree to participate, are we guaranteed an ethically sound study? Not necessarily, if the consent wasn't freely given. Suppose the subjects were prisoners. If their research participation earned them good behavior points (or even just a change in the normal routine), would this reward compromise their ability to choose to participate freely or not? If the research is risk-free, there is nothing wrong with encouraging participation by offering a reward, but what about risky research? It is considered unethical to coerce people to participate in potentially harmful research, either by force or with rewards.

In a less restrictive setting, consider the usual source of subjects in psychological research, the introductory psychology class. Students are typically required to participate in a certain number of studies to fulfill a research requirement (thus creating a convenient pool of subjects for researchers). It is believed that such participation fulfills a legitimate educational function. However, because students are not free to decline to participate under such a system, it is now common practice to provide an alternate assignment for students who do not wish to serve as research subjects. The possibility of an alternate assignment ensures that consent is truly voluntary for those who participate.

What about children? Can it be said that they are giving their consent freely when asked to participate in research? We have already examined the problems caused by children's limited understanding of the research situation. Because of the status differential between children and adults, most people recognize a degree of coercion when adults ask children to participate in research. For this reason, parental consent is required, on the assumption that since children cannot really give their own consent, this decision will be assigned to their best advocate, their parent.

How to obtain informed consent

Suppose you wish to conduct an experiment on children's reading performance in noisy versus quiet environments. You wish to test a group of second graders on their ability to locate and cross out the vowels on a page covered with letters. One-half the subjects will perform this task in a quiet room, and the other half will take the test in a room with the radio on. How should you go about obtaining informed consent?

Parental consent is best obtained in this situation with a letter. Schools vary, but the possibilities include mailing the letter to parents and receiving a reply by mail. In a large study, postage for this procedure can be expensive. Alternately, the letters can be passed out in class, and the returning consent forms collected by the teacher. This procedure is relatively inefficient, as younger children are not very reliable when it comes to carrying a letter home and returning a signed consent form to the school. Notice the possibilities for violating the rules of good sampling inherent in this procedure. If only the smarter, more mature, or more motivated students manage to return their signed consent forms, this fact will affect the results. In our experience, the most effective technique is to engage the class's interest before the letters are distributed. The researcher should visit the class, introduce himself or herself, and talk a little about the study. For example:

> Hi! I'm _____, from the University of _____. We're conducting a study to find out about second graders' reading abilities. If you want to be in the study, I'll take a bunch of you to a special room and we'll play a sort of a game involving finding letters. But first you have to have your parent's permission. I'm going to hand out a letter for you to take to your parents. It will tell them about the study. If it's OK with them, they'll sign the form on the bottom, and you should bring that back to your teacher. Everyone who brings back the letter saying it's OK with their parents will get to be in the study.

A personal approach such as this one can dramatically improve the return rate. In addition, the researcher can follow up with reminders or provide a small reward for children who return their forms.

Figure 12.1 is an example consent letter for this project. Its important features include the following. The researcher and the nature of the project are introduced. That is, the study is identified as a class project from the University of _____. Providing this information tells the parents that the study is motivated as much by the learning experience it provides the university class as it is a research study per se. The letter goes on to describe the task students will be asked to perform. Enough detail is given for parents to decide whether the task involves any risk to their child. An estimate of the length of the task is also given, so that parents can judge whether the study will have an adverse educational impact because of missed class time. The letter explains the subjects' right to refuse participation and their right to confidentiality. The letter gives the parent a way to contact the researchers to obtain further information about the study if he or she wishes. Finally, the letter gives parents the choice of saying yes or no. It is not permissible simply to declare that a child will be tested unless the parents specifically decline permission. Such practice does not fall within the definition of informed consent, because you cannot always be sure of the reasons why the consent form hasn't been returned. There is no guarantee that the parent ever received the letter in the first place.

The children in this example would most likely not be given written information about the research, because they are not proficient readers, but they would be given verbal information, and the points covered are the same as in the letter. Subjects must be told the purpose of the study, their right of refusal, and their right to confidentiality, as in this example script that may be followed on the day of testing:

Hi again. Remember me? I'm _____ from the University of _____.
Your parents have all agreed that you can be in our study, so I'd like to
tell you a little about it before we begin. We're going to play a game
trying to find certain letters on these special pages. You don't have to
play the game if you don't want to, and you won't get in trouble if you
don't play. Also, this isn't a test, and we won't be giving you or your
teacher a grade. We'd like you to try hard to do a good job though.
Now, I'll tell you about the rules of the game. . . .

Dear Parent:

As part of a class project, students from the University of _____ will soon be conducting a study at your child's school. The project investigates how children are affected by noise when they study. One-half of the children will perform a simple letter-detection task in a quiet setting, and one-half will perform the task in a room with a radio on. The children will miss approximately 15 min. of class time. Each child's participation is voluntary, and so your child will be told that he or she does not have to take part. Most children do volunteer because of the novelty and the attention they receive, and the task is designed to be fun for children of this age.

If you approve of your child's participation, and your child agrees to be in the study, your child's results are completely confidential. Because the purpose of the study is to compare group averages, no results for individual children will be released to parents or to school personnel.

Please indicate whether you approve of your child's participation by completing the attached form and sending it to school in the envelope provided. We hope your child will be able to take part in our study, and we thank you for your response. If you would like further information about this project, please don't hesitate to call _____ at [phone number].

[Researcher's signature]

- -

Child's name _____ Birthdate _____

____ Yes, I give permission for my child to participate.
____ No, I do not give permission for my child to participate.

Parent's signature _____ Date _____

- -

Figure 12.1
Sample parental consent letter

At this point, the researcher would describe the task. Before beginning the study, the researcher would give any subjects who do not wish to participate the chance to be excused.

The principles covered in this example should be adapted to whatever population is being studied. The subjects (and their advocates, if necessary) can be informed about the proposed research in writing, in person, by phone, or whatever way is most effective in a given situation.

Research not involving informed consent

Although most studies in the area of human development and family relations require some kind of informed consent of the participants, some research formats do not. For example, observation of naturally occurring behavior in public settings does not ordinarily require informing people they are being studied, provided that the observation is performed unobtrusively. That is, subjects are not aware they are being studied, are behaving in voluntary, natural ways, and are not going to be identified as research participants.

A more tricky situation involves research with participant observers, in which a researcher becomes part of a group to gather information about its normal activities. Suppose a researcher is interested in studying homeless families by posing as a homeless person, staying in a shelter to observe such families and the difficult world in which they live. Should this researcher inform fellow shelter guests that they are being studied? The answer is yes, if practically possible and if the study is not compromised by so doing. However, you can probably think of some reasons why giving such information may be harmful to the research. For example, shelter guests may feel more comfortable if they do not know they are being observed than if they are so informed. They may behave more naturally if they are not aware of the participant observer's objective.

The point is that there are circumstances, especially in observational research, under which informed consent is not required, and there are other situations in which obtaining informed consent may interfere with the observational process. Fortunately, an institutional review process (discussed later in this chapter) is usually available to help the researcher resolve sticky ethical issues involving informed consent. That is, individual researchers are not alone in making decisions about when and how informed consent is to be obtained—there are guidelines and panels of fellow researchers set up to help with such difficult decisions.

DEBRIEFING

When there has been deception in conducting the research, debriefing is necessary to fulfill our responsibility to the rights of the subjects. Even when there is no stress and virtually no possibility of harm to subjects, debriefing is given as an educational experience in exchange for the subjects' participation. This educational feature of debriefing is important whether subjects are young adult college students, older adults, or the elderly.

Milgram went to great lengths to provide a thorough debriefing session. Subjects who were obedient were told that their behavior was normal in that they had acted no differently from most other subjects. They were made aware of the strong situational pressure that was exerted on them, and efforts were made to reduce any tension they felt. Subjects were assured that no shock was actually delivered, and there was a friendly reconciliation with the confederate. Milgram also mailed a report of his research findings to his subjects and at the same time asked about their reactions to the experiment. The responses showed that 84 percent were glad that they had participated, and 74 percent said they had benefited from the experience. Only 1 percent said they were sorry they had participated. When subjects were interviewed by a psychiatrist one year later, no ill effects of participation could be detected. In this case, debriefing seems to have had its intended effect of removing any negative effects of the experience for the subjects. Other researchers who have conducted further work on the ethics of Milgram's study have reached the same conclusion (Ring, Wallston, & Corey, 1970).

What about research with children? As we discussed in Chapter 9, the question of whether it is possible to debrief children successfully depends on the age of the child. In our example study, the second graders can probably understand that the point of the study was to see whether children can find more vowels when it is quiet than when it is noisy. To children of this age, though, the point of a more sophisticated or complicated study may be more difficult to convey. In any case, the researcher's responsibility is to communicate the information about the investigation at a level commensurate with the child's level of understanding.

There are some situations in which it is possible to argue that children should not receive debriefing. A very young child may only come away with the understanding that an adult has lied or played a trick on him or her. On the other hand, it may do more harm to provide such adult role models than to forego informing the child about the true nature of the research. In other cases, debriefing may cause the child embarrassment or lowered self-esteem ("The mirror was really a trick window with a camera behind it."). Suppose the researcher had told subjects they had performed especially well or especially poorly on a test (when their performance was in fact average). The self-esteem of the children who thought they had done poorly would benefit from debriefing ("You didn't really do so badly after all."). What about the children who thought their performance was superior? Should they be left with the message that they didn't do so well after all? These questions need to be carefully weighed in deciding how to handle debriefing. Each situation brings its own special circumstances; there is no absolute rule that applies to all cases.

THE ISSUE OF NONTREATED CONTROLS

Another ethical issue arises in research designed to treat a specific existing problem. Suppose a therapist devises a special program for treatment of eating disorders in adolescents. After a program of well-designed and well-executed research, it is found that the program significantly diminishes the incidence of anorexia or bulimia in the treated group. At this point, there is an ethical duty to offer the treatment to the untreated control group.

Some kinds of research address especially compelling problems. Suppose you are testing a means of diminishing the violent self-abuse exhibited by certain autistic children, the effects of a new diet supplement on reducing infant malnutrition that results from famine in underdeveloped countries, or a new medical treatment for a devastating illness such as AIDS. In cases such as these, the researcher has the ethical dilemma of deciding just exactly when there is enough evidence to warrant the conclusion that the treatment is really effective. At that point, the ethical responsibility to offer the treatment to the control group outweighs the importance of pursuing the study to its completion.

INSTITUTIONAL REVIEW OF RESEARCH

As you can see, ethical considerations do not always provide clear-cut answers to problems. The researcher has a vested interest in the study, and thus he or she cannot be an objective judge of ethical issues. For this reason, every institution that receives funds from the Department of Health and Human Services must have an institutional review board (IRB) that helps decide whether potentially risky research may be conducted. The Department of Health and Human Services has developed regulations that attempt to categorize research according to the amount of risk imposed on the subjects. These rules are designed to be minimal standards—some universities have developed more stringent guidelines.

Research in which there is no risk is exempt from review. The following are currently considered exempt research activities:

1. Research conducted in established or commonly accepted educational settings and involving normal educational practices, such as research on instructional strategies and the effectiveness of instructional techniques, curricula, or classroom management methods.
2. Research involving the use of educational tests (cognitive, diagnostic, aptitude, achievement) if subjects cannot be identified.
3. Research involving survey or interview procedures, except where all of the following conditions exist: (a) responses are recorded in such a manner that the human subjects can be identified; (b) the subject's responses, if they become known outside the research, can reasonably place the subject at risk of criminal or civil liability or be damaging

to the subject's financial standing or employability; and (c) the research deals with sensitive aspects of the subject's own behavior, such as illegal conduct, sexual behavior, or the use of alcohol or drugs. All research involving survey or interview procedures is exempt, without exception, when the respondents are elected or appointed public officials or candidates for public office.
4. Research involving the observation of public behavior (including observation by participants), except where all the conditions identified in (3) exist.
5. Research involving the collection or study of existing data, documents, records, pathological specimens, or diagnostic specimens if the sources are publicly available or if the information is recorded by the investigator in such a manner that subjects cannot be identified.

A second type of research is called *minimal risk*, which means that the risks of harm to subjects are no greater than the risks encountered in daily life or in routine physical or psychological tests. When minimal risk research is being conducted, there is less concern for elaborate safeguards, and approval by the IRB is routine. Some of the research activities considered minimal risk are the following:

1. Recordings of data from subjects 18 years of age or older using noninvasive procedures routinely employed in clinical practice. Such recordings include the use of physical sensors that are applied to the surface of the body or used at a distance and do not involve input of matter or significant amounts of energy into the subjects or an invasion of the subject's privacy. They also include such procedures as weighing, testing sensory acuity, electrocardiography, electroencephalography, detection of naturally occurring radioactivity, diagnostic echography, and electroretinography. It does not include exposure to electromagnetic radiation outside the visible range (e.g., X-rays, microwaves).
2. Voice recordings made for research purposes such as investigations of speech defects.
3. Moderate exercise by healthy volunteers.
4. Research on individual or group behavior or characteristics of individuals, such as the study of perception, cognition, game theory, or test development in which the research investigator does not manipulate subjects' behavior and the research does not involve stress to subjects.
5. Collection of blood samples by venipuncture, in amounts not exceeding 450 ml in an eight-week period and no more often than two times per week from subjects 18 years of age or older and who are in good health and not pregnant.

Any research procedure that places participants at greater than minimal risk is subject to thorough review by the IRB. The IRB is typically composed of both scientists and nonscientists, and it may also include members of the community and legal specialists. The IRB determines whether the potential risks have been minimized as much as possible. It also judges whether the risks are reasonable in relation to the importance of the knowledge that may reasonably be expected to result from the study. Other considerations involve whether selection of subjects is equitable and noncoercive and whether informed consent procedures have been properly followed.

SUMMARY

As we have seen, the ethical issues faced by researchers who study human subjects are often difficult and complex. Researchers must be aware of the psychological as well as the physical risks to which their subjects are exposed. Behavioral research justifies exposing subjects to potentially risky situations by relying on the principle of informed consent. Various techniques are available for providing the information subjects need to make an informed decision to participate in research. Prior consent must be obtained from the subjects, their parents, or other advocates. When deception has been involved in the research situation, it is necessary to provide appropriate debriefing. Various principles have been developed that are designed to guide the researcher in devising procedures that expose the participants to the least physical and psychological risk. Institutional review boards have been created to help researchers address the ethical issues raised by their research techniques.

The Society for Research in Child Development has developed ethical standards for research activity (Figure 12.2). Whereas these standards were developed specifically for research with children, the general principles (informed consent, right to confidentiality, protection from risk, etc.) apply to any investigation involving human participants. After all, research in the behavioral sciences depends on the participation of the people we are interested in. We owe it to them to conduct our studies as ethically as possible.

Figure 12.2 Ethical standards for research with children (Society for Research in Child Development, 1973)

Children as research subjects present ethical problems for the investigator different from those presented by adult subjects. Not only are children often viewed as more vulnerable to stress but, having less knowledge and experience, they are less able to evaluate what participation in research may mean. Consent of the parent for the study of his or her child, moreover, must be obtained in addition to the child's consent. These are some of the major differences between research with children and research with adults.

1. No matter how young the child, he or she has rights that supersede the rights of the investigator. The investigator should measure each operation proposed in terms of the child's rights, and before proceeding he or she should obtain the approval of a committee of peers. Institutional peer review committees should be established in any setting where children are the subjects of the study.

Figure 12.2
(continued)

2. The final responsibility to establish and maintain ethical practices in research remains with the individual investigator. He or she is also responsible for the ethical practices of collaborators, assistants, students, and employees, all of whom, however, incur parallel obligations.

3. Any deviation from the following principles demands that the investigator seek consultation on the ethical issues to protect the rights of the research participants.

4. The investigator should inform the child of all features of the research that may affect his or her willingness to participate and the investigator should answer the child's questions in terms appropriate to the child's comprehension.

5. The investigator should respect the child's freedom to choose to participate in research or not, as well as to discontinue participation at any time. The greater the power of the investigator with respect to the participant, the greater is the obligation to protect the child's freedom.

6. The informed consent of parents or of those who act *in loco parentis* (e.g., teachers, superintendents of institutions) similarly should be obtained, preferably in writing. Informed consent requires that the parent or other responsible adult be told all features of the research that may affect his or her willingness to allow the child to participate. This information should include the profession and institutional affiliation of the investigator. Not only should the right of the responsible adult to refuse consent be respected, but he or she should be given the opportunity to refuse without penalty.

7. The informed consent of any person whose interaction with the child is the subject of the study should also be obtained. As with the child and responsible adult, informed consent requires that the person be informed of all features of the research that may affect his or her willingness to participate; any questions should be answered; and he or she should be free to choose to participate or not, and to discontinue participation at any time.

8. From the beginning of each research investigation, there should be a clear agreement between the investigator and the research participant that defines the responsibilities of each. The investigator has the obligation to honor all promises and commitments of the agreement.

9. The investigator uses no research operation that may harm the child either physically or psychologically. Psychological harm, to be sure, is difficult to define; nevertheless, its definition remains the responsibility of the investigator. When the investigator is in doubt about the possible harmful effects of the research operations, he or she seeks consultation from others. When harm seems possible, the investigator is obligated to find other means of obtaining the information or to abandon the research.

10. Although we accept the ethical ideal of full disclosure of information, particular studies may necessitate concealment or deception. Whenever concealment or deception is thought to be essential to the conduct of the study, the investigator should satisfy a committee of peers that his or her judgment is correct. If concealment or deception is practiced, adequate measures should be taken after the study to ensure the participant's understanding of the reasons for the concealment or deception.

11. The investigator should keep in confidence all information obtained about research participants. The participant's identity should be concealed in written and verbal reports of the results, as well as in informal discussions with students and colleagues. When a possibility exists that others may gain access to such information, this possibility, together with the plans for protecting confidentiality,

Figure 12.2
(continued)

should be explained to the participants as a part of the procedure for obtaining informed consent.

12. To gain access to institutional records the investigator should obtain permission from responsible individuals or authorities in charge of records. He or she should preserve the anonymity of the information and extract no information other than that for which permission was obtained. It is the investigator's responsibility to insure that these authorities do, in fact, have the confidence of the subject and that they bear some degree of responsibility in giving such permission.

13. Immediately after the data are collected, the investigator should clarify for the research participant any misconceptions that may have arisen. The investigator also recognizes a duty to report general findings to participants in terms appropriate to their understanding. Where scientific or humane values may justify withholding information, every effort should be made so that withholding the information has no damaging consequences for the participant.

14. Because the investigator's words may carry unintended weight with parents and children, caution should be exercised in reporting results, making evaluative statements, or giving advice.

15. When in the course of research, information comes to the investigator's attention that may seriously affect the child's well-being, the investigator has a responsibility to discuss the information with those expert in the field in order that the parents may arrange the necessary assistance for their child.

16. When research procedures may result in undesirable consequences for the participant that were previously unforeseen, the investigator should employ appropriate measures to correct these consequences, and should consider redesigning the procedures.

17. The investigator should be mindful of the social, political, and human implications of his or her research and should be especially careful in the presentation of the findings. This standard, however, in no way denies the investigator the right to pursue any area of research or the right to observe proper standards of scientific reporting.

18. When an experimental treatment under investigation is believed to be of benefit to children, control groups should be offered other beneficial alternative treatments, if available, instead of no treatment.

19. Teachers of courses related to children should demonstrate their concern for the rights of research participants by presenting these ethical standards to their students so that from the outset of training the participants' rights are regarded as important as substantive findings and experimental design.

20. Every investigator has a responsibility to maintain not only his or her own ethical standards but also those of his or her colleagues.

21. Editors of journals reporting investigations of children have certain responsibilities to the authors of studies they review: they should provide space where necessary for the investigator to justify the procedures and to report the precautions taken. When the procedures seem questionable, editors should ask for such information.

22. The Society and its members have a continuing responsibility to question, amend, and revise these standards.

STUDY QUESTIONS

1. Give an example of research that may place participants in physical danger. Contrast your example with an example of research that places subjects at psychological risk. How is the principle of informed consent used under such circumstances?
2. Think of a research topic that necessitates a certain degree of deception. Describe the debriefing process that should be used in that situation.
3. How would you go about obtaining informed consent in a study of children's attitudes toward television cartoon characters? Whose consent should you get? How should you get it?
4. Is informed consent necessary for an unobtrusive study of naturally occurring social behavior in a public shopping mall? Why or why not?
5. What ethical issues may arise in a proposed study of personality characteristics of hospitalized elderly Alzheimer's patients?
6. What is the "nontreated controls" issue?
7. What is an institutional review board? What kinds of materials should be submitted for review by such a panel?

APPENDIX A

A Sample Research Paper

The following is a typed manuscript of an article entitled "The influence of communication effectiveness on evaluations of younger and older adult speakers" that was originally published in the *Journal of Gerontology* (1987, 42(2), 163–164). This paper is intended to provide a useful illustration of how a research report is organized and presented.

Research journals in human development and family relations require a specific format for the presentation of research findings. One of the formats frequently used is based on the *Publication Manual of the American Psychological Association* (3rd ed., 1983). The following article was set to APA style.

Margin notes are included to point out important elements of APA style and to highlight features of the experiment. Some minor modifications were made in the paper to illustrate various style elements and different formats for presenting research results. The authors thank Dr. Ellen Ryan and the Gerontological Society of America for their gracious permission to reprint this paper.

Communication Effectiveness

1

The Influence of Communication Effectiveness on Evaluations
of Younger and Older Adult Speakers

Ellen Bouchard Ryan and Deirdre G. Johnston

Department of Psychiatry, Faculty of Health Sciences,

McMaster University

Running head: COMMUNICATION EFFECTIVENESS

APPENDIX A

Abstract begins on a new page.

The word "Abstract" is centered and not underscored.

There is no paragraph indentation in the abstract.

The abstract is usually 100 to 150 words in length.

Communication Effectiveness

Abstract

Earlier research has shown that young adults exhibit less favorable reactions to older speakers than to their peers, especially for intellectual and social competence. The present study examined the role of age in modifying the evaluations of listeners for effective and ineffective speakers. In a communication paradigm, 80 undergraduate students listened to and followed the taped instructions of a male speaker who was then evaluated. Communication effectiveness was the only significant factor for the speaker's ratings on the dimension of competence. On the benevolence dimension (e.g., trustworthiness, kindness), however, effectiveness interacted with age, such that for younger adults ineffective speakers were viewed significantly less positively than their more effective peers.

The Influence of Communication Effectiveness on
Evaluations of Younger and Older Adult Speakers

When people form impressions of individuals of contrasting ages, the social meaning of accompanying information or cues appears to be affected by the target person's age (Delia, 1976). In competence-stressing situations, younger adults frequently are rated more positively than older adults (Rubin & Brown, 1975; Stewart & Ryan, 1982). To the extent that respondents have age-based expectancies, their evaluations of specific traits or behaviors can be expected to interact with age.

Two competing hypotheses, however, can be formulated concerning the interaction pattern. One hypothesis is that disconfirmation of negative age expectations by favorable information can elicit especially positive evaluations, if the target individual is seen as an exception to the stereotype (see Jones & McGillis, 1976). This interpretation has been applied to findings of favorable reactions toward elderly persons (e.g., Crockett, Press, & Osterkamp, 1979). Alternatively, intergroup theory (Tajfel & Turner, 1979) would argue that young adults would attend less to individuating traits or behaviors of older persons than to members of their own age group. Stier and Kline (1980), for example, found that evaluations of young individuals were more sensitive to accompanying negative or positive background information than for old individuals.

APPENDIX A

This experiment was designed to test the interaction of communication effectiveness by speaker's age.

Communication Effectiveness

4

  The present study examined the role of age in modifying evaluations of effective and ineffective speakers. Earlier research has established that broad differences in age may be detected on the basis of voice cues alone and that older speakers tend to be downgraded relative to young adult speakers on competence-related traits (Ptacek & Sander, 1966; Ryan & Capadano, 1978; Stewart & Ryan, 1982). Furthermore, with a subtle manipulation of speaker competence (namely, speech rate), listeners demonstrate less sensitivity to the behavior differences in their evaluations of older adults than of young adults (Stewart & Ryan, 1982). The manipulation of communication effectiveness in this study will determine if the overall effect of speaker's age is attenuated or exaggerated by this additional information. In line with earlier research on the evaluation of speakers (Smith, Brown, Strong, & Rencher, 1975; Stewart & Ryan, 1982), judgments were examined on two major interpersonal dimensions: (a) achievement-oriented competence and (b) affiliation-oriented benevolence (i.e., trustworthiness, kindness).

Method

Subjects and Design

  Eighty university undergraduate volunteers (57 women, 23 men; mean age 19.4 years) received course credit for their participation. The experimental design was a 2 x 2 factorial with the between subjects factors of communication effectiveness (effective vs. ineffective) and speaker's age (young adult vs. older adult). The primary dependent variables evaluated were ratings of the speaker's competence and benevolence.

Method section begins immediately after the introduction (no new page). The word "Method" is centered.

Subsection headings (e.g., Subjects) are flush to the left margin, underscored, and stand alone on the line.

202

Materials & Procedure

Two scripts (approximately 150 words) describing a map route from the lobby to the X-ray department of a hypothetical hospital were used. One script was an effective message with clear, unambiguous, appropriately detailed information; the other was an ineffective message with ambiguous information and inappropriate details. Four young adult men (ages 20 to 25 years) and four older men (ages 65 to 75 years) prepared tape recordings of each message after practicing a natural presentation. For simplicity of design and consistency with previous relevant research, only male speakers were selected. The effective message was presented with confidence at a moderately fast rate (140 wpm), whereas the ineffective message was presented more slowly and hesitantly (97 wpm).

The listeners were tested in a language laboratory, and heard their 'communication partner' present a description of the map route via earphones. They drew the route on their copy of a hospital map and then rated the speaker on several 7-point Likert scales. The listeners judged how accurately they had drawn the map and, in addition, rated the speaker, as in Stewart & Ryan (1982), on two dimensions: competence (i.e., confident, intelligent, unambitious, unproductive) and benevolence (i.e., just, trustworthy, insincere, unkind). Also, speaker's age was estimated.

Results

Initially, tests were performed to check the manipulations

APPENDIX A

Marginal notes (left column):

Results section does not begin on a new page; the heading is centered and not underscored.

The experiment used a manipulation check to verify that the subjects detected the manipulations of communication effectiveness and speaker's age.

When presenting data showing statistical significance, the name of the statistical test is underscored and followed by the degrees of freedom in parentheses. Note the spacing. If your typewriter does not have a necessary symbol, write the symbol in black ink.

Most statistical symbols are underscored (e.g., $\underline{F}$, $\underline{t}$, $\underline{M}$, $\underline{p}$, $\underline{df}$).

Figures and tables, when used, must be mentioned in the text.

Communication Effectiveness
6

for age and communication effectiveness. Although the ages of the older men were underestimated substantially ($\underline{M}$ = 49.7 years), the difference in age estimates between the older and younger groups ($\underline{M}$ = 26.3 years) was highly significant, $\underline{F}(1,76)$ = 108.3, $\underline{p}$ < .001. As in Stewart and Ryan (1982), age effects on social evaluations need to be interpreted as underestimates. Message effectiveness yielded significant effects both on the objective measure of route drawing, number of correct segments out of 9 (Effective: $\underline{M}$ = 8.30 vs. Ineffective: $\underline{M}$ = 5.97), $\underline{F}(1,76)$ = 27.70, $\underline{p}$ < .001, and on subjective evaluations of accuracy (Effective: $\underline{M}$ = 5.56 vs. Ineffective: $\underline{M}$ = 3.27), $\underline{F}(1,76)$ = 43.20, $\underline{p}$ < .001.

A two-factor analysis of variance was conducted on the dependent variable of competence ratings. The main effect of speaker's age was not significant, $\underline{p}$ > .10. A significant effect for communication effectiveness was obtained showing that the effective message was rated higher in competence than the ineffective message, $\underline{F}(1,75)$ = 83.10, $\underline{p}$ < .001. As shown in Table 1, the communication effectiveness factor appears to influence the competence ratings of younger speakers more dramatically than the older speakers. However, the interaction of speaker's age by communication effectiveness was not statistically significant, $\underline{p}$ > .10.

Communication Effectiveness

Insert Table 1 about here

A second two-factor analysis of variance was conducted on the benevolence ratings. Similar to the first analysis, an age main effect was not observed, $p > .10$, while a significant main effect for communication effectiveness was detected, $F = 30.30$, $p < .001$. A significant interaction of speaker's age by communication effectiveness was obtained, $F(1,73) = 8.70$, $p < .01$. This interaction, depicted in Figure 1, shows that the influence of communication effectiveness is substantially larger for younger speakers in contrast to older speakers.

Insert Figure 1 about here

Analysis of the simple effects revealed that the benevolence ratings were significantly lower for ineffective young speakers than for effective young speakers, $F(1,38) = 40.10$, $p < .001$; but the difference between the effectiveness conditions was not significant for ratings of older speakers, $p > .10$.

Discussion

For this communication situation, manipulation of communicative effectiveness was clearly the influential factor. For the competence dimension, the concrete information conveyed about the individual speaker's abilities outweighed any initial

> Give instructions for placement of any figures and tables at the appropriate point in the text. The actual figures or tables are placed at the end of the paper.

> Discussion section immediately follows the results section. The word "Discussion" is centered and not underscored.

APPENDIX A

impressions related to age stereotyping. In other words, speakers were viewed more positively in their effective guise than in their ineffective guise. These results parallel those of Drevenstedt (1981) and Puckett et al. (1983) for written material.

On the benevolence dimension, however, communication ineffectiveness did not lead to significantly less favorable judgments of older adults as it did for younger adults. For this second interpersonal dimension, age stereotyping did attenuate the influence of behavioral evidence in a manner very similar to the findings by Stewart and Ryan (1982) for the more subtle manipulation of speech rate and by Walsh and Connor (1979) for written essays of good and poor quality. The benevolence findings of particular downgrading of the young ineffective speaker are congruent with the disconfirmation prediction discussed in the introduction (see Stier & Kline, 1980). No evidence was observed for upgrading of the older effective speaker, a pattern that would have reflected the influence of disconfirmation more strongly.

Further research concerning the role of age in modulating the social meaning of behavior should pursue the complex patterns of subtle age bias by using female target persons (see Walsh & Connor, 1979), by examining the responses of older adults, and by using more mild manipulations of communicative effectiveness.

Communication Effectiveness

References

Crockett, W. H., Press, A. N., & Osterkamp, M. (1979). The effect of deviations from stereotyped explanations upon attitudes toward older persons. Journal of Gerontology, 34, 368-374.

Delia, J. (1976). Change of meaning processes in impression formation. Communication Monographs, 13, 142-157.

Drevenstedt, J. (1981). Age bias in the evaluation of achievement: What determines? Journal of Gerontology, 36, 453-454.

Jones, E. E., & McGillis, D. (1976). Correspondent inferences and the attribution cube: A comparative reappraisal. In J. Harvey, W. Ickes, & R. Kidd (Eds.), New directions in attribution research (Vol. 1). Hillsdale, NJ: Lawrence Erlbaum Associates.

Ptacek, P. H., & Sander, E. K. (1966). Age recognition from voice. Journal of Speech and Hearing Research, 9, 273-277.

Puckett, J. M., Petty, R. E., Cacioppo, J. T., & Fischer, D. L. (1983). The relative impact of age and attractiveness stereotypes for persuasion. Journal of Gerontology, 38, 340-343.

Rubin, K. H., & Brown, I. D. R. (1975). A life-span look at person perception and its relationship to communicative interaction. Journal of Gerontology, 30, 461-468.

Ryan, E. B., & Capadano, H. L. (1978). Age perceptions and evaluative reactions toward adult speakers. Journal of Gerontology, 33, 98-102.

References begin on a new page. The first line of each reference is flush to the margin; subsequent lines are indented three spaces.

APPENDIX A

Smith, B. L., Brown, B. L., Strong, W. J., & Rencher, A. C. (1975). Effects of speech rate on personality perception. Language & Speech, 18, 145-152.

Stewart, M. A., & Ryan, E. B. (1982). Attitudes toward younger and older adult speakers: Effects of varying speech rates. Journal of Language and Social Psychology, 1, 91-109.

Stier, D. L., & Kline, D. W. (1980). Situational determinants of attitudes toward the elderly: An experimental analysis. Research on Aging, 2, 489-498.

Tajfel, H., & Turner, J. (1979). An integrative theory of intergroup conflict. In W. C. Austin & S. Worchel (Eds.), The social psychology of intergroup relations. Monterey, CA: Brooks/Cole.

Walsh, R. P., & Connor, C. L. (1979). Old men and young women: How objectively are their skills assessed? Journal of Gerontology, 3, 561-568.

Notes

This article is based on a presentation given at the annual meeting of the Gerontological Society of America. The research was partially supported by a grant from the Gerontological Research Council of Ontario.

Address correspondence to Dr. E. B. Ryan, Department of Psychiatry, Faculty of Health Sciences, McMaster University, Hamilton, Ontario, Canada L8N 3Z5.

APPENDIX A

Each table is typed on a new page. Use Arabic, not Roman, numerals to number your tables.

Table 1 shows (a) no main effect of speaker's age (bottom row marginal means), (b) a significant main effect of communication effectiveness (right-hand column marginal means), and (c) a *suggested* interaction of speaker's age by communication effectiveness that was *not* significant.

Communication Effectiveness

12

Table 1

Mean (Standard Deviation) Speaker's Competence Ratings for Communication Effectiveness by Speaker's Age

	Speaker's Age		
Communication Effectiveness	Young Adult	Older Adult	M
Effective	5.28(.94)	4.81(1.24)	5.05
Ineffective	2.82(.99)	3.19(.79)	3.00
M	4.05	4.00	

210

Communication Effectiveness

13

Figure Caption

Figure 1. Mean speaker's benevolence rating as a function of communication effectiveness by speaker's age

APPENDIX A

Each figure must go on a separate page.

Pages on which figures are drawn are not numbered nor is there a page identification. To identify the figure, write the figure number in pencil on the back of the page.

Include all necessary labels for interpreting the figure.

Draw figures carefully and make sure everything is accurate.

Note that, as in all graphs, the independent variable is placed on the horizontal axis, and the dependent variable is placed on the vertical axis.

Always draw figures in black ink.

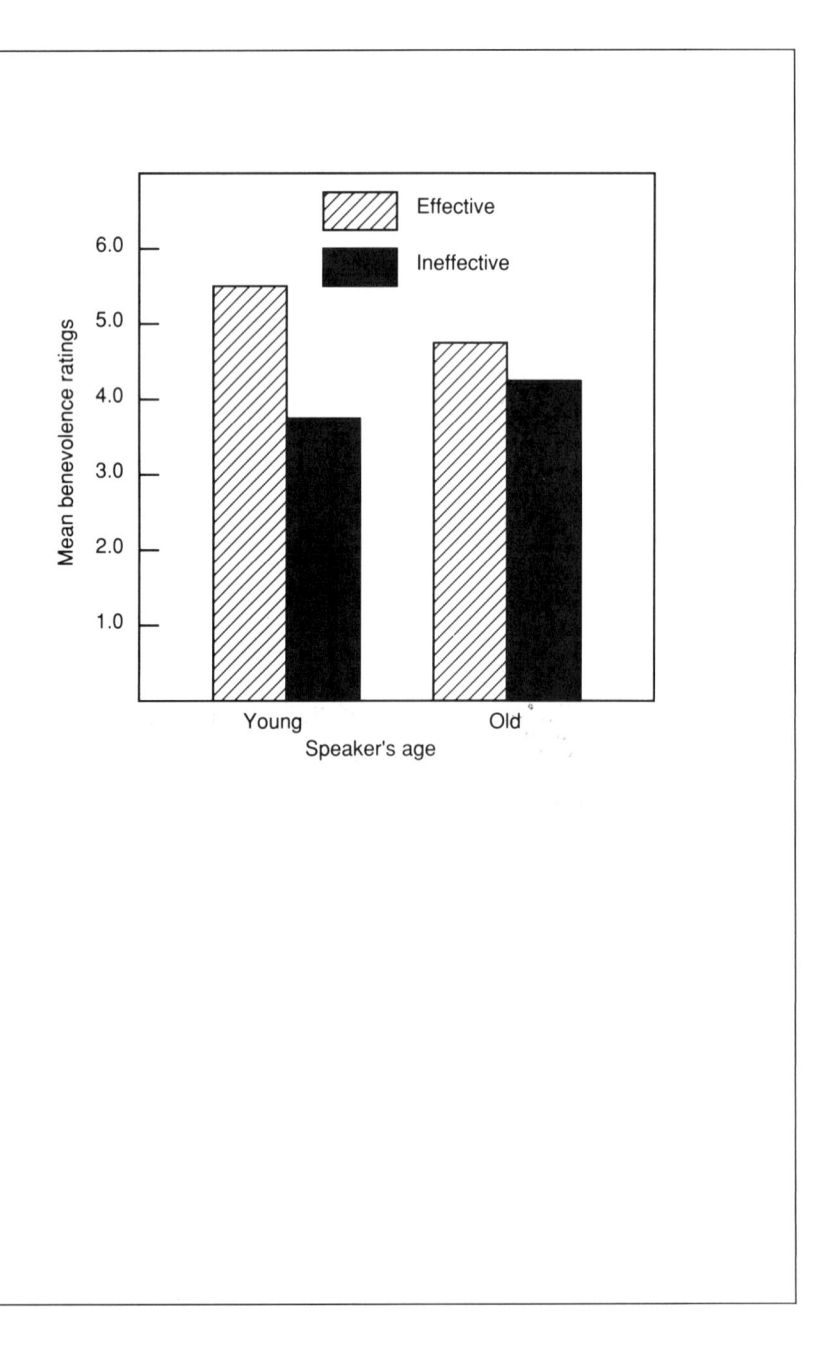

APPENDIX B

Statistical Tests

The purpose of this appendix is to provide the formulas and calculational procedures for analysis of data. All possible statistical tests are not included, but a variety of tests that should be appropriate for many of the research designs you may use are given.

We examine both descriptive and inferential statistics. Before you study the statistics, however, you should review the properties of measurement scales described in Chapter 4. Remember that there are four types of measurement scales: nominal scales, ordinal scales, interval scales, and ratio scales. *Nominal scales* have no numeric properties; *ordinal scales* provide rank order information only; and *interval scales* and *ratio scales* have equal intervals between the points on the scale. In addition, ratio scales have a true zero point. Recall from Chapter 10 that the appropriate statistical analysis is determined by the type of design and by the measurement scale that was used in the study. As we proceed, the discussion of the various statistical tests will draw to your attention the relevant measurement scale restrictions that apply.

DESCRIPTIVE STATISTICS

With a knowledge of the types of measurement scales, we can turn to a consideration of statistical techniques. We can start with two ways of describing a set of scores—central tendency and variability.

Measures of central tendency

A measure of *central tendency* gives a single number that describes how an entire group scores as a whole, or on the average. Three different central tendency measures are available—the mode, the median, and the mean.

The mode   The *mode* is the most frequently occurring score. Table B.1 shows a set of scores and the descriptive statistics that are discussed in this section. The most frequently occurring score in these data is 5: No calculations are necessary to find the mode. The mode can be used with any of the four types of measurement scales. However, it is the only measure of central tendency that can be used with nominal scale data. If you are measuring sex and find that there are 100 females and 50 males, the mode is "female,"

APPENDIX B

Table B.1 Descriptive statistics for a set of scores

Score	Descriptive statistic
1	
2	
4	Mode = 5
4	
5	Median = 5
5	$\bar{X} = \dfrac{\Sigma X}{N} = 4.5$
5	
6	
6	Range = 6
7	
$\Sigma X = 45$	$s^2 = \dfrac{\Sigma(X - \bar{X})^2}{N - 1} = \dfrac{\Sigma X^2 - N\bar{X}^2}{N - 1} = \dfrac{233 - 202.5}{9} = 3.388$
$\Sigma X^2 = 233$	
$N = 10$	$s = \sqrt{s^2} = 1.84$

because "female" is the most frequently occurring category on the nominal scale.

The median The *median* is the score that divides the group in half: 50 percent of the scores are below the median, and 50 percent are above the median. When the scores have been ordered from lowest to highest (as in Table B.1), the median is easily found. (For example, if there are 11 scores, the sixth score is the median, since there are five lower and five higher scores.) If there is an even number of scores, the median is the midpoint between the two middle scores. In the data in Table B.1, there are 10 scores, so the fifth and sixth scores are the two middle scores. To find the median, we add the two middle scores and divide by 2. Thus, in Table B.1 the median is

$$\frac{5 + 5}{2} = 5$$

The median can be used with ordinal, interval, or ratio scale data. However, it is most likely to be used with ordinal data, because calculation of the median considers only the rank ordering of scores and not the actual size of the scores.

The mean The *mean* takes into account the actual size of the scores. Thus, the mean is based on more information about the scores than either the mode or the median. However, it is appropriate only for interval or ratio scale data.

The mean is the sum of the scores in a group divided by the number of scores. The calculational formula for the mean can be expressed as

$$\bar{X} = \frac{\Sigma X}{N}$$

where $\bar{X}$ is the symbol for the mean. In this formula, X represents a score obtained by an individual, and the Σ symbol indicates that scores are to be summed. The symbol ΣX can be read as "sum of the Xs" and simply is an indication that the scores are to be added. Thus, ΣX in the data from Table B.1 is

$$1 + 2 + 4 + 4 + 5 + 5 + 5 + 6 + 6 + 7 = 45$$

The N in the formula symbolizes the number of scores in the group. In our example, $N = 10$. Thus, we can now calculate the mean:

$$\bar{X} = \frac{\Sigma X}{N} = \frac{45}{10} = 4.5$$

Measures of variability

In addition to describing the central tendency of the set of scores, we want to describe how much the scores vary among themselves. How much spread is there in the set of scores?

The range The *range* is the highest score minus the lowest score. In our example, the range is 6. The range is not a very useful statistic, however, because it is based on only two scores in the distribution. It doesn't take into account all of the information that is available in the entire set of scores.

The variance and standard deviation The variance and a related statistic called the standard deviation use all the scores to yield a measure of variability. The *variance* indicates the degree to which scores vary about the group mean. The formula for the variance (symbolized as s^2) is

$$s^2 = \frac{\Sigma (X - \bar{X})^2}{N - 1}$$

where $(X - \bar{X})^2$ is an individual score (X), minus the mean $(\bar{X})$, and then squared. Thus, $(X - \bar{X})^2$ is the squared deviation of each score from the mean. The Σ sign indicates that these squared deviation scores are to be summed. Finally, dividing by $N - 1$ gives the mean of the squared deviations. The variance, then, is the mean of the squared deviations from the group mean. (Squared deviations are used because simple deviations would add up to zero. $N - 1$ is used in most cases for statistical purposes because the scores represent a sample and not an entire population. As the sample size becomes larger, it makes little difference whether N or $N - 1$ is used.)

The data in Table B.1 can be used to illustrate calculation of the variance: $\Sigma (X - \bar{X})^2$ is equal to

$$(1 - 4.5)^2 + (2 - 4.5)^2 + (4 - 4.5)^2 + (4 - 4.5)^2 + (5 - 4.5)^2 +$$
$$(5 - 4.5)^2 + (5 - 4.5)^2 + (6 - 4.5)^2 + (6 - 4.5)^2 + (7 - 4.5)^2 =$$
$$30.50$$

The next step is to divide $\Sigma(X - \bar{X})^2$ by $N - 1$. The calculation for the variance, then, is

$$s^2 = \frac{\Sigma(X - \bar{X})^2}{N - 1} = \frac{30.50}{9} = 3.388$$

A simpler calculational formula for the variance is

$$s^2 = \frac{\Sigma X^2 - N\bar{X}^2}{N - 1}$$

where ΣX^2 is the sum of the squared individual scores and $\bar{X}^2$ is the mean squared. You can confirm that the two formulas are identical by computing the variance using this simpler formula (remember that ΣX^2 tells you to square each score and then sum the squared scores). This simpler formula is much easier to work with when there are many scores, because each deviation doesn't have to be calculated.

The *standard deviation* is the square root of the variance. Because the variance uses squared scores, the variance doesn't describe the amount of variability in the same units of measurement as the original scale. The standard deviation (s) corrects this problem.

STATISTICAL SIGNIFICANCE TESTS

This section describes several statistical significance tests. All of these tests are used to determine the probability that the outcome of the research was due to the operation of random error. All use the logic of the null hypothesis discussed in Chapter 10. We consider three significance tests in this section: the chi-square test, the Mann–Whitney U test, and the analysis of variance, or F, test.

Chi-square (X^2)

The *chi-square* (Greek letter chi, squared) *test* is used when dealing with nominal scale data. It is used when the data consist of frequencies—the number of subjects who fall into each of several categories.

Chi-square can be used with either the experimental or correlational method. It is used in conjunction with the experimental method when the dependent variable is measured on a nominal scale. It is used with the correlational method when both variables are measured on nominal scales.

Example Suppose you want to know whether there is a relationship between sex and hand dominance. To do so, you sample 50 males and 50 females and ask whether they are right-handed, left-handed, or ambidextrous (use both hands with equal skill). Your data collection involves classifying each person as male or female and as right-handed, left-handed, or ambidextrous.

Fictitious data for such a study are presented in Table B.2. The frequencies labeled as "O" in each of the six cells in the table refer to the number of male and female subjects who fall into each of the three hand-dominance categories. The frequencies labeled "E" refer to frequencies that are expected if the null hypothesis is correct. It is important that each subject falls into only one of the cells when using chi-square (i.e., no subject can be counted as both male and female or both right-handed and left-handed).

Table B.2
Data for hypothetical study on sex and hand dominance: chi-square test

Sex of Subject	Hand dominance Right	Hand dominance Left	Ambidextrous	Row totals
Male	$O_1 = 15$ $E_1 = 25$	$O_2 = 30$ $E_2 = 20$	$O_3 = 5$ $E_3 = 5$	50
Female	$O_4 = 35$ $E_4 = 25$	$O_5 = 10$ $E_5 = 20$	$O_6 = 5$ $E_6 = 5$	50
Column totals	50	40	10	$N = 100$

Computations:

Cell number	$\frac{(O - E)^2}{E}$
1	4.00
2	5.00
3	0.00
4	4.00
5	5.00
6	0.00
$\Sigma =$	18.00

$$X^2 = \Sigma \frac{(O - E)^2}{E} = 18.00$$

The chi-square test examines the extent to which the frequencies that are actually observed in the study differ from the frequencies that are expected if the null hypothesis is correct. The null hypothesis states that there is no relationship between sex and hand dominance: Males and females do not differ on this characteristic.

The formula for computing chi-square is

$$X^2 = \Sigma \frac{(O - E)^2}{E}$$

where O is the *observed frequency* in each cell, E is the *expected frequency* in each cell, and the symbol Σ refers to summing over all cells. The steps in calculating the value of X^2 are the following:

Step 1. Arrange the observed frequencies in a table such as Table B.2. Note that in addition to the observed frequencies in each cell, the table presents row totals, column totals, and the total number of observations (N).

Step 2. Calculate the expected frequencies for each of the cells in the table. The expected frequency formula is

$$E = \frac{\text{Row total} \times \text{column total}}{N}$$

where the row total refers to the row total for the cell and the column total refers to the column total for the cell. Thus, the expected frequency for Cell 1 (male right-handedness) is

APPENDIX B

$$E_1 = \frac{50 \times 50}{100} = 25$$

The expected frequencies for each of the cells are shown in Table B.2 below the observed frequencies.

Step 3. Calculate the quantity $(O - E)^2/E$ for each cell. For Cell 1, this quantity is

$$\frac{(15 - 25)^2}{25} = \frac{100}{25} = 4.00$$

Step 4. Find the value of X^2 by summing the $(O - E)^2/E$ values found in step 3. The calculations for obtaining X^2 for the example data are shown in Table B.2.

Significance of chi-square   The significance of the obtained X^2 value can be evaluated by consulting a table of critical values of X^2. A table of critical X^2 values is presented in Appendix C (Table C.3). The critical X^2 values indicate the value that the *obtained* X^2 must equal or exceed to be significant at the .10 level, the .05 level, and the .01 level.

To be able to use the X^2 table of critical values as well as most other statistical tables, you must understand the concept of *degrees of freedom* (*df*), which refers to the number of scores that are free to vary. In the table of categories for a chi-square test, the number of degrees of freedom is the number of cells in which the frequencies are free to vary once we know the row totals and column totals. The degrees of freedom for chi-square are easily calculated:

$$df = (R - 1)(C - 1)$$

where R is the number of rows in the table and C is the number of columns. In Table B.1, there are two rows and three columns, thus there are 2 degrees of freedom. In a study with three rows and three columns, there are 4 degrees of freedom, and so on.

To use Table C.3, find the correct number of degrees of freedom and then determine the critical value of X^2 necessary to reject the null hypothesis at the chosen significance level. With 2 degrees of freedom, the obtained X^2 value must be *equal to or greater than* the critical value of 5.991, say, to be significant at the .05 level. There is only a .05 probability that a X^2 of 5.991 will occur if only random error is operating. Because the obtained X^2 from Table B.2 is 18.00, we can reject the null hypothesis that there is no relationship between sex and hand dominance. (The chi-square was based on fictitious data, but it would be relatively easy for you to determine for yourself whether there is in fact a relationship.)

Concluding remarks   The chi-square test is extremely useful and is used frequently in all of the behavioral sciences. The calculational formula described is generalizable to expanded studies in which there are additional categories on either of the variables. One note of caution, however: When both variables have only two categories, so that there are only two rows and two columns, the formula for calculating chi-square changes slightly. In such cases, the formula is

$$X^2 = \sum \frac{(|O - E|) - .5)^2}{E}$$

where $|O - E|$ is the absolute value of $O - E$ and .5 is a constant that is subtracted for each cell.

Mann–Whitney U test

The *Mann–Whitney U test* is used to test whether there is a significant difference between two groups when the subjects are measured on an ordinal scale. The two groups may have been formed using either the experimental or the correlational method. However, the Mann–Whitney U test can only be used with an independent groups design, in which the two groups are made up of different subjects.

Example Suppose you want to test the hypothesis that only children are less aggressive than children who have at least one brother or sister. To collect data, you go to an elementary school class and determine which pupils are only children and which have siblings. You also ask the teacher to rate each child's aggressiveness on a scale of 1 to 25 (least aggressive to most aggressive). Before collecting your data, you determine that your aggression measure is really an ordinal scale, so you decide to use the Mann–Whitney U test to evaluate your results.

Table B.3 shows fictitious results for such a study. The table shows the score the teacher gave to each child, the rank ordering of these scores, and the basic calculations for the Mann–Whitney U test. It is important to keep in mind that it is the *rank order* of scores that is crucial in the U test, not the size of the actual scores on the measurement scale.

Finding the value of U involves making two calculations:

$$N_1 N_2 + \frac{N_1(N_1 + 1)}{2} - R_1$$

$$N_1 N_2 + \frac{N_2(N_2 + 1)}{2} - R_2$$

where R_1 is the sum of the ranks in the first group, R_2 is the sum of the ranks in the second group, and N_1 and N_2 refer to the number of subjects in the groups, respectively. The value of U is the *smaller* of these two quantities. To calculate U, follow these steps:

Step 1. Arrange the scores in each group from lowest to highest, as is done in Table B.3. Assign a rank to each of the scores. The smallest score receives a rank of 1, the next highest score receives a rank of 2, and so on. Ranks are assigned on the basis of lowest to highest, regardless of which group the subject is in. When there are tied scores, each subject receives the mean of the rank he or she occupies. For example, in Table B.3, two subjects received a score of 2. Since these subjects occupy the second and third ranks, each receives the same mean rank of 2.5.

Step 2. Calculate the sum of ranks for each of the groups.

**Table B.3
Data for hypothetical experiment on only children and aggression: Mann–Whitney U test**

Only children		Children with siblings	
Score	Rank	Score	Rank
1	1	5	6.5
2	2.5	5	6.5
2	2.5	9	11
3	4	10	12
4	5	11	13
6	8	13	15
7	9	14	16
8	10	16	18
12	14	19	19
15	17	23	20
	$R_1 = 73$		$R_2 = 137$

$$N_1 N_2 + \frac{N_1(N_1 + 1)}{2} - R_1 \qquad N_1 N_2 + \frac{N_2(N_2 + 1)}{2} - R_2$$

$$= (10)(10) + \frac{(10)(11)}{2} - 73 \qquad = (10)(10) + \frac{(10)(11)}{2} - 137$$

$$= 82 \qquad\qquad\qquad\qquad = 18$$

Since (2) is the smaller calculation, $U = 18$

Step 3. Calculate the two quantities described in the preceding equations. The value of U is the smaller of these two quantities.

Significance of U Critical values for determining the significance of U are shown in Appendix C (Table C.4). To use this table, first determine your significance level. The table in Appendix C is made up of three smaller tables (A, B, and C) for significance levels of .10, .05, and .01.

If you choose a .05 level of significance, use the table marked (B). Find the critical value of U for N_1 and N_2 in your study. In our example, $N_1 = 10$ and $N_2 = 10$. The critical value of U at the .05 level, then, is 23. To be significant, the obtained value of U must be *equal to or smaller than* the critical value. Since the obtained value of U (18) is smaller than the critical value (23), we conclude that the results are significant at the .05 level.

A note of caution: The significance of U is determined by whether the obtained U is smaller than the critical value. This procedure is directly opposite to the procedures used with most other significance tests (e.g., the chi-square test). With most tests, the obtained value must *exceed* the critical value to be significant.

Concluding remarks The Mann–Whitney U test is useful when the data are of an ordinal scale type and an independent groups design has been used. However, other tests must be used when the study uses a repeated measures design. Such tests may be found in statistics texts.

Analysis of variance (F test)

The *analysis of variance*, or *F test*, is used to determine whether there is a significant difference between groups that have been measured on either interval or ratio scales. The groups may have been formed using either the experimental or the correlational method; what is important is that an interval scale measure is used. The analysis of variance may be used with either independent groups or repeated measures designs. Procedures for calculating F for both types of designs are presented.

Analysis of variance: One independent variable

To illustrate the use of the analysis of variance, let's consider a hypothetical experiment on vividness and children's picture book reading activity. You think that children will be less distracted and will pay more attention to picture books that are illustrated in vivid detail. To test this idea, you conduct an experiment with three different versions of the same picture book: One version is illustrated in vivid detail; a second is illustrated with routine drawings; the third includes only simple line drawings. Subjects are seated at a small table and given one of the three books to read at their own pace. The version of the book read is the independent variable manipulation. Subjects are randomly assigned to the three book conditions. Distraction, the dependent variable, is measured by recording the number of seconds the child looks away from the book while reading.

Fictitious data for such an experiment are shown in Table B.4. Note that this design is an independent groups design with five subjects in each group.

Table B.4 Data for hypothetical experiment on vividness and children's picture book reading: Analysis of variance

	Picture Detail (A)	
Vivid (A1)	Routine (A2)	Simple (A3)
33	21	20
24	25	13
31	19	15
29	27	10
34	26	14
$T_{A1} = 151$	$T_{A2} = 118$	$T_{A3} = 72$
$n_{A1} = 5$	$n_{A2} = 5$	$n_{A3} = 5$
$\overline{X}_{A1} = 30.20$	$\overline{X}_{A2} = 23.60$	$\overline{X}_{A3} = 14.40$
$\Sigma X_{A1}^2 = 4623$	$\Sigma X_{A2}^2 = 2832$	$\Sigma X_{A3}^2 = 1090$
$T^2 = 22801$	$T^2 = 13924$	$T^2 = 5184$

$$SS_{TOTAL} = \Sigma X^2 - \frac{G^2}{N} = (4623 + 2832 + 1090) - \frac{(151 + 118 + 72)^2}{15}$$
$$= 8545 - 7752.07$$
$$= 792.93$$

$$SS_A = \Sigma \frac{T_a^2}{n_a} - \frac{G^2}{N} = \left[\frac{(151)^2}{5} + \frac{(118)^2}{5} + \frac{(72)^2}{5}\right] - 7752.07$$
$$= 8381.80 - 7752.07$$
$$= 629.73$$

$$SS_{ERROR} = \Sigma X^2 - \Sigma \frac{T_a^2}{n_a} = 8545 - 8381.80$$
$$= 163.20$$

The calculations of the systematic variance and error variance involve computing the sum of squares for the different types of variance.

Sum of squares *Sum of squares* stands for the *sum of squared deviations from the mean*. Computing an analysis of variance for the data in Table B.4 involves three sums of squares: (1) SS_{TOTAL}, the sum of squared deviations of each individual score from the grand mean; (2) SS_A, the sum of squared deviations of each of the group means from the grand mean; and (3) SS_{ERROR}, the sum of squared deviations of the individual scores from their respective group means. A in SS_A is used to indicate that we are dealing with the systematic variance associated with independent variable A.

The three sums of squares are deviations from a mean (recall that we calculated such deviations earlier when discussing the variance in a set of scores). We can calculate the deviations directly with the data in Table B.4, but such calculations are hard to work with, so we use simplified formulas for computational purposes:

$$SS_{TOTAL} = \Sigma X^2 - \frac{G^2}{N}$$

$$SS_A = \Sigma \frac{T_a^2}{n_a} - \frac{G^2}{N}$$

$$SS_{ERROR} = \Sigma X^2 - \Sigma \frac{T_a^2}{n_a}$$

Note that $SS_{TOTAL} = SS_A + SS_{ERROR}$. The actual computations are shown in Table B.4.

SS_{TOTAL} The formula for SS_{TOTAL} is

$$\Sigma X^2 - \frac{G^2}{N}$$

where ΣX^2 is the sum of the squared scores of all subjects in the experiment. Each of the scores is squared first and then added. Thus, for the data in Table B.4, ΣX^2 is $33^2 + 24^2 + 31^2$, and so on, until all of the scores have been squared and added. If you are making these calculations by hand or with a pocket calculator, it may be convenient to find the ΣX^2 for the scores in each group and then add these for your final computation. The G in the formula stands for the grand total of all of the scores, which involves adding the scores for all subjects. The grand total is then squared and divided by N, the total number of subjects in the experiment. When computing the sum of squares, you should always keep the calculations clearly labeled, because you can simplify later calculations by referring to these earlier ones. Once you have computed SS_{TOTAL}, SS_A can be calculated.

SS_A The formula for SS_A is

$$\Sigma \frac{T_a^2}{n_a} - \frac{G^2}{N}$$

where T_a refers to the total of the scores in Group *a* of independent variable A. (T_a is a shorthand notation for ΣX in each group [recall the computation of ΣX from our discussion of the mean]. T_a is used to avoid having to deal with too many Σ signs in our calculational procedures.) The a is used to symbolize the group number; thus, T_a is a general symbol for T_1, T_2, and T_3. Looking at our data in Table B.4, $T_1 = 151$, $T_2 = 118$, and $T_3 = 72$. These are the sums of the scores in each of the groups. After T_a has been calculated, T_a^2 is found by squaring T_a. Now, T_a^2 is divided by n_a, the number of subjects in Group a. Once the quantity T_a^2/n_a has been computed for each group, the quantities are summed as indicated by the Σ symbol.

Notice that the second part of the formula, G^2/N, is calculated when SS_{TOTAL} is obtained. Since we already have this quantity, it needn't be recalculated when computing SS_A. After obtaining SS_A, we can compute SS_{ERROR}.

SS_{ERROR} The formula for SS_{ERROR} is

$$\Sigma X^2 - \Sigma \frac{T_a^2}{n_a}$$

All of these quantities were already calculated when we obtained SS_{TOTAL} and SS_A in the preceding sections. To obtain SS_{ERROR}, we merely have to subtract these quantities. As a check on the calculations, we can make sure that $SS_{TOTAL} = SS_A + SS_{ERROR}$.

The next step in the computation of the analysis of variance is to find the mean square for each of the sums of squares. We can then find the value of F. The necessary computations are shown in an analysis of variance summary (Table B.5). Constructing a summary table is the easiest way to complete the computations.

Mean squares After obtaining the sum of squares, it is necessary to compute the *mean squares* (*MS*), which stands for the *mean of the sum of the squared deviations from the mean*, or more simply, the *mean of the sum of squares*. The mean square is the sum of squares divided by the degrees of freedom. The degrees of freedom are determined by the number of scores in the sum of squares that are free to vary. The mean squares are the variances that are used in computing the value of F.

From Table B.5, you can see that the mean squares that concern us are the mean square for A (systematic variance) and the mean square for error (error variance). The formulas are as follows:

$$MS_A = SS_A/df_A$$
$$MS_{ERROR} = SS_{ERROR}/df_{ERROR}$$

Table B.5 Analysis of variance summary table

Source of variance	Sum of squares	df	Mean square	F
A	SS_A	$a - 1$	SS_A/df_A	MS_A/MS_{ERROR}
Error	SS_{ERROR}	$N - a$	SS_{ERROR}/df_{ERROR}	
Total	SS_{TOTAL}	$N - 1$		
A	629.73	2	314.87	23.15
Error	163.20	12	13.60	
Total	792.93	14		

where $df_A = a - 1$ (number of groups $-$ 1) and $df_{ERROR} = N - a$ (total number of subjects $-$ number of groups).

Obtaining the F value   The obtained F for the data in Table B.4 is found by dividing MS_A by MS_{ERROR}. If only random error is operating, the expected value of F is 1.0. The greater the F value, the lower the probability that the results of the experiment are due to chance error.

Significance of F   To determine the significance of the obtained F value, it is necessary to compare the obtained F to a critical value of F. Appendix C (Table C.6) shows critical values of F for significance levels of .10, .05, and .01. To find the critical value of F, locate on the table the degrees of freedom for the numerator of the ratio (the systematic variance) and the degrees of freedom for the denominator of the F ratio (the error variance). The intersection of these two degrees of freedom is the critical F value.

The appropriate degrees of freedom for our sample data are 2 and 12 (see Table B.5). The critical F value from Appendix C is 3.89 for a .05 level of significance. For the results to be significant, the obtained F value must be *equal to or greater than* the critical value. Since the obtained value of F in Table B.5 is greater than the critical value, we conclude that the results are significant, and we reject the null hypothesis that the means of the groups are equal in the population.

Concluding remarks   The analysis of variance for one independent variable with an independent groups design can be used when there are two or more groups in the experiment. The general formulas described are appropriate for all such designs. Also, the calculations are the same whether the experimental or the correlational method is used to form the groups. In addition, the formulas are applicable to cases in which the number of subjects in each group is not equal.

When the design of the experiment includes more than two levels of the independent variable (as in our example experiment, which has three groups), the obtained F value doesn't tell us whether any two specific groups are significantly different from one another. One way to examine the difference between two groups in such a study is to use the formula for SS_A to compute the sum of squares and the mean square for the two groups (the df in this case is $2 - 1$). When making this calculation, the previously calculated MS_{ERROR} should be used as the error variance term for computing F. More complicated procedures for evaluating the difference between two groups in such designs are available, but these are beyond the scope of this book. Once the basic analysis of variance technique is understood, it is not difficult to extend the analysis to designs with more than one independent variable.

Analysis of variance: Two independent variables

In this section, we describe the computations for analysis of variance with a factorial design containing two independent variables. The formulas apply to an $A \times B$ factorial design with any number of levels of the independent variables. The formulas apply only to a completely independent groups design with different subjects in each group, and the number of subjects in each group must be equal. However, once you understand this analysis, you should have little trouble understanding the analysis for more complicated designs with repeated measures or unequal numbers of subjects. With these limitations in mind, let's consider example data from a hypothetical experiment.

Table B.6 shows hypothetical data for an experiment that uses a 2×2 factorial design. Variable A is the type of counseling provided, and variable B is age level of persons in a residential care facility. Counseling provided is either group or individual. Subjects are assigned to the different levels of this independent variable randomly. Age level is a subject variable on which individuals are selected to represent persons ages 65 to 70 in contrast to persons ages 70 to 75. After a 6-week counseling period, residents rated their satisfaction with their treatment at the facility.

The table shows data for five subjects in each condition. This design allows us to evaluate three effects—the main effect of A, the main effect of

Table B.6 Data for hypothetical experiment on influence of counseling and age level on rated satisfaction with residential care: Analysis of variance

	Age (B)		
	65–70 (B1)	70–75 (B2)	
Group counseling (A1)	75 70 69 72 68	90 95 89 85 91	
	$T_{A1B1} = 354$ $\Sigma X^2_{A1B1} = 25094$ $n_{A1B1} = 5$ $\overline{X}_{A1B1} = 70.80$	$T_{A1B2} = 450$ $\Sigma X^2_{A1B2} = 40552$ $n_{A1B2} = 5$ $\overline{X}_{A1B2} = 90.00$	$T_{A1} = 804$ $n_{A1} = 10$ $\overline{X}_{A1} = 80.40$
Individual counseling (A2)	85 87 83 90 89	87 94 93 89 92	
	$T_{A2B1} = 434$ $\Sigma X^2_{A2B1} = 37704$ $n_{A2B1} = 5$ $\overline{X}_{A2B1} = 86.80$	$T_{A2B2} = 455$ $\Sigma X^2_{A2B2} = 41439$ $n_{A2B2} = 5$ $\overline{X}_{A2B2} = 91.00$	$T_{A2} = 889$ $n_{A2} = 10$ $\overline{X}_{A2} = 88.90$
	$T_{B1} = 788$ $n_{B1} = 10$ $\overline{X}_{B1} = 78.80$	$T_{B2} = 905$ $n_{B2} = 10$ $\overline{X}_{B2} = 90.50$	

APPENDIX B

B, and the A × B interaction. The main effect of A is whether one type of counseling is superior to the other; the main effect of B is whether older subjects rated their satisfaction differently than younger subjects do; the A × B interaction examines whether the effect of one independent variable is different depending on the level of the other variable.

The computation of the analysis of variance starts with calculation of the sum of squares for the following sources of variance in the data: SS_{TOTAL}, SS_A, SS_B, $SS_{A \times B}$, and SS_{ERROR}. The procedures for calculation are similar to the calculations performed for the analysis of variance with one independent variable, and the calculations for the example data are shown in Table B.7. We can now consider each of these calculations.

SS_{TOTAL} The SS_{TOTAL} is computed in the same way as in the previous analysis:

$$SS_{TOTAL} = \Sigma X^2 - \frac{G^2}{N}$$

where ΣX^2 is the sum of the squared scores of all subjects in the experiment, G is the grand total of all of the scores, and N is the total number of subjects. It is usually easiest to calculate ΣX^2 and G in smaller steps by calculating subtotals separately for each group in the design. The subtotals are then added. The calculations presented in Tables B.6 and B.7 follow this procedure.

Table B.7 Computations for analysis of variance with two independent variables

$$SS_{TOTAL} = \Sigma X^2 - \frac{G^2}{N} = (25094 + 40552 + 37704 + 41439)$$
$$- \frac{(354 + 450 + 434 + 455)^2}{20}$$
$$= 144789 - 143312.45$$
$$= 1476.55$$

$$SS_A = \frac{\Sigma T_a^2}{n_a} - \frac{G^2}{N} = \frac{(804)^2 + (889)^2}{10} - 143312.45$$
$$= 143673.70 - 143312.45$$
$$= 361.25$$

$$SS_B = \frac{\Sigma T_b^2}{n_b} - \frac{G^2}{N} = \frac{(788)^2 + (905)^2}{10} - 143312.45$$
$$= 143996.90 - 143312.45$$
$$= 684.45$$

$$SS_{A \times B} = \frac{\Sigma T_{ab}^2}{n_{ab}} - \frac{G^2}{N} - SS_A - SS_B = \frac{(354)^2 + (450)^2 + (434)^2 + (455)^2}{5}$$
$$- 143312.45 - 361.25 - 684.45$$
$$= 144639.40 - 143312.45 - 361.25 - 684.45$$
$$= 281.25$$

$$SS_{ERROR} = \Sigma X^2 - \frac{\Sigma T_{ab}^2}{n_{ab}} = 144789 - 144639.40$$
$$= 149.60$$

SS$_A$ The formula for SS_A is

$$SS_A = \frac{\Sigma T_a^2}{n_a} - \frac{G^2}{N}$$

where ΣT_a^2 is the sum of the squared totals of the scores in each of the groups of independent variable A and n_a is the number of subjects in each level of independent variable A. When calculating SS_A, we only consider the groups of independent variable A without considering the level of B. In other words, the totals for each group of the A variable are obtained by considering all subjects in that level of A, irrespective of which condition of B the subject may be in. The quantity of G^2/N was calculated in the preceding section for SS_{TOTAL}.

SS$_B$ The formula for SS_B is

$$SS_B = \frac{\Sigma T_b^2}{n_b} - \frac{G^2}{N}$$

where SS_B is calculated in the same manner as SS_A; the only difference is that we are calculating totals of the groups of independent variable B.

SS$_{A \times B}$ The formula for $SS_{A \times B}$ is

$$SS_{A \times B} = \frac{\Sigma T_{ab}^2}{n_{ab}} - \frac{G^2}{N} - SS_A - SS_B$$

The sum of squares for the $A \times B$ interaction is computed by first calculating the quantity ΣT_{ab}^2, which involves squaring the total of the scores in each of the ab conditions in the experiment. In our example experiment in Table B.6, there are four conditions; the interaction calculation considers *all* of the groups. Each of the group totals is squared, and then the sum of the squared totals is obtained. This sum is divided by n_{ab}, the number of subjects in each group. The other quantities in the formula for $SS_{A \times B}$ have already been calculated, so the computation of $SS_{A \times B}$ is relatively straightforward.

SS$_{ERROR}$ The quantities involved in the SS_{ERROR} formula have already been calculated, so we merely have to perform the proper subtraction to complete the calculation:

$$SS_{ERROR} = \Sigma X^2 - \frac{\Sigma T_{ab}^2}{n_{ab}}$$

At this point, you may want to practice calculating the sums of squares using the data in Table B.6. As a check on the calculations, make sure that $SS_{TOTAL} = SS_A + SS_B + SS_{A \times B} + SS_{ERROR}$.

After obtaining the sums of squares, the next step is to find the mean square for each of the sources of variance. The easiest way to accomplish this task is to use an analysis of variance summary table like the one in Table B.8.

Mean square The mean square for each of the sources of variance is the sum of squares divided by the degrees of freedom. The formulas for the

Table B.8 Analysis of variance summary table: Two independent variables

Source of variance	Sum of squares	df	Mean square	F
A	SS_A	$a-1$	SS_A/df_A	MS_A/MS_{ERROR}
B	SS_B	$B-1$	SS_B/df_B	MS_B/MS_{ERROR}
A × B	$SS_{A \times B}$	$(a-1)(b-1)$	$SS_{A \times B}/df_{A \times B}$	$MS_{A \times B}/MS_{ERROR}$
Error	SS_{ERROR}	$N-ab$	SS_{ERROR}/df_{ERROR}	
Total	SS_{TOTAL}			
A	361.25	1	361.25	38.64
B	684.45	1	684.45	73.20
A × B	281.25	1	281.25	30.08
Error	149.60	16	9.35	
Total	1476.55	19		

degrees of freedom and the mean square are shown in the top portion of Table B.8; the computed values are shown in the bottom portion.

Obtaining the F value The F value for each of the three sources of systemic variance (main effects for A and B and the interaction) is obtained by dividing the appropriate mean square by the MS_{ERROR}. We now have three obtained F values and can evaluate the significance of the main effects and the interaction.

Significance of F To determine whether an obtained F is significant, we need to find the critical value of F from Table C.6. For all of the Fs in Table B.8, the degrees of freedom are 1 and 16. Let's assume that a .01 significance level for rejecting the null hypothesis is chosen. The critical F at .01 for 1 and 16 degrees of freedom is 8.53. If the obtained F is larger than 8.53, we can say that the results are significant at the .01 level. By referring to the obtained Fs in Table B.8, you can see that the main effects and the interaction are all significant. We leave it to you to interpret the main effect means and to graph the interaction. If you don't recall this procedure, you should review the material in Chapters 7 and 10.

Analysis of variance: Repeated measures and matched subjects

The analysis of variance computations considered thus far have been limited to independent groups designs. This section considers the computations for analysis of variance of a repeated measures or a matched random assignment design with one independent variable.

Fictitious data for a hypothetical experiment using a repeated measures design are presented in Table B.9. The experiment examines the influence of a job candidate's sex on judgments of the candidate's competence. The levels of the independent variable are male versus female; the dependent variable is judged competence on a 10-point scale. Subjects in the experiment view two videotapes of a man and a woman performing routine child-care activities associated with nannies. Both videotape participants perform equally

Table B.9
Data for hypothetical experiment on sex and judged competence: Repeated measures analysis of variance

Subjects (or subject pairs)	Male candidate (A1)	Female candidate (A2)	T_s	T_s^2
1	6	8	14	196
2	5	6	11	121
3	5	9	14	196
4	7	6	13	169
5	4	6	10	100
6	3	5	8	64
7	5	5	10	100
8	4	7	11	121

$T_{A1} = 39$ $T_{A2} = 52$ $\Sigma T_s^2 = 1067$
$\Sigma X_{A1}^2 = 201$ $\Sigma X_{A2}^2 = 352$
$n_{A1} = 8$ $n_{A2} = 8$
$\overline{X}_{A1} = 4.88$ $\overline{X}_{A2} = 6.50$

$$SS_{TOTAL} = \Sigma X^2 - \frac{G^2}{N} = (201 + 352) - \frac{(39+52)^2}{16}$$
$$= 553 - 517.56$$
$$= 35.44$$

$$SS_A = \frac{\Sigma T_a^2}{n_a} - \frac{G^2}{N} = \frac{(39)^2 + (52)^2}{8} - 517.56$$
$$= 528.13 - 517.56$$
$$= 10.57$$

$$SS_{SUBJECTS} = \frac{\Sigma T_s^2}{n_s} - \frac{G^2}{N} = \frac{1067}{2} - 517.56$$
$$= 533.50 - 517.56$$
$$= 15.94$$

$$SS_{ERROR} = SS_{TOTAL} - SS_A - SS_{SUBJECTS} = 35.44 - 10.57 - 15.94$$
$$= 8.93$$

well. The order of presentation of the two tapes is counterbalanced to control for order effects.

The main difference between the repeated measures analysis of variance and the independent groups analysis described earlier is that the effect of subject differences becomes a source of variance. There are four sources of variance in the repeated measures analysis of variance, thus four sums of squares are calculated:

$$SS_{TOTAL} = \Sigma X^2 - \frac{G^2}{N}$$

$$SS_A = \frac{\Sigma T_a^2}{n_a} - \frac{G^2}{N}$$

$$SS_{SUBJECTS} = \frac{\Sigma T_s^2}{n_a} - \frac{G^2}{N}$$

$$SS_{ERROR} = SS_{TOTAL} - SS_A - SS_{SUBJECTS}$$

APPENDIX B

The calculations for these sums of squares are shown in the lower portion of Table B.9. The quantities in the formulas should be familiar to you by now. The only new quantity involves the calculation of $SS_{SUBJECTS}$. The term T_s^2 refers to the squared total score of each subject—that is, the squared total of the scores that each subject gives when measured in the different groups in the experiment. The quantity ΣT_s^2 refers to the sum of these squared totals for all subjects. The calculation of $SS_{SUBJECTS}$ is completed by dividing ΣT_s^2 by n_s and then subtracting by G^2/N. The term n_s refers to the number of scores that each subject gives. Since our hypothetical experiment has two groups, $n_s = 2$. The total for each subject is based on two scores.

An analysis of variance summary table is shown in Table B.10. The procedures for computing the mean squares and obtaining F are similar to our previous calculations. Note that the mean square and F for the subjects' source of variance are not computed. There is usually no reason to know or care whether subjects differ significantly from each other. The ability to calculate this source of variance does have the advantage of reducing the amount of error variance—in an independent groups design, subject differences are part of the error variance. Because there is only one score per subject in the independent groups design, it is impossible to estimate the influence of subject differences.

You can use the summary table and the table of critical F values in Table C.6 to determine whether or not the difference between the two groups is significant. The procedures are identical to those discussed previously.

Analysis of variance: Conclusion

The analysis of variance is a useful test that can be extended to any type of factorial design, including those that use both independent groups and repeated measures in the same design. The method of computing analysis of variance is much the same regardless of the complexity of the design. A section on analysis of variance as brief as this one cannot hope to cover all of the many aspects of such a general statistical technique. However, you should now have the background to compute an analysis of variance and to

Table B.10 Analysis of variance summary table: Repeated measures design

Source of variance	Sum of squares	df	Mean square	F
A	SS_A	$a - 1$	SS_A/df_A	MS_A/MS_{ERROR}
Subjects	$SS_{SUBJECTS}$	$s - 1$		
Error	SS_{ERROR}	$(a - 1)(s - 1)$	SS_{ERROR}/df_{ERROR}	
Total	SS_{TOTAL}	$N - 1$		
A	10.57	1	10.57	8.26
Subjects	15.94	7		
Error	8.93	7	1.28	
Total	35.44	15		

understand the more detailed discussions of analysis of variance in advanced statistics texts.

MEASURES OF STRENGTH OF ASSOCIATION

Finally, we discuss several measures of the strength of association between two variables. These measures are called *correlation coefficients*. Three correlation coefficients are considered here: the contingency coefficient, the Spearman rank order correlation coefficient, and the Pearson product-moment correlation coefficient.

Contingency coefficient

The *contingency coefficient* (C) is a measure of strength of association for nominal data. It is computed after obtaining the value of chi-square. The formula is

$$C = \sqrt{\frac{X^2}{N + X^2}}$$

Thus, the value of C for the sex and hand-dominance study analyzed in Table B.2 is

$$C = \sqrt{\frac{18}{100 + 18}} = \sqrt{.153} = .39$$

Because the significance of the obtained chi-square value has already been determined in Table C.2, no further significance testing of C is necessary.

Spearman rank order correlation coefficient

The *Spearman rank order correlation coefficient* (rho) is used to measure the strength of association between pairs of variables measured on an ordinal scale. To use rho, pairs of observations must be made on each subject. These observations must be in terms of ranks; if scores rather than ranks are obtained from each subject, the scores must be converted to ranks.

Example Suppose you are interested in the dominance rankings of a group of boys in an institutional care setting. You wish to know whether the dominance ranks during the day shift are related to the dominance ranks during the night shift, when different staff members are present. To obtain pairs of observations, you determine the dominance rank of each boy during the day shift and again during the night shift.

Fictitious data for such a study, along wtih calculations for Spearman's rho, are presented in Table B.11. The seven subjects in the study are assigned ranks ranging from 1 (highest in dominance) to 7 (lowest in dominance).

APPENDIX B

Table B.11
Data for hypothetical study on the relationship between dominance rank during the day and night shifts: Spearman rho

Subject (initials)	Rank during day shift	Rank during night shift	d	d^2
B.W.	2	1	1	1
G.N.	4	3	1	1
S.P.	1	2	−1	1
R.A.	6	5	1	1
D.G.	7	7	0	0
C.M.	5	6	−1	1
J.J.	3	4	−1	1
				$\Sigma d^2 = 6$

Computation:
$$rho = 1 - \frac{6\Sigma d^2}{N^3 - N} = 1 - \frac{(6)(6)}{343 - 7}$$
$$= 1 - \frac{36}{336}$$
$$= 1 - .107$$
$$= .893$$

The calculational formula for *rho* is

$$rho = 1 - \frac{6\Sigma d^2}{N^3 - N}$$

where d is the difference between each subject's rank on the first observation and the rank on the second observation. The quantity d^2 is obtained by squaring each subject's rank difference. The quantity Σd^2 is simply the total of all subjects' squared rank differences. N refers to the number of paired ranks, and N^3 is N cubed, or $N \times N \times N$. Once the value of *rho* has been obtained, the significance of *rho* can be determined.

Significance of *rho* To test the null hypothesis that the correlation in the population is 0.00, we can consult a table of critical values of *rho*. Appendix C (Table C.2) shows critical values for .10, .05, and .01 significance levels. To use the table, find the critical value of *rho* for N, the number of paired observations. The obtained value of *rho* must be *greater than* the critical value to be significant. The critical value at the .05 level for our example data ($N = 7$) is .786 (plus or minus). Since the obtained value of *rho* is larger than the critical value, we conclude that the dominance rankings are significantly correlated.

Pearson product-moment correlation coefficient

The *Pearson product-moment correlation coefficient* (r) is used to find the strength of the relationship between two variables that have been measured on interval scales.

Example Suppose you want to know how certain variables are related to attendance of meetings of single-parent groups. You've noticed that some people come to every meeting and others come only occasionally. In your study, you measure participants in a single-parent group on the variables of need for affiliation (a personality trait) and the number of meetings attended. The affiliation variable is measured by giving a personality test at the first meeting of a group that will meet weekly for 15 weeks. During the 15-week period, you keep a record of the number of meetings attended by each participant. After obtaining the pairs of observations for each member of the group, a Pearson r can be computed to measure the strength of the relationship between affiliation need and attendance at group meetings.

Table B.12 presents fictitious data from such a study along with the calculations for r. The calculational formula for r is

$$r = \frac{N\Sigma XY - \Sigma X \Sigma Y}{\sqrt{N\Sigma X^2 - (\Sigma X)^2} \sqrt{N\Sigma Y^2 - (\Sigma Y)^2}}$$

where X refers to a subject's score on variable X and Y is a subject's score on variable Y. In Table B.12, the affiliation personality test is variable X, and the attendance score is variable Y. In the formula, N is the number of paired observations, that is, the number of subjects measured on both variables.

Table B.12 Data for hypothetical study on need for affiliation and attendance at group meetings: Pearson r

Subject identification number	Affiliation score (X)	Meetings attended (Y)	XY
01	4	10	40
02	6	15	90
03	7	8	56
04	8	9	72
05	8	7	56
06	12	10	120
07	14	15	210
08	15	13	195
09	15	15	225
10	17	14	238
	$\Sigma X = 106$	$\Sigma Y = 116$	$\Sigma XY = 1302$
	$\Sigma X^2 = 1308$	$\Sigma Y^2 = 1434$	
	$(\Sigma X)^2 = 11236$	$(\Sigma Y)^2 = 13456$	

Computation:

$$r = \frac{N\Sigma XY - \Sigma X \Sigma Y}{\sqrt{N\Sigma X^2 - (\Sigma X)^2} \sqrt{N\Sigma Y^2 - (\Sigma Y)^2}}$$

$$= \frac{10(1302) - (106)(116)}{\sqrt{10(1308) - 11236} \sqrt{10(1434) - 13456}}$$

$$= \frac{13020 - 12296}{\sqrt{13080 - 11236} \sqrt{14340 - 13456}}$$

$$= \frac{724}{\sqrt{1844} \sqrt{884}}$$

$$= \frac{724}{1276.61}$$

$$= .567$$

The calculation of r requires a number of arithmetic operations on the X and Y scores. ΣX is simply the sum of the scores on variable X. ΣX^2 is the sum of the squared scores on X (each score is first squared and then the sum of the squared scores is obtained). The quantity $(\Sigma X)^2$ is the square of the sum of the scores: The total of the X scores (ΣX) is first calculated and then this total is squared. It is important not to confuse the quantities ΣX^2 and $(\Sigma X)^2$. The same calculations are made using the Y scores to obtain ΣY, ΣY^2, and $(\Sigma Y)^2$. To find ΣXY, each subject's X score is multiplied by the score on Y; these values are then summed for all subjects. When these calculations have been made, r is computed by using the formula given.

At this point, you may wish to examine carefully the calculations shown in Table B.12 to familiarize yourself with the procedures for computing r. Appendix C (Table C.8) contains a table of critical values of r.

Significance of r To test the null hypothesis that the population correlation coefficient is in fact 0.00, we consult a table of critical values of r. The table in Appendix C shows critical values of r for .10, .05, and .01 levels of significance. To find the critical value, you first need to determine the degrees of freedom. The *df* for the significance test for r is $N - 2$. In our example study on affiliation and group attendance, the number of paired observations is 10, so the *df* = 8. For 8 degrees of freedom, the critical value of r at the .05 level of significance is .632 (plus or minus). The obtained r must be *greater than* the critical r to be significant. Since our obtained r (from Table B.12) of .567 is less than the critical value, we do not reject the null hypothesis.

Notice that we do not reject the null hypothesis in this case, even though the magnitude of r is fairly large. It is possible, however, that a significant correlation may be obtained with a larger sample size.

CONCLUSION

You now have a basis for computing a number of statistical tests. The basic calculations for these tests are not difficult, but the calculations become tedious with large amounts of data. The development of computer analysis of research data has reduced much of the labor involved in making the calculations. If you are planning to pursue advanced studies in human development or family relations, you will probably want to become familiar with the use of statistical analysis programs for computers.

APPENDIX C

Statistical Tables

This appendix provides a number of tables that are frequently used in research on human development and family relations.

The *random number table* can be used to select data when an arbitrary sequence of numbers is needed. To obtain a series of random numbers, enter the table at any arbitrary point and read in sequence either across or down.

To use the random number table, first order your subjects in some way, perhaps by name or by assigning a number to each subject. Suppose that you have three groups and want five subjects per group, for a total of 15 subjects. Table C.1 presents a list of 15 subjects ordered from first to 15th. Enter the random number table and assign a number to each subject (if there is a duplicate number, ignore it and use the next number in the sequence). In our example, the table is entered in the upper left-hand corner and is read downward. Now assign the subjects to groups: The five subjects who receive the lowest random numbers are assigned to Group 1, the next five subjects are assigned to Group 2, and the five subjects with the highest numbers are assigned to Group 3. These general procedures can be followed with any number of groups in an experiment.

Table C.1 Fifteen subjects ordered from 1–15, their random number, and their group assignment

Subject order	Random number	Group assignment
1	10	1
2	37	2
3	08	1
4	09	1
5	12	1
6	66	2
7	31	2
8	85	3
9	63	2
10	73	2
11	98	3
12	11	1
13	83	2
14	88	3
15	99	3

APPENDIX C

To use the random number table for random sampling, first make a list of all members of your population. Enter the random number table and assign a number to each member of the population. Determine your desired sample size (N). Your sample, then, will be comprised of the first N individuals. For example, if you want to take a random sample of 15 faculty members at your school, use the random number table to give each faculty member a number. The 15 faculty with the lowest numbers would be selected for the sample.

Table C.2 Random number table

10 09 73 25 33	76 52 01 35 86	34 67 35 48 76	80 95 90 91 17	39 29 27 49 45
37 54 20 48 05	64 89 47 42 96	24 80 52 40 37	20 63 61 04 02	00 82 29 16 65
08 42 26 89 53	19 64 50 93 03	23 20 90 25 60	15 95 33 47 64	35 08 03 36 06
99 01 90 25 29	09 37 67 07 15	38 31 13 11 65	88 67 67 43 97	04 43 62 76 59
12 80 79 99 70	80 15 73 61 47	64 03 23 66 53	98 95 11 68 77	12 17 17 68 33
66 06 57 47 17	34 07 27 68 50	36 69 73 61 70	65 81 33 98 85	11 19 92 91 70
31 06 01 08 05	45 57 18 24 06	35 30 34 26 14	86 79 90 74 39	23 40 30 97 32
85 26 97 76 02	02 05 16 56 92	68 66 57 48 18	73 05 38 52 47	18 62 38 85 79
63 57 33 21 35	05 32 54 70 48	90 55 35 75 48	28 46 82 87 09	83 49 12 56 24
73 79 64 57 53	03 52 96 47 78	35 80 83 42 82	60 93 52 03 44	35 27 38 84 35
98 52 01 77 67	14 90 56 86 07	22 10 94 05 58	60 97 09 34 33	50 50 07 39 98
11 80 50 54 31	39 80 82 77 32	50 72 56 82 48	29 40 52 42 01	52 77 56 78 51
83 45 29 96 34	06 28 89 80 83	13 74 67 00 78	18 47 54 06 10	68 71 17 78 17
88 68 54 02 00	86 50 75 84 01	36 76 66 79 51	90 36 47 64 93	29 60 91 10 62
99 59 46 73 48	87 51 76 49 69	91 82 60 89 28	93 78 56 13 68	23 47 83 41 13
65 48 11 76 74	17 46 85 09 50	58 04 77 69 74	73 03 95 71 86	40 21 81 65 44
80 12 43 56 35	17 72 70 80 15	45 31 82 23 74	21 11 57 82 53	14 38 55 37 63
74 35 09 98 17	77 40 27 72 14	43 23 60 02 10	45 52 16 42 37	96 28 60 26 55
69 91 62 68 03	66 25 22 91 48	36 93 68 72 03	76 62 11 39 90	94 40 05 64 18
09 89 32 05 05	14 22 56 85 14	46 42 75 67 88	96 29 77 88 22	54 38 21 45 98
91 49 91 45 23	68 47 92 76 86	46 16 28 35 54	94 75 08 99 23	37 08 92 00 48
80 33 69 45 98	26 94 03 68 58	70 29 73 41 35	53 14 03 33 40	42 05 08 23 41
44 10 48 19 49	85 15 74 79 54	32 97 92 65 75	57 60 04 08 81	22 22 20 64 13
12 55 07 37 42	11 10 00 20 40	12 86 07 46 97	96 64 48 94 39	28 70 72 58 15
63 60 64 93 29	16 50 53 44 84	40 21 95 23 63	43 65 17 70 82	07 20 73 17 90
61 19 69 04 46	26 45 74 77 74	51 92 43 37 29	65 39 45 95 93	42 58 26 05 27
15 47 44 52 66	95 27 07 99 53	59 36 78 38 48	82 39 61 01 18	33 21 15 94 66
94 55 72 85 73	67 89 75 43 87	54 62 24 44 31	91 19 04 25 92	92 92 74 59 73
42 48 11 62 13	97 34 40 87 21	16 86 84 87 67	03 07 11 20 59	25 70 14 66 70
23 52 37 83 17	73 20 88 98 37	68 93 59 14 16	26 25 22 96 63	05 52 28 25 62
04 49 35 24 94	75 24 63 38 24	45 86 25 10 25	61 96 27 93 35	65 33 71 24 72
00 54 99 76 54	64 05 18 81 39	96 11 96 38 96	54 69 28 23 91	23 28 72 95 29
35 96 31 53 07	26 89 80 93 54	33 35 13 54 62	77 97 45 00 24	90 10 33 93 33
59 80 80 83 91	45 42 72 68 42	83 60 94 97 00	13 02 12 48 92	78 56 52 01 06
46 05 88 52 36	01 39 00 22 86	77 28 14 40 77	93 91 08 36 47	70 61 74 29 41
32 17 90 05 97	87 37 92 52 41	05 56 70 70 07	86 74 31 71 57	85 39 41 18 38
69 23 46 14 06	20 11 74 52 04	15 95 66 00 00	18 74 39 24 23	97 11 89 63 38
19 56 54 14 30	01 75 87 53 79	40 41 92 15 85	66 67 43 68 06	84 96 28 52 07
45 15 51 49 38	19 47 60 72 46	43 66 79 45 43	59 04 79 00 33	20 82 66 95 41
94 86 43 19 94	36 18 81 08 51	34 88 88 15 53	01 54 03 54 56	05 01 45 11 76

Table C.2
(continued)

09 18 82 00 97	32 82 53 95 27	04 22 08 63 04	83 38 98 73 74	64 27 85 80 44	
90 04 58 54 97	51 98 15 06 54	94 93 88 19 97	91 87 07 61 50	68 47 68 46 59	
73 18 95 02 07	47 67 72 62 69	62 29 06 44 64	27 12 46 70 18	41 36 18 27 60	
75 76 87 64 90	20 97 18 17 49	90 42 91 22 72	95 37 50 58 71	93 82 34 31 78	
54 01 64 40 56	66 28 13 10 03	00 68 22 73 98	20 71 45 32 95	07 70 61 78 13	
08 35 86 99 10	78 54 24 27 85	13 66 15 88 73	04 61 89 75 53	31 22 30 84 20	
28 30 60 32 64	81 33 31 05 91	40 51 00 78 93	32 60 46 04 75	94 11 90 18 40	
53 84 08 62 33	81 59 41 36 28	51 21 59 02 90	28 46 66 87 93	77 76 22 07 91	
91 75 75 37 41	61 61 36 22 69	50 26 39 02 12	55 78 17 65 14	83 48 34 70 55	
89 41 59 26 94	00 39 75 83 91	12 60 71 76 46	48 94 27 23 06	94 54 13 74 08	
77 51 30 38 20	86 83 42 99 01	68 41 48 27 74	51 90 81 39 80	72 89 35 55 07	
19 50 23 71 74	69 97 92 02 88	55 21 02 97 73	74 28 77 52 51	65 34 46 74 15	
21 81 85 93 13	93 27 88 17 57	05 68 67 31 56	07 08 28 50 46	31 85 33 84 52	
51 47 46 64 99	68 10 72 38 21	94 04 99 13 45	42 83 60 91 91	08 00 74 54 49	
99 55 96 83 31	62 53 52 41 70	69 77 71 28 30	74 81 97 81 42	43 86 07 28 34	
33 71 34 80 07	93 58 47 28 69	51 92 66 47 21	58 30 32 98 22	93 17 49 39 72	
85 27 48 68 93	11 30 32 92 70	28 83 43 41 37	73 51 59 04 00	71 14 84 36 43	
84 13 38 96 40	44 03 55 21 66	73 85 27 00 91	61 22 26 05 61	62 32 71 84 23	
56 73 21 62 34	17 39 59 61 31	10 12 39 16 22	85 49 65 75 60	81 60 41 88 80	
65 13 85 66 06	87 64 88 52 61	34 31 36 58 61	45 87 52 10 69	85 64 44 72 77	
38 00 10 21 78	81 71 91 17 11	71 60 29 29 37	74 21 96 40 49	65 58 44 96 98	
37 40 29 63 97	01 30 47 75 86	56 27 11 00 65	47 32 46 26 05	40 03 03 74 38	
97 12 54 03 48	87 08 33 14 17	21 81 53 92 50	75 23 76 20 47	15 50 12 95 78	
21 82 64 11 34	47 14 33 40 72	64 63 88 59 02	49 13 90 64 41	03 85 65 45 52	
73 13 54 27 42	95 71 90 90 35	85 79 47 42 96	08 78 98 81 56	64 69 11 92 02	
07 63 87 79 29	03 06 11 80 72	96 20 74 41 56	23 82 19 95 38	04 71 36 69 94	
60 52 88 34 41	07 95 41 98 14	59 17 52 06 95	05 53 35 21 39	61 21 20 64 55	
83 59 63 56 55	06 95 89 29 83	05 12 80 97 19	77 43 35 37 83	92 30 15 04 98	
10 85 06 27 46	99 59 91 05 07	13 49 90 63 19	53 07 57 18 39	06 41 01 93 62	
39 82 09 89 52	43 62 26 31 47	64 42 18 08 14	43 80 00 93 51	31 02 47 31 67	
59 58 00 64 78	75 56 97 88 00	88 83 55 44 86	23 76 80 61 56	04 11 10 84 08	
38 50 80 73 41	23 79 34 87 63	90 82 29 70 22	17 71 90 42 07	95 95 44 99 53	
30 69 27 06 68	94 68 81 61 27	56 19 68 00 91	82 06 76 34 00	05 46 26 92 00	
65 44 39 56 59	18 28 82 74 37	49 63 22 40 41	08 33 76 56 76	96 29 99 08 36	
27 26 75 02 64	13 19 27 22 94	07 47 74 46 06	17 98 54 89 11	97 34 13 03 58	
91 30 70 69 91	19 07 22 42 10	36 69 95 37 28	28 82 53 57 93	28 97 66 62 52	
68 43 49 46 88	84 47 31 36 22	62 12 69 84 08	12 84 38 25 90	09 81 59 31 46	
48 90 81 58 77	54 74 52 45 91	35 70 00 47 54	83 82 45 26 92	54 13 05 51 60	
06 91 34 51 97	42 67 27 86 01	11 88 30 95 28	63 01 19 89 01	14 97 44 03 44	
10 45 51 60 19	14 21 03 37 12	91 34 23 78 21	88 32 58 08 51	43 66 77 08 83	
12 88 39 73 43	65 02 76 11 84	04 28 50 13 92	17 97 41 50 77	90 71 22 67 69	
21 77 83 09 76	38 80 73 69 61	31 64 94 20 96	63 28 10 20 23	08 81 64 74 49	
19 52 35 95 15	65 12 25 96 59	86 28 36 82 58	69 57 21 37 98	16 43 59 15 29	
67 24 55 26 70	35 58 31 65 63	79 24 68 66 86	76 46 33 42 22	28 65 59 08 02	
60 58 44 73 77	07 50 03 79 92	45 13 42 65 29	26 76 08 36 37	41 32 64 43 44	

Source: From tables of the Rand Corporation from *A Million Random Digits with 100,000 Normal Deviates* (New York: The Free Press, 1955) by permission of the Rand Corporation.

APPENDIX C

**Table C.3
Critical values of chi-square**

Degrees of freedom	Probability level .10	Probability level .05	Probability level .01
1	2.706	3.841	6.635
2	4.605	5.991	9.210
3	6.251	7.815	11.345
4	7.779	9.488	13.277
5	9.236	11.070	15.086
6	10.645	12.592	16.812
7	12.017	14.067	18.475
8	13.362	15.507	20.090
9	14.684	16.919	21.666
10	15.987	18.307	23.209
11	17.275	19.675	24.725
12	18.549	21.026	26.217
13	19.812	22.362	27.688
14	21.064	23.685	29.141
15	22.307	24.996	30.578
16	23.542	26.296	32.000
17	24.769	27.587	33.409
18	25.989	28.869	34.805
19	27.204	30.144	36.191
20	28.412	31.410	37.566

Source: Table adapted from *Statistical Tables for Biological, Agricultural, and Medical Research*, 6th ed. by Fisher and Yates, 1974 (London: Longman). Reprinted by permission.

**Table C.4
Critical values of the Mann–Whitney U**

(A)
.10 probability level

N_2 \ N_1	7	8	9	10	11	12	13	14	15	16	17	18	19	20
3	2	3	3	4	5	5	6	7	7	8	9	9	10	11
4	4	5	6	7	8	9	10	11	12	14	15	16	17	18
5	6	8	9	11	12	13	15	16	18	19	20	22	23	25
6	8	10	12	14	16	17	19	21	23	25	26	28	30	32
7	11	13	15	17	19	21	24	26	28	30	33	35	37	39
8	13	15	18	20	23	26	28	31	33	36	39	41	44	47
9	15	18	21	24	27	30	33	36	39	42	45	48	51	54
10	17	20	24	27	31	34	37	41	44	48	51	55	58	62
11	19	23	27	31	34	38	42	46	50	54	57	61	65	69
12	21	26	30	34	38	42	47	51	55	60	64	68	72	77
13	24	28	33	37	42	47	51	56	61	65	70	75	80	84
14	26	31	36	41	46	51	56	61	66	71	77	82	87	92
15	28	33	39	44	50	55	61	66	72	77	83	88	94	100
16	30	36	42	48	54	60	65	71	77	83	89	95	101	107
17	33	39	45	51	57	64	70	77	83	89	96	102	109	115
18	35	41	48	55	61	68	75	82	88	95	102	109	116	123
19	37	44	51	58	65	72	80	87	94	101	109	116	123	130
20	39	47	54	62	69	77	84	92	100	107	115	123	130	138

Table C.4 *(continued)*

(B)
.05 probability level

N_2	N_1	7	8	9	10	11	12	13	14	15	16	17	18	19	20
3		1	2	2	3	3	4	4	5	5	6	6	7	7	8
4		3	4	4	5	6	7	8	9	10	11	11	12	13	13
5		5	6	7	8	9	11	12	13	14	15	17	18	19	20
6		6	8	10	11	13	14	16	17	19	21	22	24	25	27
7		8	10	12	14	16	18	20	22	24	26	28	30	32	34
8		10	13	15	17	19	22	24	26	29	31	34	36	38	41
9		12	15	17	20	23	26	28	31	34	37	39	42	45	48
10		14	17	20	23	26	29	33	36	39	42	45	48	52	55
11		16	19	23	26	30	33	37	40	44	47	51	55	58	62
12		18	22	26	29	33	37	41	45	49	53	57	61	65	69
13		20	24	28	33	37	41	45	50	54	59	63	67	72	76
14		22	26	31	36	40	45	50	55	59	64	67	74	78	83
15		24	29	34	39	44	49	54	59	64	70	75	80	85	90
16		26	31	37	42	47	53	59	64	70	75	81	86	92	98
17		28	34	39	45	51	57	63	67	75	81	87	93	99	105
18		30	36	42	48	55	61	67	74	80	86	93	99	106	112
19		32	38	45	52	58	65	72	78	85	92	99	106	113	119
20		34	41	48	55	62	69	76	83	90	98	105	112	119	127

(C)
.01 probability level

N_2	N_1	7	8	9	10	11	12	13	14	15	16	17	18	19	20
3		—	—	0	0	0	1	1	1	2	2	2	2	3	3
4		0	1	1	2	2	3	3	4	5	5	6	6	7	8
5		1	2	3	4	5	6	7	7	8	9	10	11	12	13
6		3	4	5	6	7	9	10	11	12	13	15	16	17	18
7		4	6	7	9	10	12	13	15	16	18	19	21	22	24
8		6	7	9	11	13	15	17	18	20	22	24	26	28	30
9		7	9	11	13	16	18	20	22	24	27	29	31	33	36
10		9	11	13	16	18	21	24	26	29	31	34	37	39	42
11		10	13	16	18	21	24	27	30	33	36	39	42	45	48
12		12	15	18	21	24	27	31	34	37	41	44	47	51	54
13		13	17	20	24	27	31	34	38	42	45	49	53	56	60
14		15	18	22	26	30	34	38	42	46	50	54	58	63	67
15		16	20	24	29	33	37	42	46	51	55	60	64	69	73
16		18	22	27	31	36	41	45	50	55	60	65	70	74	79
17		19	24	29	34	39	44	49	54	60	65	70	75	81	86
18		21	26	31	37	42	47	53	58	64	70	75	81	87	92
19		22	28	33	39	45	51	56	63	69	74	81	87	93	99
20		24	30	36	42	48	54	60	67	73	79	86	92	99	105

APPENDIX C

Table C.5
Critical values of t

$N_1 + N_2 - 2$ (df)	Significance Level*			
	.05 / .10	.025 / .05	.01 / .02	.005 / .01
1	6.314	12.706	31.821	63.657
2	2.920	4.303	6.965	9.925
3	2.353	3.182	4.541	5.841
4	2.132	2.776	3.747	4.604
5	2.015	2.571	3.365	4.032
6	1.943	2.447	3.143	3.707
7	1.895	2.365	2.998	3.499
8	1.860	2.306	2.896	3.355
9	1.833	2.262	2.821	3.250
10	1.812	2.228	2.764	3.169
11	1.796	2.201	2.718	3.106
12	1.782	2.179	2.681	3.055
13	1.771	2.160	2.650	3.012
14	1.761	2.145	2.624	2.977
15	1.753	2.131	2.602	2.947
16	1.746	2.120	2.583	2.921
17	1.740	2.110	2.567	2.898
18	1.734	2.101	2.552	2.878
19	1.729	2.093	2.539	2.861
20	1.725	2.086	2.528	2.845
21	1.721	2.080	2.518	2.831
22	1.717	2.074	2.508	2.819
23	1.714	2.069	2.500	2.807
24	1.711	2.064	2.492	2.797
25	1.708	2.060	2.485	2.787
26	1.706	2.056	2.479	2.779
27	1.703	2.052	2.473	2.771
28	1.701	2.048	2.467	2.763
29	1.699	2.045	2.462	2.756
30	1.697	2.042	2.457	2.750
40	1.684	2.021	2.423	2.704
60	1.671	2.000	2.390	2.660
120	1.658	1.980	2.358	2.617
∞	1.645	1.960	2.326	2.576

*Use the top significance level when you have predicted a specific directional difference (e.g., Group 1 will be greater than Group 2). Use the bottom significance level when you have only predicted that Group 1 will differ from Group 2 without specifying the direction of the difference.

Table C.6
Critical values of F

df for denominator (error)	α	\multicolumn{12}{c}{df for numerator (systematic)}
		1	2	3	4	5	6	7	8	9	10	11	12
1	.25	5.83	7.50	8.20	8.58	8.82	8.98	9.10	9.19	9.26	9.32	9.36	9.41
	.10	39.9	49.5	53.6	55.8	57.2	58.2	58.9	59.4	59.9	60.2	60.5	60.7
	.05	161	200	216	225	230	234	237	239	241	242	243	244
2	.25	2.57	3.00	3.15	3.23	3.28	3.31	3.34	3.35	3.37	3.38	3.39	3.39
	.10	8.53	9.00	9.16	9.24	9.29	9.33	9.35	9.37	9.38	9.39	9.40	9.41
	.05	18.5	19.0	19.2	19.2	19.3	19.3	19.4	19.4	19.4	19.4	19.4	19.4
	.01	98.5	99.0	99.2	99.2	99.3	99.3	99.4	99.4	99.4	99.4	99.4	99.4
3	.25	2.02	2.28	2.36	2.39	2.41	2.42	2.43	2.44	2.44	2.44	2.45	2.45
	.10	5.54	5.46	5.39	5.34	5.31	5.28	5.27	5.25	5.24	5.23	5.22	5.22
	.05	10.1	9.55	9.28	9.12	9.01	8.94	8.89	8.85	8.81	8.79	8.76	8.74
	.01	34.1	30.8	29.5	28.7	28.2	27.9	27.7	27.5	27.3	27.2	27.1	27.1
4	.25	1.81	2.00	2.05	2.06	2.07	2.08	2.08	2.08	2.08	2.08	2.08	2.08
	.10	4.54	4.32	4.19	4.11	4.05	4.01	3.98	3.95	3.94	3.92	3.91	3.90
	.05	7.71	6.94	6.59	6.39	6.26	6.16	6.09	6.04	6.00	5.96	5.94	5.91
	.01	21.2	18.0	16.7	16.0	15.5	15.2	15.0	14.8	14.7	14.5	14.4	14.4
5	.25	1.69	1.85	1.88	1.89	1.89	1.89	1.89	1.89	1.89	1.89	1.89	1.89
	.10	4.06	3.78	3.62	3.52	3.45	3.40	3.37	3.34	3.32	3.30	3.28	3.27
	.05	6.61	5.79	5.41	5.19	5.05	4.95	4.88	4.82	4.77	4.74	4.71	4.68
	.01	16.3	13.3	12.1	11.4	11.0	10.7	10.5	10.3	10.2	10.1	9.96	9.89
6	.25	1.62	1.76	1.78	1.79	1.79	1.78	1.78	1.77	1.77	1.77	1.77	1.77
	.10	3.78	3.46	3.29	3.18	3.11	3.05	3.01	2.98	2.96	2.94	2.92	2.90
	.05	5.99	5.14	4.76	4.53	4.39	4.28	4.21	4.15	4.10	4.06	4.03	4.00
	.01	13.7	10.9	9.78	9.15	8.75	8.47	8.26	8.10	7.98	7.87	7.79	7.72
7	.25	1.57	1.70	1.72	1.72	1.71	1.71	1.70	1.70	1.69	1.69	1.69	1.68
	.10	3.59	3.26	3.07	2.96	2.88	2.83	2.78	2.75	2.72	2.70	2.68	2.67
	.05	5.59	4.74	4.35	4.12	3.97	3.87	3.79	3.73	3.68	3.64	3.60	3.57
	.01	12.2	9.55	8.45	7.85	7.46	7.19	6.99	6.84	6.72	6.62	6.54	6.47
8	.25	1.54	1.66	1.67	1.66	1.66	1.65	1.64	1.64	1.63	1.63	1.63	1.62
	.10	3.46	3.11	2.92	2.81	2.73	2.67	2.62	2.59	2.56	2.54	2.52	2.50
	.05	5.32	4.46	4.07	3.84	3.69	3.58	3.50	3.44	3.39	3.35	3.31	3.28
	.01	11.3	8.65	7.59	7.01	6.63	6.37	6.18	6.03	5.91	5.81	5.73	5.67
9	.25	1.51	1.62	1.63	1.63	1.62	1.61	1.60	1.60	1.59	1.59	1.58	1.58
	.10	3.36	3.01	2.81	2.69	2.61	2.55	2.51	2.47	2.44	2.42	2.40	2.38
	.05	5.12	4.26	3.86	3.63	3.48	3.37	3.29	3.23	3.18	3.14	3.10	3.07
	.01	10.6	8.02	6.99	6.42	6.06	5.80	5.61	5.47	5.35	5.26	5.18	5.11
10	.25	1.49	1.60	1.60	1.59	1.59	1.58	1.57	1.56	1.56	1.55	1.55	1.54
	.10	3.29	2.92	2.73	2.61	2.52	2.46	2.41	2.38	2.35	2.32	2.30	2.28
	.05	4.96	4.10	3.71	3.48	3.33	3.22	3.14	3.07	3.02	2.98	2.94	2.91
	.01	10.0	7.56	6.55	5.99	5.64	5.39	5.20	5.06	4.94	4.85	4.77	4.71

APPENDIX C

Table C.6 (continued)

df for denominator (error)	α	\multicolumn{12}{c}{df for numerator (systematic)}
		1	2	3	4	5	6	7	8	9	10	11	12
11	.25	1.47	1.58	1.58	1.57	1.56	1.55	1.54	1.53	1.53	1.52	1.52	1.51
	.10	3.23	2.86	2.66	2.54	2.45	2.39	2.34	2.30	2.27	2.25	2.23	2.21
	.05	4.84	3.98	3.59	3.36	3.20	3.09	3.01	2.95	2.90	2.85	2.82	2.79
	.01	9.65	7.21	6.22	5.67	5.32	5.07	4.89	4.74	4.63	4.54	4.46	4.40
12	.25	1.46	1.56	1.56	1.55	1.54	1.53	1.52	1.51	1.51	1.50	1.50	1.49
	.10	3.18	2.81	2.61	2.48	2.39	2.33	2.28	2.24	2.21	2.19	2.17	2.15
	.05	4.75	3.89	3.49	3.26	3.11	3.00	2.91	2.85	2.80	2.75	2.72	2.69
	.01	9.33	6.93	5.95	5.41	5.06	4.82	4.64	4.50	4.39	4.30	4.22	4.16
13	.25	1.45	1.55	1.55	1.53	1.52	1.51	1.50	1.49	1.49	1.48	1.47	1.47
	.10	3.14	2.76	2.56	2.43	2.35	2.28	2.23	2.20	2.16	2.14	2.12	2.10
	.05	4.67	3.81	3.41	3.18	3.03	2.92	2.83	2.77	2.71	2.67	2.63	2.60
	.01	9.07	6.70	5.74	5.21	4.86	4.62	4.44	4.30	4.19	4.10	4.02	3.96
14	.25	1.44	1.53	1.53	1.52	1.51	1.50	1.49	1.48	1.47	1.46	1.46	1.45
	.10	3.10	2.73	2.52	2.39	2.31	2.24	2.19	2.15	2.12	2.10	2.08	2.05
	.05	4.60	3.74	3.34	3.11	2.96	2.85	2.76	2.70	2.65	2.60	2.57	2.53
	.01	8.86	6.51	5.56	5.04	4.69	4.46	4.28	4.14	4.03	3.94	3.86	3.80
15	.25	1.43	1.52	1.52	1.51	1.49	1.48	1.47	1.46	1.46	1.45	1.44	1.44
	.10	3.07	2.70	2.49	2.36	2.27	2.21	2.16	2.12	2.09	2.06	2.04	2.02
	.05	4.54	3.68	3.29	3.06	2.90	2.79	2.71	2.64	2.59	2.54	2.51	2.48
	.01	8.68	6.36	5.42	4.89	4.56	4.32	4.14	4.00	3.89	3.80	3.73	3.67
16	.25	1.42	1.51	1.51	1.50	1.48	1.47	1.46	1.45	1.44	1.44	1.44	1.43
	.10	3.05	2.67	2.46	2.33	2.24	2.18	2.13	2.09	2.06	2.03	2.01	1.99
	.05	4.49	3.63	3.24	3.01	2.85	2.74	2.66	2.59	2.54	2.49	2.46	2.42
	.01	8.53	6.23	5.29	4.77	4.44	4.20	4.03	3.89	3.78	3.69	3.62	3.55
17	.25	1.42	1.51	1.50	1.49	1.47	1.46	1.45	1.44	1.43	1.43	1.42	1.41
	.10	3.03	2.64	2.44	2.31	2.22	2.15	2.10	2.06	2.03	2.00	1.98	1.96
	.05	4.45	3.59	3.20	2.96	2.81	2.70	2.61	2.55	2.49	2.45	2.41	2.38
	.01	8.40	6.11	5.18	4.67	4.34	4.10	3.93	3.79	3.68	3.59	3.52	3.46
18	.25	1.41	1.50	1.49	1.48	1.46	1.45	1.44	1.43	1.42	1.42	1.41	1.40
	.10	3.01	2.62	2.42	2.29	2.20	2.13	2.08	2.04	2.00	1.98	1.96	1.93
	.05	4.41	3.55	3.16	2.93	2.77	2.66	2.58	2.51	2.46	2.41	2.37	2.34
	.01	8.29	6.01	5.09	4.58	4.25	4.01	3.84	3.71	3.60	3.51	3.43	3.37
19	.25	1.41	1.49	1.49	1.47	1.46	1.44	1.43	1.42	1.41	1.41	1.40	1.40
	.10	2.99	2.61	2.40	2.27	2.18	2.11	2.06	2.02	1.98	1.96	1.94	1.91
	.05	4.38	3.52	3.13	2.90	2.74	2.63	2.54	2.48	2.42	2.38	2.34	2.31
	.01	8.18	5.93	5.01	4.50	4.17	3.94	3.77	3.63	3.52	3.43	3.36	3.30
20	.25	1.40	1.49	1.48	1.46	1.45	1.44	1.43	1.42	1.41	1.40	1.39	1.39
	.10	2.97	2.59	2.38	2.25	2.16	2.09	2.04	2.00	1.96	1.94	1.92	1.89
	.05	4.35	3.49	3.10	2.87	2.71	2.60	2.51	2.45	2.39	2.35	2.31	2.28
	.01	8.10	5.85	4.94	4.43	4.10	3.87	3.70	3.56	3.46	3.37	3.29	3.23

Table C.6
(continued)

df for denominator (error)	α	\multicolumn{12}{c}{df for numerator (systematic)}
		1	2	3	4	5	6	7	8	9	10	11	12
22	.25	1.40	1.48	1.47	1.45	1.44	1.42	1.41	1.40	1.39	1.39	1.38	1.37
	.10	2.95	2.56	2.35	2.22	2.13	2.06	2.01	1.97	1.93	1.90	1.88	1.86
	.05	4.30	3.44	3.05	2.82	2.66	2.55	2.46	2.40	2.34	2.30	2.26	2.23
	.01	7.95	5.72	4.82	4.31	3.99	3.76	3.59	3.45	3.35	3.26	3.18	3.12
24	.25	1.39	1.47	1.46	1.44	1.43	1.41	1.40	1.39	1.38	1.38	1.37	1.36
	.10	2.93	2.54	2.33	2.19	2.10	2.04	1.98	1.94	1.91	1.88	1.85	1.83
	.05	4.26	3.40	3.01	2.78	2.62	2.51	2.42	2.36	2.30	2.25	2.21	2.18
	.01	7.82	5.61	4.72	4.22	3.90	3.67	3.50	3.36	3.26	3.17	3.09	3.03
26	.25	1.38	1.46	1.45	1.44	1.42	1.41	1.39	1.38	1.37	1.37	1.36	1.35
	.10	2.91	2.52	2.31	2.17	2.08	2.01	1.96	1.92	1.88	1.86	1.84	1.81
	.05	4.23	3.37	2.98	2.74	2.59	2.47	2.39	2.32	2.27	2.22	2.18	2.15
	.01	7.72	5.53	4.64	4.14	3.82	3.59	3.42	3.29	3.18	3.09	3.02	2.96
28	.25	1.38	1.46	1.45	1.43	1.41	1.40	1.39	1.38	1.37	1.36	1.35	1.34
	.10	2.89	2.50	2.29	2.16	2.06	2.00	1.94	1.90	1.87	1.84	1.81	1.79
	.05	4.20	3.34	2.95	2.71	2.56	2.45	2.36	2.29	2.24	2.19	2.15	2.12
	.01	7.64	5.45	4.57	4.07	3.75	3.53	3.36	3.23	3.12	3.03	2.96	2.90
30	.25	1.38	1.45	1.44	1.42	1.41	1.39	1.38	1.37	1.36	1.35	1.35	1.34
	.10	2.88	2.49	2.28	2.14	2.05	1.98	1.93	1.88	1.85	1.82	1.79	1.77
	.05	4.17	3.32	2.92	2.69	2.53	2.42	2.33	2.27	2.21	2.16	2.13	2.09
	.01	7.56	5.39	4.51	4.02	3.70	3.47	3.30	3.17	3.07	2.98	2.91	2.84
40	.25	1.36	1.44	1.42	1.40	1.39	1.37	1.36	1.35	1.34	1.33	1.32	1.31
	.10	2.84	2.44	2.23	2.09	2.00	1.93	1.87	1.83	1.79	1.76	1.73	1.71
	.05	4.08	3.23	2.84	2.61	2.45	2.34	2.25	2.18	2.12	2.08	2.04	2.00
	.01	7.31	5.18	4.31	3.83	3.51	3.29	3.12	2.99	2.89	2.80	2.73	2.66
60	.25	1.35	1.42	1.41	1.38	1.37	1.35	1.33	1.32	1.31	1.30	1.29	1.29
	.10	2.79	2.39	2.18	2.04	1.95	1.87	1.82	1.77	1.74	1.71	1.68	1.66
	.05	4.00	3.15	2.76	2.53	2.37	2.25	2.17	2.10	2.04	1.99	1.95	1.92
	.01	7.08	4.98	4.13	3.65	3.34	3.12	2.95	2.82	2.72	2.63	2.56	2.50
120	.25	1.34	1.40	1.39	1.37	1.35	1.33	1.31	1.30	1.29	1.28	1.27	1.26
	.10	2.75	2.35	2.13	1.99	1.90	1.82	1.77	1.72	1.68	1.65	1.62	1.60
	.05	3.92	3.07	2.68	2.45	2.29	2.17	2.09	2.02	1.96	1.91	1.87	1.83
	.01	6.85	4.79	3.95	3.48	3.17	2.96	2.79	2.66	2.56	2.47	2.40	2.34
200	.25	1.33	1.39	1.38	1.36	1.34	1.32	1.31	1.29	1.28	1.27	1.26	1.25
	.10	2.73	2.33	2.11	1.97	1.88	1.80	1.75	1.70	1.66	1.63	1.60	1.57
	.05	3.89	3.04	2.65	2.42	2.26	2.14	2.06	1.98	1.93	1.88	1.84	1.80
	.01	6.76	4.71	3.88	3.41	3.11	2.89	2.73	2.60	2.50	2.41	2.34	2.27
∞	.25	1.32	1.39	1.37	1.35	1.33	1.31	1.29	1.28	1.27	1.25	1.24	1.24
	.10	2.71	2.30	2.08	1.94	1.85	1.77	1.72	1.67	1.63	1.60	1.57	1.55
	.05	3.84	3.00	2.60	2.37	2.21	2.10	2.01	1.94	1.88	1.83	1.79	1.75
	.01	6.63	4.61	3.78	3.32	3.02	2.80	2.64	2.51	2.41	2.32	2.25	2.18

APPENDIX C

Table C.7
Critical values of rho (Spearman rank order correlation coefficient)

N	Level of significance α*		
	.10	.05	.01
5	.90	1.00	
6	.83	.89	1.00
7	.71	.79	.93
8	.64	.74	.88
9	.60	.68	.83
10	.56	.65	.79
11	.52	.61	.77
12	.50	.59	.75
13	.47	.56	.71
14	.46	.54	.69
15	.44	.52	.66
16	.42	.51	.64
17	.41	.49	.62
18	.40	.48	.61
19	.39	.46	.60
20	.38	.45	.58
21	.37	.44	.56
22	.36	.43	.55
23	.35	.42	.54
24	.34	.41	.53
25	.34	.40	.52
26	.33	.39	.51
27	.32	.38	.50
28	.32	.38	.49
29	.31	.37	.48
30	.31	.36	.47

*α is halved for a one-sided test.

**Table C.8
Critical values of *r*
(Pearson product-moment correlation coefficient)**

df	Level of significance for two-tailed test		
	.10	.05	.01
1	.988	.997	.9999
2	.900	.950	.990
3	.805	.878	.959
4	.729	.811	.917
5	.669	.754	.874
6	.622	.707	.834
7	.582	.666	.798
8	.549	.632	.765
9	.521	.602	.735
10	.497	.576	.708
11	.476	.553	.684
12	.458	.532	.661
13	.441	.514	.641
14	.426	.497	.623
15	.412	.482	.606
16	.400	.468	.590
17	.389	.456	.575
18	.378	.444	.561
19	.369	.433	.549
20	.360	.423	.537
25	.323	.381	.487
30	.296	.349	.449
35	.275	.325	.418
40	.257	.304	.393
45	.243	.288	.372
50	.231	.273	.354
60	.211	.250	.325
70	.195	.232	.303
80	.183	.217	.283
90	.173	.205	.267
100	.164	.195	.254

Glossary

Age-related difference
: Observed differences on a dependent variable from a cross-sectional developmental comparison. The difference is *not* attributed to age per se because (1) cause and effect should not be assumed when the independent variable is *not* manipulated and (2) other factors that vary with age may be responsible such as maturation and experience.

Analysis of variance
: *See* F test.

Applied research
: Research conducted to address a practical problem and to suggest solutions.

Archival data
: Currently existing sources of information that are available to a researcher.

Area sampling
: The random selection of a sample of geographic areas from a population of such areas.

Attention control group
: A control group that receives an equal amount of attention as the group receiving the manipulation, but does not receive the independent variable treatment.

Bar graph (histogram)
: Graphic display of the scores in a frequency distribution; vertical or horizontal bars represent the frequencies of each score.

Baseline
: In a single-subject design, the subject's behavior during a control period before introduction of the experimental manipulation.

Basic research
: Research designed to uncover evidence about fundamental behavioral processes.

Between-subjects design
: *See* independent groups design.

Blind procedure
: A procedure in which the subject does not know which group he or she has been assigned to (e.g., in medical research when the patient does not know whether a pill is actual medication or a placebo). *See* double-blind procedure.

Carry-over effect
: A problem that may occur in repeated measures designs if the effects of one treatment are still present when the next treatment is given.

Case study
: A descriptive account of the behavior, past history, and other relevant factors concerning a specific individual.

Ceiling effect
: A dependent measure (i.e., a task that is too easy) resulting in performance at or near the maximum possible in one or more groups of subjects. *See* floor effect.

Central tendency
: A single number or value that describes the typical or central score among a set of scores.

Coding system
: In systematic observation and content analysis, a set of categories used to code data.

Cohort
: A group of subjects defined by a common characteristic, usually age.

Confederate
: A person posing as a subject in an experiment who is actually part of the experiment.

Confounding
: Failure to control for the effects of a third variable in an experimental design.

Construct validity
: The degree to which a measurement device accurately measures the theoretical construct it is designed to measure.

Content analysis
: Systematic analysis of the content of documents such as speeches, letters, or mass communications.

Correlation coefficient
: An index of how strongly two variables are related to each other in a group of subjects.

Correlational method
: A method of determining whether two variables are related by measurement or observation of the variables.

Counterbalancing
: A method of controlling for order effects in a repeated measures design by either including all orders of treatment presentation or randomly determining the order for each subject.

Criterion validity
: The degree to which a measurement device accurately predicts behavior on a criterion measure.

Criterion variable
: A behavior that a researcher wishes to predict using a predictor variable.

Cross-cultural research
: Research that studies the relationship between variables across different cultures.

Cross-sectional method
: A developmental research method in which persons of different ages are studied at only one point in time; conceptually similar to an independent groups design.

Debriefing
: Explanation of the purposes of the research that is given to subjects following their participation in the research.

Deception
: A research situation in which participants are deliberately not told about all aspects of the research.

Degrees of freedom (*df*)
: The number of observations that are free to vary given that there are certain restrictions placed on the set of observations.

Demand characteristics
: Cues that inform the subject how he or she is expected to behave.

Dependent variable
: The variable that is the subject's response to, and dependent on, the level of the manipulated independent variable.

Descriptive statistics
: Statistical measures that describe the results of a study; descriptive statistics include measures of central tendency (e.g., mean), variability (e.g., standard deviation), and correlation (e.g., Pearson *r*).

Double-blind procedure
: A procedure in which both the subject and the investigator are unaware of the treatment or group to which the subject has been assigned. *See* blind procedure.

Error variance
: Random variability in a set of scores that is not the result of the independent variable. Statistically, the variability of each score from its group mean.

Event manipulation
: A manipulation of the independent variable in an experiment involving a staged event, usually with one or more confederates.

Experimental method
: A method of determining whether variables are related in which the researcher manipulates the independent variable and controls all other variables either by randomization or by direct experimental control.

Experimenter bias (expectancy)
: Any intentional or unintentional influence that the experimenter exerts on subjects to confirm the hypothesis under investigation.

External validity
: The degree to which the results of an experiment may be generalized.

F test (analysis of variance)
: A statistical significance test for determining whether two or more means are significantly different. *F* is the ratio of systematic variance to error variance.

Face validity
: The degree to which a measurement device appears to measure a variable accurately.

Factorial design
: A design in which all levels of each independent variable are combined with all levels of the other independent variables. A factorial design allows investigation of the separate main effects and interactions of two or more independent variables.

Field observation
: A nonexperimental research method in which observations are made in a natural setting over an extended period.

Filler items
: Items included in a questionnaire measure to help disguise the true purpose of the measure.

Floor effect
: A dependent measure (i.e., a task that is too difficult) resulting in performance at or near the minimum possible in one or more groups of subjects. *See* ceiling effect.

Frequency distribution
: An arrangement of a set of scores from lowest to highest that indicates the number of times each score is obtained.

Frequency polygon
: A graphic display of a frequency distribution in which the frequency of each score is plotted on the vertical axis, with the plotted points connected by straight lines.

Functional design
: An experiment that contains many levels of the independent variable to determine the exact functional relationship between the independent and dependent variables.

Generalization
: A goal of research; that results obtained for a sample of subjects will be representative of the population from which that sample is drawn.

Haphazard sampling
: Selecting subjects in a haphazard manner, usually on the basis of availability, and not with regard to having a representative sample of the population; a type of nonprobability sampling.

Hawthorne effect
: A change in performance (usually improvement) related to knowledge that research is being conducted. *See* reactivity.

Histogram
: *See* bar graph.

History
: As a threat to the internal validity of an experiment, refers to any outside event that is not part of the manipulation that could be responsible for the results.

Hypothesis
: A statement that makes an assertion about what is true in a specific situation; often, a statement asserting that two or more variables are related to one another.

Independent variable
: The variable that is manipulated to observe its effect on the dependent variable.

Independent groups design
: An experiment in which different subjects are assigned to each group. Also called between-subjects design.

Inferential statistics
: Statistics designed to determine whether results based on sample data are generalizable to a population.

Informed consent
: In research ethics, the principle that subjects in a study be informed in advance of all aspects of the research that may influence their decision to participate.

Institutional review board (IRB)
: A committee in an institution designed to review research projects to determine whether or not they adhere to ethical principles of research with human subjects.

Instructional manipulation
  A manipulation of the independent variable in an experiment accomplished by giving different sets of instructions to different experimental groups.

Instrument decay
  As a threat to internal validity, the possibility that a change in the characteristics of the measurement instrument is responsible for the results.

Interaction effect
  The differing effect of one independent variable on the dependent variable, depending on the level of another independent variable.

Internal validity
  The certainty with which results of an experiment can be attributed to the manipulation of the independent variable rather than to some other confounding variable.

Interval scale
  A scale of measurement in which the intervals between numbers on the scale are all equal in size.

Interviewer bias
  Intentional or unintentional influence exerted by an interviewer in such a way that the actual or interpreted behavior of respondents is consistent with the interviewer's expectations.

Longitudinal method
  A developmental research method in which the same persons are observed repeatedly as they grow older; conceptually similar to a repeated measures design.

Main effect
  The direct effect of an independent variable on a dependent variable.

Manipulation check
  A measure used to determine whether the manipulation of the independent variable has had its intended effect on a subject.

Matched random assignment
  A method of assigning subjects to groups in which pairs of subjects are first matched on some characteristic and then individually assigned randomly to groups.

Maturation
  As a threat to internal validity, the possibility that any naturally occurring change within the individual is responsible for the results.

Maturation control group
  A control group that receives no treatment but is tested at the end of the study to see whether or not any changes were produced by the physical or mental maturation of the subjects.

Mean
  A measure of central tendency, obtained by summing scores and then dividing the sum by the number of scores.

Measurement error
  The degree to which a measurement deviates from the true score value.

Median
  A measure of central tendency; the middle score in a distribution of scores that divides the distribution in half.

Mode
: A measure of central tendency; the most frequent score in a distribution of scores.

Monotonic relationship
: Any relationship between variables in which increases in the independent variable are accompanied by consistent increases in the dependent variable.

Mortality
: The loss of subjects who decide to leave an experiment. Mortality is a threat to internal validity when the mortality rate is related to the nature of the experimental manipulation.

Multiple correlation
: A correlation between one variable and a combined set of predictor variables.

Nominal scale
: A scale of measurement with two or more categories that have numeric (less than, greater than) properties.

Nonmonotonic relationship
: Any relationship between two variables in which increases in the independent variable are accompanied by both increases and decreases in the dependent variable.

Nonprobability sampling
: Type of sampling procedure in which one cannot specify the probability that any member of the population will be included in the sample.

Nonsignificant results
: Results that are probably due to error factors and are indicative of a decision not to reject the null hypothesis.

Nontreated control
: A control group in an experiment that does not receive a potentially beneficial treatment. Ethical principles hold that such subjects deserve to receive the treatment if it is found to be of benefit.

Null hypothesis
: The hypothesis, used for statistical purposes, that the variables under investigation are not related in the population, that any observed effect based on sample results is due to random error.

Objectives of science
: Objectives include (1) description of behavior, (2) identification of causes of behavior, (3) advancement of explanations of behavior, and (4) prediction of behavior.

Operational definition
: Definition of a concept that specifies the operation used to measure or manipulate the concept.

Order effect
: In a repeated measures design, the effect that the order of introducing treatment has on the dependent variable.

Panel design
: In survey research, a design in which the same individuals are surveyed at two or more points in time.

Partial correlation
: The correlation between two variables with the influence of a third variable statistically controlled for.

Participant observer
: In field observation, an observer who is an active participant in the social setting being studied.

Pilot study
: A small-scale study conducted prior to conducting an actual experiment; designed to test and refine procedures.

Placebo group
: In drug research, a group given an inert substance to assess the psychological effect of receiving a treatment.

Population
: The defined group of individuals from which a sample is drawn.

Prediction
: A statement that makes an assertion concerning what will occur in a specific research investigation.

Predictor variable
: A measure that is used to predict behavior on another measure.

Probability
: The likelihood that a given event (among a specific set of events) will occur.

Probability sampling
: Type of sampling procedure in which one is able to specify the probability that any member of the population will be included in the sample.

Program evaluation
: Research designed to evaluate programs (e.g., social reforms, innovations) that hope to produce certain changes or outcomes in a target population.

Projective measure
: A measure consisting of an ambiguous stimulus to which subjects respond and thus "project" elements of their personality, values, and so on.

Quota sampling
: A sampling procedure in which the sample is chosen to reflect the numerical composition of various subgroups in the population. A haphazard sampling technique is used to obtain the sample.

Random assignment
: Assigning subjects to groups in a random manner such that assignment is determined entirely by chance.

Random error
: An unexplained and unsystematic variability from a true score.

Random time-series design
: A design in which the effectiveness of a randomly introduced treatment is determined by examining a series of measurements made over an extended time period both before and after the treatment is introduced.

Randomization
: Controlling for the effects of extraneous variables by ensuring that the variables operate in a manner determined entirely by chance.

Reactivity
: A problem of measurement in which the measure changes the behavior being observed.

Regression equation
: A mathematical equation that allows prediction of one behavior when the score on another variable is known.

Reliability
: The degree to which a measure is consistent.

Repeated measures design
: An experiment in which the same subjects are assigned to each group. Also called within-subjects design.

Replication
: Repeating a research study to determine whether the results can be duplicated.

Research hypothesis
: The hypothesis that the variables under investigation are related in the population, that the observed effect based on sample data is true in the population.

Research proposal (prospectus)
: A brief report providing the background and methodology to be used in a proposed study. Commonly used to apply for grants, human subjects' approval, and for preliminary review of master's and doctoral theses.

Response set
: A pattern of individual response to questions on a self-report measure that is not related to the content of the questions.

Reversal design
: Also called an ABA design. A time series experiment beginning with a baseline period, followed by a manipulation or treatment period, and then a second baseline period (the reversal or withdrawal phase).

Sampling
: The process of choosing members of a population to be included in a sample.

Selection differences
: Differences in the type of subjects who comprise each group in an experimental design; this situation occurs when subjects elect which group they are to be assigned to.

Self-report measure
: A dependent measure in which subjects provide information about themselves, for example, by filling out a questionnaire.

Sensitivity
: The ability of a measure to detect differences between groups.

Sequential design
: An experimental design incorporating both cross-sectional and longitudinal components.

Significance level
: The probability of rejecting the null hypothesis when it is true.

Significant result
: An outcome of a study that has a low probability of occurrence if the null hypothesis is true; a result that leads to a decision to reject the null hypothesis.

Simple random sampling
: A sampling procedure in which each member of the population has an equal probability of being included in the sample.

Single-subject experiment
: An experiment in which the effect of the independent variable is assessed using data from a single subject.

Social desirability
: A response set in which respondents attempt to answer questions in a socially desirable or approved manner.

Staged manipulation
: *See* event manipulation.

Standard deviation
: The square root of the variance.

Statistical regression
: The tendency of extreme scores on a measure to become less extreme (regress toward the mean) when the measurement is made a second time.

Stratified random sampling
: A sampling procedure in which the population is divided into strata followed by random sampling from each stratum.

Stratum (*pl.* strata)
: Subdivision of a population based on specified characteristics of its members.

Systematic observation
: Careful observation of one or more behaviors in a specific setting.

Systematic variance
: Variability in a set of scores that is the result of the independent variable; statistically, the variability of each group mean from the grand mean of all subjects.

Time-lagged correlation
: The correlation between one variable measured at Time 1 and another variable measured at Time 2.

Time-series experiment
: A procedure involving systematically presenting and withdrawing the independent variable and observing changes in the dependent variable.

Theoretical internal validity
: The certainty with which the results of an experiment can be attributed to an underlying theoretical construct used to explain those results.

True score
: An individual's actual score on a variable being measured, as opposed to the score the individual obtained on the measure itself.

Type I error
: An incorrect decision to reject the null hypothesis when it is true.

Type II error
: An incorrect decision to accept the null hypothesis when it is false.

Unobtrusive measure
: A measure of behavior that is made without the subject's awareness.

Validity
: The degree to which a measurement instrument measures what it is intended to measure.

Variability
: The amount of dispersion of scores about some central value.

Variable
: A general class or category of objects, events, or situations within which specific instances are found to vary.

Variance
: A measure of the variability of scores about a mean; the mean of the sum of squared deviations of scores from the group mean.

Within-subjects design
: *See* repeated measures design.

References

Adams, L. T., & Worden, P. E. (1986). Script development and memory organization in preschool and elementary school children. *Discourse Processes*, *9*, 149–166.

Ainsworth, M. D. S., Blehar, M. C., Waters, E., & Wall, S. (1978). *Patterns of attachment: A psychological study of the strange situation*. Hillsdale, NJ: Lawrence Erlbaum Associates.

Allen, K. E., Hart, B., Buell, J. S., Harris, F. R., & Wolf, M. M. (1964). Effects of social reinforcement on isolate behavior of a nursery school child. *Child Development*, *35*, 511–518.

Andrew, C., Hartwell, S. W., Hutt, M. L., & Walton, B. E. (1953). *The Michigan Picture Test*. New York: Science Research Association.

Anyan, W. R., Jr., & Quillian, W. W. (1971). The naming of primary colors by children. *Child Development*, *42*, 1629–1632.

Bahrick, H. P., Bahrick, P. O., & Wittlinger, R. P. (1975). Fifty years of memory for names and faces: A cross-generational approach. *Journal of Experimental Psychology: General*, *104*, 54–75.

Bakeman, R., & Brownlee, J. R. (1980). The strategic use of parallel play: A sequential analysis. *Child Development*, *51*, 873–878.

Bakeman, R., & Gottman, J. M. (1986). *Observing interaction*. Cambridge, Eng.: Cambridge University Press.

Bales, R. F. (1970). *Personality and interpersonal behavior*. New York: Holt, Rinehart, & Winston.

Ballmer, H. B., & Cozby, P. C. (1981). Family environments of women who return to college. *Sex Roles*, *7*, 1019–1026.

Baltes, P. B., Dittmann-Kohli, F., & Dixon, R. A. (1984). New perspectives on the development of intelligence in adulthood: Toward a dual-process conception and a model of selective optimization with compensation. In P. B. Baltes & O. G. Brim, Jr. (Eds.), *Life-span development and behavior* (Vol. 6). New York: Academic Press.

Bandura, A., Grusec, J. E., & Menlove, F. L. (1966). Observational learning as a function of symbolization and incentive set. *Child Development*, *37*, 499–506.

Bandura, A., Ross, D., & Ross, S. A. (1961). Transmission of aggression through imitation of aggressive models. *Journal of Abnormal and Social Psychology*, *63*, 375–382.

Bandura, A., Ross, D., & Ross, S. A. (1963). Imitation of film-mediated aggressive models. *Journal of Abnormal and Social Psychology*, *66*, 3–11.

Barlow, D. H., & Hersen, M. (1984). *Single-case experimental designs*. New York: Pergamon Press.

Barton, E. M., Baltes, M. M., & Orzech, M. J. (1980). Etiology of dependence in nursing home residents during morning care: The role of staff behavior. *Journal of Personality and Social Psychology*, *38*, 423–431.

REFERENCES

Bathurst, K., & Gottfried, A. W. (1987). Untestable subjects in child development research: Developmental implications. *Child Development, 58,* 1135–1144.

Baumrind, D. (1971). Current patterns of parental authority. *Developmental Psychology Monograph, 4.*

Bayley, N. (1969). *Bayley Scales of Infant Development: Birth to two years.* New York: The Psychological Corporation.

Becker, H. S. (1963). *Outsiders: Studies in the sociology of deviance.* New York: Free Press.

Bellak, L., & Bellak, S. S. (1949). *Children's Apperception Test (animal figures).* Larchmont, NY: C.P.S.

Bellak, L., & Bellak, S. S. (1965). *Children's Apperception Test (human figures).* Larchmont, NY: C.P.S.

Bem, S. L. (1974). The measurement of psychological androgyny. *Journal of Consulting and Clinical Psychology, 42,* 155–162.

Benson, J., & Hocevar, D. (1985). The impact of item phrasing on the validity of attitude scales for elementary school children. *Journal of Educational Measurement, 22,* 231–240.

Bouchard, T. J., Jr., & McGue, M. (1981). Familial studies of intelligence: A review. *Science, 212,* 1055–1059.

Bradley, R. H., & Caldwell, B. M. (1980). The relation of home environment, cognitive competence, and IQ among males and females. *Child Development, 51,* 1140–1148.

Brainerd, C. J. (1976). *Piaget's theory of intelligence.* Englewood Cliffs, NJ: Prentice-Hall.

Brazelton, T. B. (1973). *Neonatal Behavioral Assessment Scale.* London: Spastics International Medical Publications.

Bryant, B. K. (1982). An index of empathy for children and adolescents. *Child Development, 53,* 412–425.

Burington, R. S., & May, D. C. (1970). *Handbook of probability and statistics with tables.* New York: McGraw-Hill.

Buros, O. K. (Ed.). (1978). *Mental measurements yearbook* (Vols. 1 & 2). (8th ed.) Highland Park, NJ: Gryphon Press.

Byrne, D., Ervin, C. R., & Lamberth, J. (1970). Continuity between the experimental study of attraction and real-life computer dating. *Journal of Personality and Social Psychology, 16,* 157–165.

Campbell, D. T. (1968). Quasi-experimental design. In D. L. Gillis (Ed.), *International encyclopedia of the social sciences* (Vol. 5). New York: Macmillan and Free Press.

Campbell, D. T. (1969). Reforms as experiments. *American Psychologist, 24,* 409–429.

Campbell, D. T., & Stanley, J. C. (1966). *Experimental and quasi-experimental designs for research.* Chicago: Rand-McNally.

Cantor, G. N. (1968). Effects of a "boredom" treatment on children's simple RT performance. *Psychonomic Science, 10,* 299–300.

Cavan, S. (1966). *Liquor license: An ethnography of bar behavior.* Chicago: Aldine.

Cazden, C. (1972). *Child language and education.* New York: Holt, Rinehart, & Winston.

Ceci, S. (1987). *Handbook of cognitive, social, and neuropsychological aspects of learning disabilities*. Hillsdale, NJ: Erlbaum.

Ceci, S. J., & Bronfenbrenner, U. (1985). "Don't forget to take the cupcakes out of the oven": Prospective memory, strategic time-monitoring, and context. *Child Development, 56*, 152–164.

Clarke-Stewart, K. A. (1973). Interactions between mothers and their young children: Characteristics and consequences. *Monographs of Society for Research in Child Development, 38* (No. 153).

Cohn, J. F., & Tronick, E. Z. (1983). Three-month-old infants' reaction to simulated maternal depression. *Child Development, 54*, 185–193.

Cook, T. D., & Campbell, D. T. (1979). *Quasi-experimentation: Design and analysis issues for field settings*. Chicago: Rand-McNally.

Coopersmith, S. (1967). *The antecedents of self-esteem*. San Francisco: W. H. Freeman.

Crandall, V. C., & Battle, E. S. (1970). The antecedents and adult correlates of academic and intellectual achievement effort. In J. Hill (Ed.), *Minnesota Symposia on Child Development* (Vol. 4). Minneapolis: University of Minnesota Press.

Curtiss, S. (1977). *Genie: A psycholinguistic study of a modern day "wild child."* New York: Academic Press.

Dawson, G., Finley, C., Phillips, S., & Galpert, L. (1986). Hemispheric specialization and the language abilities of autistic children. *Child Development, 57*, 1440–1453.

de Charms, R., & Moeller, G. H. (1962). Values expressed in American children's readers: 1800–1900. *Journal of Abnormal and Social Psychology, 64*, 136–142.

Donovan, W. L., & Leavitt, L. A. (1985). Simulating conditions of learned helplessness: The effects of interventions and attributions. *Child Development, 56*, 594–603.

Douglas, J. D. (1976). *Investigative social research: Individual and team field research*. Beverly Hills, CA: Sage.

Dunn, L. M., & Dunn, L. M. (1981). *Peabody Picture Vocabulary Test—Revised*. Circle Pines, MN: American Guidance Service.

Fantz, R. L. (1961). The origin of form perception. *Scientific American, 204*, 66–72.

Fantz, R. L. (1963). Pattern vision in newborn infants. *Science, 140*, 296–297.

Feshbach, N. D., & Roe, K. (1968). Empathy in six- and seven-year-olds. *Child Development, 39*, 133–145.

Flavell, J. (1985). *Cognitive development*. Englewood Cliffs, NJ: Prentice-Hall.

Flavell, J. H., Speer, J. R., Green, F. L., & August, D. L. (1981). The development of comprehension monitoring and knowledge about communication. *Monographs of the Society for Research in Child Development, 46* (Whole No. 192).

Foellinger, D. B., & Trabasso, T. (1977). Seeing, hearing, and doing: A developmental study of memory for actions. *Child Development, 48*, 1482–1489.

Gans, H. (1962). *Urban villagers*. New York: Free Press.

Garrett, C. S., Ein, P. L., & Tremaine, L. (1977). The development of gender stereotyping of adult occupations in elementary school children. *Child Development, 48*, 507–512.

Gibbs, J. C., Widaman, K. F., & Colby, A. (1982). Construction and validation of a simplified, group-administered equivalent to the moral judgment interview. *Child Development, 53*, 895–910.

REFERENCES

Goethals, G. R., & Reckman, R. F. (1973). The perception of consistency in attitudes. *Journal of Experimental Social Psychology, 9,* 491–501.

Gottfried, A. E., & Gottfried, A. W. (1988). *Maternal employment and children's development: Longitudinal research.* New York: Plenum Press.

Green, J., & Wallat, C. (1981). *Ethnography and language in educational settings.* New York: Ablex Publishing.

Gregg, L. W. (1978). Spatial concepts, spatial names, and the development of egocentric representations. In R. S. Siegler (Ed.), *Children's thinking: What develops?* Hillsdale, NJ: Erlbaum.

Gunzenhauser, N., & Caldwell, B. M. (1986). *Group care for young children: Considerations for child care and health professionals, providers, policy makers and parents.* Skillman, NJ: Johnson and Johnson.

Gwaltney-Gibbs, P. A. (1986). The institutionalization of premarital cohabitation: Estimates from marriage license applications, 1970 and 1980. *Journal of Marriage and the Family, 48,* 423–434.

Hall, J. A., & Halberstadt, A. G. (1980). Masculinity and femininity in children: Development of the Children's Personal Attributes Questionnaire. *Developmental Psychology, 16,* 270–280.

Harter, S. (1981). A new self-report scale of intrinsic versus extrinsic orientation in the classroom: Motivational and informational components. *Developmental Psychology, 17,* 300–312.

Harter, S. (1982). The perceived competence scale for children. *Child Development, 53,* 87–97.

Henle, M., & Hubbell, M. B. (1938). "Egocentricity" in adult conversation. *Journal of Social Psychology, 9,* 227–234.

Hill, C. T., Rubin, Z., & Peplau, L. A. (1976). Breakups before marriage: The end of 103 affairs. *Journal of Social Issues, 32,* 147–168.

Holmes, T. H., & Rahe, R. H. (1967). The Social Readjustment Rating Scale. *Journal of Psychosomatic Research, 11,* 213–218.

Holsti, O. R. (1969). *Content analysis for the social sciences and humanities.* Reading, MA: Addison-Wesley.

Istomina, Z. M. (1975). The development of voluntary memory in preschool-age children. *Soviet Psychology, 13,* 5–64.

Jourard, S. M. (1969). The effects of experimenters' self-disclosure on subjects' behavior. In C. Spielberger (Ed.), *Current topics in community and clinical psychology.* New York: Academic Press.

Kagan, J., Rosman, B. L., Day, D., Albert, J., & Phillips, W. (1964). Information processing in the child: Significance of analytic and reflective attitudes. *Psychological Monographs, 78* (Whole No. 578).

Kenny, D. A. (1975). A quasi-experimental approach to assessing treatment effects in the nonequivalent control group design. *Psychological Bulletin, 82,* 345–362.

Kidder, L. H., & Judd, C. M. (1986). *Research methods in social relations* (5th ed.). New York: Holt, Rinehart, & Winston.

Kubose, S. K. (1972). Motivational effects of boredom on children's response speeds. *Developmental Psychology, 6,* 302–305.

Langer, E. J., & Rodin, J. (1976). The effects of choice and enhanced personal responsibility for the aged: A field experiment in an institutional setting. *Journal of Personality and Social Psychology, 34*, 191–198.

Levin, J. R. (1983). Pictorial strategies for school learning: Practical illustrations. In M. Pressley & J. R. Levin (Eds.), *Cognitive strategy research: Educational applications* (pp. 213–238). New York: Springer-Verlag.

Levin, J. R. (1985). Some methodological and statistical "bugs" in research on children's learning. In M. Pressley & C. J. Brainerd (Eds.), *Cognitive learning and memory in children: Progress in cognitive development research*. New York: Springer-Verlag.

Levin, J. R., Morrison, C. R., McGivern, J. E., Mastropieri, M. A., & Scruggs, T. E. (1986). Mnemonic facilitation of text-embedded science facts. *American Educational Research Journal, 23*, 489–506.

Locke, H. J., & Wallace, K. M. (1959). Short marital adjustment and prediction tests: Their reliability and validity. *Marriage and Family Living, 21*, 251–255.

Lofland, J. (1971). *Analyzing social settings*. Belmont, CA: Wadsworth.

Lofland, J. (1976). *Doing social life: The qualitative study of human interaction in natural settings*. New York: Wiley.

Mandler, J. M., & Johnson, N. S. (1976). Some of the thousand words a picture is worth. *Journal of Experimental Psychology: Human Learning and Memory, 2*, 529–540.

Mandler, J. M., & Ritchey, G. H. (1977). Long-term memory for pictures. *Journal of Experimental Psychology: Human Learning and Memory, 3*, 386–396.

Mandler, J. M., & Robinson, C. A. (1978). Developmental changes in picture recognition. *Journal of Experimental Child Psychology, 26*, 122–136.

Mangen, D. J., & Peterson, W. A. (1982a). *Research instruments in social gerontology, Vol. 1: Clinical and social gerontology*. Minneapolis: University of Minnesota Press.

Mangen, D. J., & Peterson, W. A. (1982b). *Research instruments in social gerontology, Vol. 2: Social roles and social participation*. Minneapolis: University of Minnesota Press.

Markman, E. M. (1977). Realizing you don't understand: A preliminary investigation. *Child Development, 46*, 986–992.

Marsh, H. W. (1986). Negative item bias in ratings scales for preadolescent children: A cognitive-developmental phenomenon. *Developmental Psychology, 22*, 37–49.

Mayo, E. (1946). *The human problems of an industrial civilization*, (2nd ed.). New York: Macmillan.

McDaniel, M., & Pressley, M. (1987). *Imagery and related mnemonic processes: Theories, individual differences, and application*. New York: Springer-Verlag.

Milgram, S. (1963). Behavioral study of obedience. *Journal of Abnormal and Social Psychology, 67*, 371–378.

Milgram, S. (1964). Group pressure and action against a person. *Journal of Abnormal and Social Psychology, 69*, 137–143.

Milgram, S. (1965). Some conditions of obedience and disobedience to authority. *Human Relations, 18*, 57–76.

REFERENCES

Milosky, L. M., Wilkinson, L. C., Chiang, C., Lindow, J., & Salmon, D. (1986). School-age children's understanding of explanation adequacy. *Journal of Educational Psychology, 78,* 334, 340.

Mischel, W., & Ebbesen, E. B. (1970). Attention in delay of gratification. *Journal of Personality and Social Psychology, 16,* 329–337.

Mischel, W., Ebbesen, E. B., & Zeiss, A. (1972). Cognitive and attentional mechanisms in delay of gratification. *Journal of Personality and Social Psychology, 21,* 204–218.

Mitchell, J. (1985). *The ninth mental measurements yearbook.* Lincoln, NE: Buros Institute of Mental Measurements.

Moos, R. H., & Moos, B. S. (1981). *Family Environment Scale manual.* Palo Alto, CA: Consulting Psychologist Press.

Neugarten, B. L., Havighurst, R. J., & Tobin, S. S. (1961). The measurement of life satisfaction. *Journal of Gerontology, 16,* 134–143.

Nickerson, R. S., & Adams, M. J. (1979). Long-term memory for a common object. *Cognitive Psychology, 11,* 287–307.

Nisbett, R. E., & Ross, L. (1980). *Human inference: Strategies and shortcomings of social judgment.* Englewood Cliffs, NJ: Prentice-Hall.

Nisbett, R. E., & Wilson, T. D. (1977). Telling more than we can know: Verbal reports on mental processes. *Psychological Review, 84,* 231–259.

Novak, M. A., & Harlow, H. F. (1975). Social recovery of monkeys isolated for the first year of life: Rehabilitation and therapy. *Developmental Psychology, 11,* 453–465.

Patterson, G. R., & Moore, D. (1979). Interactive patterns as units of behavior. In M. E. Lamb, S. J., Sumoi, & G. R. Stephenson (Eds.), *Social interaction analysis: Methodological issues* (pp. 77–96). Madison: University of Wisconsin Press.

Perry, D. G., & Bussey, K. (1977). Self-reinforcement in high- and low-aggressive boys following acts of aggression. *Child Development, 48,* 653–657.

Perry, D. G., & Perry, L. C. (1974). Denial of suffering in the victim as a stimulus to violence in aggressive boys. *Child Development, 45,* 55–62.

Peterson, J. L., & Zill, N. (1986). Marital disruption, parent–child relationships, and behavior problems in children. *Journal of Marriage and the Family, 48,* 295–307.

Piaget, J. (1952). *The origins of intelligence in children.* New York: International Universities Press.

Piers, E., & Harris, D. (1969). *The Piers–Harris Children's Self-Concept Scale.* Nashville, TN: Counselor Recordings and Tests.

Potts, R., Huston, A. C., & Wright, J. C. (1986). The effects of television form and violent content on boys' attention and social behavior. *Journal of Experimental Child Psychology, 41,* 1–17.

Pressley, M., Levin, J. R., & Delaney, H. D. (1982). The mnemonic keyword method. *Review of Educational Research, 52,* 61–91.

Rest, J. R. (1979). *Development in judging moral issues.* Minneapolis: University of Minnesota Press.

Ring, K., Wallston, K., & Corey, M. (1970). Mode of debriefing as a factor affecting subjects' reaction to a Milgram-type obedience experiment: An ethical inquiry. *Representative Research in Social Psychology, 1,* 67–68.

Robbins, L. C. (1963). The accuracy of parental recall of aspects of child development and of child-rearing practices. *Journal of Abnormal and Social Psychology, 66,* 261–270.

Robinson, J. P., & Shaver, P. R. (1973). *Measures of social psychological attitudes.* Ann Arbor, MI: Institute for Social Research.

Rodin, J., & Langer, E. J. (1977). Long-term effects of a control-relevant intervention with the institutionalized aged. *Journal of Personality and Social Psychology, 35,* 897–902.

Rogoff, B. (1981). Schooling and the development of cognitive skills. In H. C. Triandis & H. A. Heron (Eds.), *Handbook of cross-cultural psychology* (Vol. 4). Boston: Allyn & Bacon.

Rohwer, W. D., Jr. (1973). Elaboration and learning in childhood and adolescence. In H. W. Reese (Ed.), *Advances in child development and behavior* (Vol. 3). New York: Academic Press.

Rohwer, W. D., Jr. (1976). An introduction to research on individual and developmental differences in learning. In W. K. Estes (Ed.), *Handbook of learning and cognitive processes* (Vol. 3). Hillsdale, NJ: Erlbaum.

Rosenbaum, J., & Prinsky, L. (1987). Sex, violence, and rock 'n' roll: Youth's perceptions of popular music. *Popular Music and Society, 11,* 384–397.

Rosenblatt, P. C., & Cleaves, W. T. (1981). Family behavior in public places: Interaction patterns within and across generations. *Merrill-Palmer Quarterly, 27,* 257–269.

Rosenblatt, P. C., & Cozby, P. C. (1972). Courtship patterns associated with freedom of choice of spouse. *Journal of Marriage and the Family, 34,* 689–695.

Rosenblatt, P. C., de Mik, L., Anderson, R. M., & Johnson, P. A. (1985). *The family in business.* San Francisco: Jossey-Bass.

Rosenhan, D. (1973). On being sane in insane places. *Science, 179,* 250–258.

Rosenthal, R. (1966). *Experimenter effects in behavioral research.* New York: Appleton-Century-Crofts.

Rosenthal, R., & Fode, K. L. (1963). The effect of experimenter bias on the performance of the albino rat. *Behavioral Science, 8,* 183–189.

Ross, R. T., Begab, M. J., Dondis, E. H., Giampiccolo, J. S., & Myers, C. E. (1985). *Lives of the mentally retarded: A forty-year follow-up study.* Stanford, CA: Stanford University Press.

Ross, L. E., & Ward, T. B. (1978). The processing of information from short-term visual store: Developmental and intellectual level differences. In N. R. Ellis (Ed.), *International review of research in mental retardation* (Vol. 9). New York: Academic Press.

Rossi, P. H., Freeman, H. E., & Wright, S. R. (1979). *Evaluation: A systematic approach.* Beverly Hills, CA: Sage.

Rubin, Z. (1970). Measurement of romantic love. *Journal of Personality and Social Psychology, 16,* 265–273.

Rubin, Z. (1973). *Liking and loving: An invitation to social psychology.* New York: Holt, Rinehart, & Winston.

Rubin, K. H., Fein, G. G., & Vandenberg, B. (1983). Play. In P. Mussen (Ed.), *Manual of child psychology* (Vol. 4). New York: Wiley.

REFERENCES

Schaie, K. W. (1986). Beyond calendar definitions of age, time, and cohort: The general developmental model revisited. *Developmental Review, 6*, 252–277.

Schreiber, F. R. (1973). *Sybil.* Chicago: Regency.

Sebald, H. (1986). Adolescents' shifting orientation toward parents and peers: A curvilinear trend over recent decades. *Journal of Marriage and the Family, 48*, 5–13.

Seeley, T. T., Abramson, P. R., Perry, L. B., Rothblatt, A. B., & Seeley, D. M. (1980). Thermographic measurement of sexual arousal: A methodological note. *Archives of Sexual Behavior, 9*, 77–85.

Serbin, L. A., O'Leary, K. D., Kent, R. N., & Tonick, I. J. (1973). A comparison of teacher response to the pre-academic and problem behavior of boys and girls. *Child Development, 44*, 796–804.

Sheingold, K., & Tenney, Y. J. (1982). Memory for a salient childhood event. In U. Neisser (Ed.), *Memory observed: Remembering in natural contexts.* San Francisco: W. H. Freeman.

Shneidman, E. S. (1952). *Manual for the make-a-picture story method: Project monograph 2.* Portland, OR: The Society for Projective Techniques and Rorschach Institute.

Skinner, B. F. (1953). *Science and human behavior.* New York: Macmillan.

Sigel, I. E. (1982). The relationship between parental distancing strategies and the child's cognitive behavior. In L. M. Laosa & I. E. Sigel (Eds.), *Families as learning environments for children.* New York: Plenum Press.

Society for Research in Child Development (1973, Winter). Ethical standards for research with children. Newsletter 3–5.

Solomon, I. L., & Starr, B. D. (1968). *School apperception method.* New York: Springer-Verlag.

Spanier, G. B. (1976). Measuring dyadic adjustment: New scales for assessing the quality of marriage and similar dyads. *Journal of Marriage and the Family, 38*, 15–28.

Spence, J. T., & Helmreich, R. L. (1978). *Masculinity and femininity: Their psychological dimensions, correlates, and antecedents.* Austin: University of Texas Press.

Squire, L. R., & Slater, P. C. (1975). Forgetting in very long-term memory as assessed by an improved questionnaire technique. *Journal of Experimental Psychology: Human Learning and Memory, 104*, 50–54.

Terman, L. M., & Merrill, M. A. (1973). *Stanford–Binet Intelligence Scale.* Boston: Houghton Mifflin.

Toner, I. J., Holstein, R. B., & Hetherington, E. M. (1977). Reflection-impulsivity and self-control in preschool children. *Child Development, 48*, 239–245.

Viney, L. L. (1983). The assessment of psychological states through content analysis of verbal communications. *Psychological Bulletin, 94*, 542–563.

Webb, E. J., Campbell, D. T., Schwartz, R. D., Sechrest, R., & Grove, J. B. (1981). *Nonreactive measures in the social sciences* (2nd ed.). Boston: Houghton Mifflin.

Wechsler, D. (1967). *Wechsler Preschool and Primary Scale of Intelligence.* New York: The Psychological Corporation.

Wechsler, D. (1974). *Wechsler Intelligence Scale for Children—Revised.* New York: The Psychological Corporation.

Wechsler, D. (1981). *Wechsler Adult Intelligence Scale—Revised.* New York: The Psychological Corporation.

Weissberg, J. A., & Paris, S. G. (1986). Young children's remembering in different contexts: A reinterpretation of Istomina's study. *Child Development, 57,* 1123–1129.

Weissert, W. G. (1986). Hard choices: Targeting long-term care to the "at risk" aged. *Journal of Health, Politics, Policy, and Law, 11,* 463–481.

Woll, S. B., & Cozby, P. C. (1976). Categories of moral judgment and attitudes toward amnesty and the Nixon pardon. *Personality and Social Psychology Bulletin, 2,* 183–186.

Worden, P. E., & Sherman-Brown, S. (1983). A word-frequency cohort effect in young vs. elderly adults' memory for words. *Developmental Psychology, 19,* 521–530.

Yin, R. K. (1984). *Case study research: Design and methods.* Beverly Hills, CA: Sage.

Zajonc, R. B. (1975). Birth order and intellectual development. *Psychological Review, 82,* 74–82.

Index

ABA design, 82–83
Abstract of report, 20–22, 24, 200
Age-related differences, 92
Analysis of variance, 162–163, 169, 220–229
Applied research, 8–9
Archival research, 125–127
Area sampling, 144
Artificiality, 39
Authority, 6
Author's notes (research report), 209

Baseline, 83–86
Basic research, 8–9
Behavioral measures, 47–48
Between-subjects design (see *independent groups design*)
Blind techniques, 138

Carry-over effect, 76
Case study, 118–119
Cause and effect, 34–36, 38, 96
Central tendency, 154–156, 213–215, 216–219
Chi-square, 168–169, 216–219
Closed-ended questions, 46–47
Coding systems, 116–117, 127
Cohort effects, 78–80
Confounding, 60, 80
Construct validity, 52–53
Content analysis, 127
Contingency coefficient, 231
Control group, 64–66, 137–140, 192

Correlational method, 34–36
  and correlation coefficients, 172–173
  direction of cause and effect, 34–35
  prediction, 40
  third variables, 35–36, 177–178
  uses of, 39–40
Correlation coefficient, 51, 173–175, 231–234, 245
Counterbalancing, 75–76
Criterion validity, 52
Cross-cultural research, 127, 143
Cross-sectional design, 77–80
Curvilinear relationship, 33, 99, 176–177

Debriefing, 146–147, 190
Deception, 146, 186
Degrees of freedom, 218
Demand characteristics, 77
Dependent variable, 38, 102
Description, 4, 111
Descriptive statistics, 153–156, 213–216
Design
  factorial, 90–97, 224–228
  independent groups, 72–74, 97
  mixed factorial, 97–98
  multiple-baseline, 84–86
  nonequivalent control group, 64–65
  nonequivalent control group pretest-posttest, 68–69
  posttest only, 66–68
  pretest-posttest, 66–68
  quasi-experimental, 68–69

267

INDEX

Design *continued*
  repeated measures, 72–77, 96–98, 228–230
  reversal, 82
  single-subject, 82–86
Discussion section of research report, 24–25, 205
Distractor, 14
Double-blind technique, 138

Electroencephalograph (EEG), 48
Electromyograph (EMG), 48
Error
  measurement, 50
  Type I, 164
  Type II, 165
Error variance, 73–74, 162
Ethical principles, 192–196
  and correlational method, 39–40
  children, 141, 191, 194–196
  deception, 146, 186
  informed consent, 185, 187–190
Evaluation research (see *program evaluation*)
Event manipulation, 135
Experimental control, 37, 59
Experimental method, 36–37, 59
Experimenter expectancies, 138–139
Explanation, 4
External validity, 60–61, 115 (see also *generalization*)

F test (see *analysis of variance*)
Face validity, 52
Factorial design, 90–97, 224–228
  interactions, 92–93, 95, 101–102, 224–228
  main effects, 91–92, 147–148, 224–228
  mixed, 96–98
Field experiments, 39
Field observation, 112–116
Figures (in research reports), 212
Floor effect, 137
Frequency distribution, 153
Frequency polygon, 153–154
Functional design, 99

Galvanic skin response (GSR), 48
Generalization, 60–61, 115, 143
Goals of science, 3–5
Graphing relationships among variables, 32–33, 156, 174–176

Haphazard sampling, 142–143
Hawthorne effect, 139
Histogram, 153–154
History effects, 63
Human Relations Area Files, 127

Ideas, sources of, 13–17
Independent groups design, 72–74, 97–98
Independent variables, 38
Inferential statistics, 157–162
Informed consent, 185–190
Institutional Review Board (IRB), 186, 192–193
Instructional manipulation, 135
Instrument decay, 63
Interaction, 92–93, 95, 101–102, 224–228
Internal consistency reliability, 51
Internal validity, 60
  threats to, 63–65, 67, 69
Interrater reliability, 51, 118
Interval scales, 54–55, 168–169
Interviewer bias, 122
Introduction section of research report, 24, 201
Intuition, 6

Journals, 18–20

Literature review, 20–23
Longitudinal design, 77–80

Main effect, 91–92, 147–148, 224–228
Mann–Whitney *U* test, 168, 219–220
Matched random assignment, 73–74, 228–230
Maturation, 63, 140
Mean, 154, 214–215
Measurement scales, 53–55, 168–169
Median, 154, 214
Method section of research report, 24, 202
Minimal risk research, 193
Mixed factorial design, 96–98
Mode, 154, 213–214
Mortality, 67, 81
Multiple baseline design, 84–86
Multiple correlation, 179

Negative case analysis, 115
Negative relationship, 33, 175
Nominal scale, 54, 168–169

268

Nonequivalent control group design, 64–65
Nonequivalent control group pretest-posttest design, 68–69
Nonprobability sampling, 142–143
Null hypothesis, 158, 164–168

Observation, 15, 112–118
One-group pretest-posttest design, 62–64
One-shot case study, 62
Open-ended questions, 46–47
Operational definition, 30–31
Order effect, 75
Ordinal scale, 54, 168–169
Outcome evaluation, 10–11

Panel study, 121
Partial correlation, 178
Participant observer, 113–115
Pearson r, 173–175, 232–234
Physiological measures, 48–49
Pilot study, 147–148
Placebo group, 138
Population, 141–142
Positive relationship, 33, 175
Posttest-only design, 66–68
Prediction, 5, 40, 178–179
Preferential looking technique, 47
Pretest-posttest design, 66–68
Pretests, 67–68
Probability, 158–160
Probability sampling, 142
Professional societies, 17–18
Program evaluation, 9–11
Psychological Abstracts, 21

Quasi-experimental designs, 68–69
Questionnaires, 118–120
Quota sampling, 142–143

Random assignment, 37, 59, 72–73, 235
Randomization, 37, 59, 157
Random number table, 72–73, 235–237
Range, 215
Ratio scale, 55, 168–169
Reactivity, 49–50, 118, 139
Reference section of research report, 24–25, 207–208
Regression equation, 178–179
Relationships between variables, 31–34
　curvilinear, 33, 99, 176–177
　negative, 33, 175
　positive, 33, 175

Reliability, 49, 50–52, 118, 136
Repeated measures design, 72–77, 96–98, 228–230
Research hypothesis, 164
Research proposal, 131–132
Response sets, 123
Restriction of range, 176
Results section of research report, 22–24, 203
Retrospective memory, 124–125
Reversal design, 82
Risk to subject, 182

Sampling, 119, 121–122, 142–144
　area, 144
　haphazard, 142–143
　nonprobability, 142–143
　probability, 142
　quota, 142–143
　random, 144
　stratified random, 144
Scatterplot, 174–176
Scientific method, 6–7
Selection differences, 64–65
Self-report measures, 40–47
Sensitivity of measures, 136
Sequential design, 82
Setting the stage, 145
Significance, 157–159
Single-subject design, 82–96
Social desirability, 123
Social Science Citation Index, 22–23
Spearman *rho*, 231–232
Split-half reliability, 51
Stage theories, 16
Staged manipulation, 135–136
Standard deviation, 156, 215–216
Statistical records, 125
Statistical regression, 63–64
Straightforward manipulation, 135
Stratified random sample, 144
Strength of manipulation, 133
Stress, 183–184
Subject variables, 40, 96
Survey archives, 126
Survey research, 119–125
Systematic observation, 116–118
Systematic variance, 162

Tables (in reports), 210
Testing effects, 63
Test-retest reliability, 51
Theories, 15
Third variable problem, 35–36, 177–178

Time series, 82–86
Title page (research report), 199
True score, 50
t test, 160–161, 168, 240
Type I error, 164
Type II error, 165

Unobtrusive measures, 49–50

Validity of measures, 49, 52–53
Variability, 73–74, 155–156, 215–216

Variables, 29–30
   dependent, 38, 136–137
   independent, 38, 133–136
   relationships between, 31–34
Variance
   as descriptive statistic, 156, 215–216
   error, 162
   systematic, 162

Within-subjects design (see *repeated measures design*)